AMERICAN MUSIC

Culture and Society Series—CS1

AMERICAN MUSIC:
FROM STORYVILLE
TO WOODSTOCK

edited by

Charles Nanry

with a foreword by

Irving Louis Horowitz

*trans*action *books*
New Brunswick, New Jersey
Distributed by E. P. Dutton and Company

*trans*action *books*
Rutgers University
New Brunswick, New Jersey 08903

Library of Congress Catalog Card Number: 71-164978
ISBN: 0-87855-007-0 (cloth); 0-87855-506-4 (paper)

Printed in the United States of America

To Jacqueline

RECIPE

Blend & merge a clear
    tune with dangerous
drummer pounding &
    pulsating a plastic
beat and pausing to let
    you feel freedom.
    Wind a length of
caring around clarinet.
It stands so straight.
    Bend it! Wipe out
    its mind with wind
    soaked trills and slides.
Open wide the mellow throb
Open & pierce with fierce
    f-sharps and no flats
Fake it (if you have to)
But play it 'til nomore
    notes come. Play it! 'til
    your crazy conceited
    song, or you, dies.

Judy Shepps

Contents

Foreword

IRVING LOUIS HOROWITZ

Where art exists, analysis is sure to follow. Artists may be thoroughly dismayed by attempts to characterize and consume their efforts; like most human beings, artists—and musicians in particular—do not like to be studied. They see themselves as sui generis: creatures who come into the world to do their thing, in their own time and their own way. Indeed, the cult of individualism is so great that it not only forms the basis of much behavior in the jazz world, but is in itself a prime illustration of the tendency of all culture to resist easy classification. Indeed, if classification were simple, if styles of performance could easily by typed, the very reason for an audience would be largely obviated. If, for example, a Sonny Stitt sounded exactly like a Charlie Parker, you would have a curiosity, not an achievement. Further, sensitive musicians like the aforementioned Mr. Stitt spent a not inconsequential amount of time moving beyond imitation and mimesis into the highest level of art, creation.

Then, along comes the interpreter of music. First the discographers who codify; then the commentators who solidify tastes; then the critics who offer comparisons, invidious and otherwise; and finally, the sociologists who create models of cosmopolitans and locals, bureaucratic and charismatic types. And this entire barrage of words and meanings derives from an art that ultimately must rest on transgressing the meanings of words and finding meanings through sounds. In effect, the processes of musical classification and musical creation are at cross purposes; but a dialectical series of cross purposes that makes it possible for both the musician and his audience to understand the larger society illumined by the smaller musical culture. It is the great merit of Charles Nanry's volume that in its own right and in its choice of other papers, it displays a sensitive awareness that in the beginning come the hymns of the life process, in the middle comes the analysis, and in the end we go out to the mass of paradise—lost and found.

One reason that people like to write about musicians, especially those in the field of jazz and rock, is that musicians share with intellectuals a concern for high moral principles; they are dedicated to an art form, to the traditions from which it emanates, to the furtherance of that tradition and to a living constituency that is small and itself deeply committed. What gives musicians a special appeal is the ways they differ from the intellectuals who write of them: musicians exhibit a lack of self-consciousness, a familiarity and an ease with living in a world of ordinary people, and an ability to achieve a certain level of fame and notoriety that provides them with the glitter and glamour of mass culture without somehow detracting from their sense of high principle. Perhaps this is why musicians and analysts alike are so terribly concerned with problems of biography—of "selling out," of "imitating" and "stealing" and all of the human foibles that become superhuman fables when they become part of the legend of the musician. In short, the history of American music as distinct from the history of music in America is unique because the artistry derives, for the first time, from lower class and racially distinctive constituencies.

American music, whatever else it turns out to be, represents a decisive break with the aristocratic tradition that conceived of music as a "court" activity of captive intellects. American music is also distinct from the music of the bourgeoisie that substituted orchestral size and sound for song and simplicity. Furthermore, it is not a churchly music, a music based on distinguishing itself from the profane chores of the ordinary world. In fact, only when America produced its unique combination of folk, pop and jazz—or what might be called a tri-track system—was a successful break made with the European modality of musical representation.

It is for these reasons that American music always was and remains closely related to the American masses. So much of this volume is taken up with problems of artist and audience precisely because of the mass character of the music and the unique blend of culture and commerce it represents. If music in America never achieved the synthetic qualities of its European counterparts, it has nonetheless managed to infuse the twentieth century with a sense of the changing relationships between musical values and cultural values. The new balance of rhythmic and harmonic components (with an accent on the rhythmic)not only coincided with the origins of jazz in Afro-European roots, but also coincided with the experience of urban industrial life and the sense of accelerated process.

However, the point of this foreword is not to present yet another discourse, but simply to note that the phrase "American music" means more than geography. It implies a range of social and economic considerations unique to the American experience and to its particularly oppressed minorities, that somehow strangely enough reflect the divided sensibilities and bifurcated loyalties of the American public.

Just as very few people can make a living playing marginal musics like jazz, rock or even classical idioms, even fewer can make a living writing about music. With the exception of the shrunken opportunity area of writing liner notes for recording companies and critical columns for newspapers and magazines, opportunities for writing about music are severely limited. This volume includes the essays of people who are expert in fields as varied as engineering and sociology, but who share an avocational rather than vocational concern for the contemporary music scene. This perhaps is as it should be: a living music attracts odd listening types—thwarted amateur musicians, scholars who see their interests in black liberation best expressed through music, and those for whom music is the most ubiquitous yet most potent expression of the peaks and troughs of American civilization.

Just as one can observe that the professionalization of American music has been a slow and painful experience, and not entirely satisfactory from a technical standpoint, so too can this be said about criticism of American music. Attempts to professionalize criticism have resulted in an arid, formalistic period of criticism, in which the essential issues of musicology have simply gone unexamined. Thus it is that, like the music itself, criticism has been experimental, engaged in by diverse sectors of the intellectual community, and is effective when most defiant of established trends and tendencies. It is the supreme merit of this collection that it has been true to the music and to the musicians, by drawing together a fine list of experimental and engaging writings on the art of music and the craft of musicians.

Rutgers University
New Brunswick, N. J.
September 25, 1971

Acknowledgments

The Editor wishes to acknowledge the former Dean of the Extension Division of Rutgers University, Ernest McMahon, and his successor Hamilton Stillwell for their support in developing the Rutgers Institute of Jazz Studies and for their encouragement in organizing the conference "Jazz and All that Sociology"; its papers constitute the heart of this volume.

I wish to also thank the conference participants for their contributions. They were: Walter Allen, Howard S. Becker, Donald Heckman, Irving Louis Horowitz, Neil Leonard, Richard Peterson, Ernest Smith, Robert Stebbins, Richard Stephenson, William Weinberg and Christopher White.

The help of David Cayer and William Weinberg of the Institute of Jazz Studies Executive Committee during my dissertation research and in planning the conference is gratefully acknowledged. Mary Prioli and Richard Seidel of the Institute staff helped immeasurably in executing both the conference and this book. My colleague, Phillip Hughes, through his insightful criticism and patient discussion has constantly clarified my thinking about sociology and about jazz.

Morroe Berger, the father of the sociology of jazz, has been a constant source of inspiration. This book is Irving Louis Horowitz's "baby" as much as my own; he has been a wellspring of help and encouragement. Mary Curtis has played the role of editor's editor. Her knowledgeable and cogent editing contributed greatly to the clarity of the final manuscript.

This volume is dedicated to my wife Jacqueline. The idea of a conference was hers and her intelligence and good sense is the Polaris by which I am guided.

Introduction

Any collection of materials such as this one could be either twice as long or half as long. In my research on music and musicians I discovered a rather large and substantial analytical literature with sociological significance. The selection in this volume represents a very small portion of that literature. Some of the materials presented here are original and were developed out of papers presented at a symposium on the interfaces of jazz and sociology sponsored by the Rutgers Institute of Jazz Studies and held in Newark in the fall of 1970. Additional essays have been added to the symposium material, especially some papers pertaining to the development of rock.

Jazz and rock represent the mainstream of American popular music over the last 50 years. Other forms have certainly reached audiences during this period—for example, ethnic and folk music, country and western music, and so-called "classical" music—but on the whole jazz and rock have been the major forms exploited for the mass American (and world) audience. The popularity of "folk" music in the early sixties and the rather consistent appearance of country and western tunes in the "top 40" charts attest to the fact that jazz and rock have not completely dominated American

1

popular music. But some form of either jazz or rock has held center stage in this country since the "jazz age" of the "roaring twenties."

Of course I do not wish to imply that the best of jazz and rock became popular or commercial mass music. On the contrary, the most creative and innovative music and musicians have often failed to get a hearing. But we are speaking here of influence. Jazzman Billy Taylor once said to me that he rarely heard a radio or TV commercial or listened to a studio band that was not primarily jazz based. Even the most casual listener must realize how quickly advertisers attempt to achieve product identification with popular rock tunes.

This book describes the important sociohistorical process that shaped and still shapes American popular music, through analyses of the jazz and rock phenomenon/ The first part of the book centers attention on jazz, the second on rock. The presentation of material is roughly chronological, covering aspects of jazz from the twenties through the fifties and rock in the fifties through the sixties. This period, from the twenties into the seventies, was a time of incredible growth in American technology and industry. In a unique way jazz and rock have reflected these changes in American life. Both art forms have "folk" origins, especially in the black South, but their development has depended on technology and urbanism. Transportation and communication media have also played a vital role in developing the two forms. Both jazz and rock owe their vitality to the creative combination of older forms yielding newer ones.

The development of jazz in America is a fascinating case study in the evolution of an art form through the conjoining of literally hundreds of cultural elements and traits from several continents shaped by the vagaries of historical accident. African polyrhythm, for example, was tenaciously retained through generations of cruel slavery and combined with European melodic and instrument development. And

2   INTRODUCTION

the call and response pattern was a part of both African tribal and European religious music. Many other examples of fortuitous historical accidents could be given. The evolution of rock provides yet another case study of a creative historical amalgam. As was the case with jazz, the black rural South provided the wellspring for rock. As it developed, other forms were drawn into the vortex of creativity: Indian, American Indian, country and western and so forth. Both jazz and rock are restless art forms. They use other forms of music and the technology that environs them in a bewildering kaleidoscope of embracement and discard. At their best both forms can delight the listener by drawing him into the crucible of improvisation. Whitney Balliett's characterization of jazz as the "sound of surprise" applies as well to the best of rock.

Jazz and rock have abandoned the security of the folk tradition with its stress on the familiar and on amateurism and boldly seek to make music for (though not necessarily from) the masses. Unlike "classical" music which can always rely on form and an educated elite for support, jazz and rock look to the marketplace for attention. They are both survival musics in the sense that they usually will change rather than die. Both forms are of great interest to the social scientist because of their intimate relationship to urbanism, technology (try to imagine a rock band that is not "plugged in") and mass society. Failure to recognize that jazz and rock represent something new in the arts—a deliberate search for creative *and* popular music—is to miss the sociohistorical lesson that the two forms can provide about ourselves and about the society that we live in.

What follows is a careful selection of material that should lead to a better understanding of American popular music. I have tried to select material that is both lively and scholarly. The major purpose of this collection is to stimulate the reader into further investigation of these two companion arts and the society which generated them.

Part I:
Bix Lives
to Bird Lives:
The Jazz
Phenomena

Jazz has its roots in the expression of an oppressed people. It began in the field chants of black slaves so constricted by their cruel environment that only a primal cry could be their emotional outlet. Slaves from many distinctive African cultures, often speaking in tongues foreign to each other as well as to their oppressors, were forced to reach deep within themselves in order to find common modes of association, shaped always by the repressive social structure which channeled, restricted and directed the breadth if not the depth of their expression.

Those field chants, coupled later with work songs, spirituals and the blues, created an amalgam within the American black social world that interacted with forms already present in the larger society. Jazz was born. This lusty offspring of crosscultural fertilization, this slave child of the arts, was to achieve heights rarely paralleled in the history of music. Born in America at the turn of the century, in something less than the biblical four score and ten years jazz has grown to maturity. It has produced offspring, most notably rock. One can hardly understand musical America without knowing its biography.

In what I think is the best single piece of work done by a social scientist on the adolescence of jazz, Morroe Berger chronicles the repressive treatment accorded black jazz in white America. Using jazz as a case study Berger marshals evidence to "confirm the hypothesis that in the diffusion process the prestige of the donors has considerable bearing on the way in which a borrowing group reacts to cultural traits of other groups." He convincingly argues that the low social status of blacks in America colored the evaluation of their contribution to the arts. The jazz musician is an "invisible man," contributing mightily to American cultural life yet usually rewarded with facelessness and anonymity. Professor Berger also documents effectively the negative reaction of American guardians of morality to "sinful" jazz. Vested interest groups in other forms of music joined in the antijazz crusade. "Jazz: Resistance to the Diffusion of a Culture-Pattern" is a moving chronicle of yet another facet of American racism as well as a sociohistorical document on American music.

In his book, *Jazz and the White Americans,* Neil Leonard applies the principle of dialectical development to jazz. He summarizes this position in the conclusion of that book.

> A new art form or style, touching upon the basic assumptions of a culture-system, usually provokes controversy. Traditionalists, that is, those who hold strongly to conventional values (esthetic and non-esthetic), tend to disregard or oppose the innovation. On the other hand, modernists, who find that the innovation satisfies esthetic and other needs, react against traditionalist opposition by drawing together in an area of understanding or brotherhood and often ignore or flout important traditional values. Before long, a group of moderates arises and tries to bridge the gap between the sensibilities of the camps.

In the section reprinted here, "The Impact of Mechanization," Professor Leonard discusses the impact of recording, film and radio on the development of jazz. He tells us that the acceptance of jazz in the mass media was won through a compromise which involved suppressing some of the more vigorous elements of black jazz in favor of a "refined" or "symphonic" jazz that certain moral entrepreneurs felt would be more acceptable to mass audiences.

Howard S. Becker's contribution is a distillation of his classic analysis of dance band musicians from the book *Outsiders*. Becker contrasts jazz (free self-expression) with commercial music (influenced by outside, nonmusic, pressures). Some musicians playing in dance bands are frustrated because they hold jazz values and yet are forced to play commercial music. The discussion presented here, "The Culture and Career of the Dance Musician," is summarized by Becker:

> ... the emphasis of musicians on freedom from the interference inevitable in their work creates a new dimension of professional prestige which conflicts with the previously discussed job prestige in such a way that one cannot rank high in both. The greatest rewards are in the hands of those who have sacrificed their artistic independence, and who demand a similar sacrifice from those they recruit for these higher positions. This creates a dilemma for the individual musician, and his response determines the future course of his career. Refusing to submit means that all hope of achieving jobs of high prestige and income must be abandoned, while giving in to commercial pressures opens the way to success for them.

In deft and bold strokes Nat Hentoff outlines the changes that occurred in jazz's professional elite up to the advent of modern rock. His book, *The Jazz Life,* from which "Paying Dues" is excerpted, is written with passion, authority and style and avoids pedantry and sentimentality. Although the advent of modern rock undoubtedly has reduced the potential jazz audience, his description of jazz's new self-awareness as serious music is most accurate. "Most of the younger players now approach jazz as a career with as much seriousness as apprentices in classical music."

While Hentoff is concerned primarily with the jazz elite, Robert Stebbins focuses his attention on local jazz enclaves. Professor Stebbins concludes "that the jazz community lacks institutional completeness: its solutions to the collective problems of socialization, mastery of nature, and social control are inadequate in that the existence of the jazz community and its members is constantly threatened. For this reason, it is better to refer to the jazz community as a 'semicommunity,' a tendency toward community formation which, because of the conditions of its origin, cannot become total."

Richard Peterson (in an essay prepared for this volume) elaborates a process model of jazz history. Professor Peterson's discussion of the evolution of jazz brings to mind the metaphor of a flowing river. Like an active river the art form leaves residues behind on the terrain it traverses. The schematic presentation on page 138 represents Peterson's view of how jazz has changed and developed.

In another essay prepared for this volume and presented at the Rutgers Institute of Jazz Studies Symposium Neil Leonard discusses the influence of jazz on artists working in other media. His work provides a glimpse of the enormous impact that jazz has had on American culture and on art in general. As Professor Leonard says: "I am suggesting here that jazz was an important element in the sensibility of the Atlantic community in the first part of this century and that the new music, however diluted, found its way into the works of artists who did not necessarily like it, or its derivatives."

In the final chapter in Part I, I have reviewed some of the jazz literature and have attempted to develop a typology that may aid in understanding some of the controversy that has grown up around sociological writings on jazz. In it, I offer some suggestions for future research based on a division of the jazz literature into two types. Much confusion has grown up because writers are often not clear about whether they are discussing jazz from the broad perspective of macrosociology (the assimilationists) or from that of circumscribed groups of musicians (the subculturists).

Jazz:
Resistance to the
Diffusion of
a Culture Pattern

MORROE BERGER

The purpose of this chapter is to examine the implications, for the diffusion of jazz, of the fact that Negroes, with whom jazz is correctly associated, are a low-status group in the United States. The evidence to be presented will confirm the hypothesis that in the diffusion process the prestige of the donors has considerable bearing on the way in which a borrowing group reacts to cultural traits of other groups. Thus mere exposure to certain influences does not insure acceptance of them.

From this hypothesis and the fact of the Negroes' inferior status, the following facts may be expected to follow:

1) Leaders and representatives of the white community, especially those who concern themselves with "public morality" and education, opposed the acceptance of jazz music and the dances accompanying it. The basic reason for this opposition is the identification of jazz with crime, vice and greater sexual freedom than is countenanced by the common rules of morality. Certain leaders among the Negroes could be expected to take a similar position.

11

2) The musicians (and those on the periphery of the profession) associated with "classical" music and forms of popular music other than jazz, also opposed the introduction of jazz, since it was produced by musicians who were not educated in the familiar tradition, and did not conform to rules of public conduct developed by centuries of the concert stage.

3) The white South did not accept jazz to the same degree as the white North, since in the South the Negro is in a lower status position than in the North.

4) Throughout the United States, jazz was not so readily accepted as other forms of Negro music, especially spirituals, since they are associated with religious fevor and, in the eyes of white persons at least, show the Negro in a submissive rather than exuberant role.

A review of the relevant data will show that each of the four implications is correct.

OPPOSITION OF COMMUNITY LEADERS

By an analysis of news items, feature articles and letters on jazz that appeared in the *New York Times* between 1919 and 1944, a picture of the sources of opposition to the introduction of jazz may be obtained. For present purposes this survey may be confined to the period 1919-1927, the years in which jazz was making its first major penetration of white society in America as the effects of the wanderings of New Orleans jazz players and the production of their recordings were being felt. During this nine-year span only three items reported favorable statements on jazz by community leaders, church leaders or educators, while 18 items reported unfavorable statements by them. The three favorable statements, however, were not unqualified. Two of them came in 1924 from Otto Kahn, businessman and then Chairman of the Board of Directors of the Metropolitan Opera Company. Early in 1924, his son, Roger Wolf Kahn, had startled polite society by announcing his intention to form a jazz orchestra.[1] Under the influence of the youth, the elder Kahn became interested in jazz, and in November of 1924 he said in a talk to the Brooklyn Chamber of Commerce: "There is a vast amount of talent among players and composers of jazz. It will have to purge itself of crudities, it will have to frown upon vulgarity . . .it will have to aim, as some of its leaders do, at evolution from its present stage. We should try to help and hasten that process."[2]

The last of the three favorable statements came in 1927, from the President of the National Federation of Music Clubs. This too was only qualified toleration of jazz, rather than acceptance of it. Stating that the music clubs were sympathetic to jazz but opposed to jazz treatment of the classics, the president remarked, in what appears to have been a mood of resignation: "We have no fight with any new movements, but the music clubs . . . are anxious to see that the great classical compositions are undisturbed."[3]

Both of these remarks exemplify an attitude toward jazz that will be discussed later in this chapter. This attitude is that jazz must be made less vulgar and more refined, and must keep its "proper" place. It was at once a feeling that jazz was something for the masses for whom classical music was too highbrow, yet it must not debase the wide number of persons attracted to it; jazz was simultaneously to have its standards raised and its place fixed below that of traditionally accepted music.

Those who opposed jazz with no qualification whatever saw in it an appeal to sensuousness, a return to primitive forms, and described it as the music of persons without any training. Calling jazz an "agency of the devil," the pastor of the Calvary Baptist Church in New York said in 1926: "Jazz, with its . . . appeal to the sensuous, should be stamped out."[4] The rector of the Episcopal Church of the Ascension in New York said in 1922: "Jazz is retrogression. It is going to the African jungle for our music."[5] A professor of romance languages at an eastern university said in 1925: "Most of the jazz music, like jazz literature and jazz thinking, is the product of an untrained mind. . . ."[6] Henry Ford identified jazz dancing with urban life. Opening a campaign with Mrs. Ford in 1925 to drive out jazz dances and revive polkas, waltzes and quadrilles, he said: "It is only in the cities that jazz has taken its place."[7] The lengths to which opponents of jazz went is revealed by a law suit, brought in Cincinnati in 1926, by the Salvation Army to prevent the building of a movie house next to one of its homes for girls. It was argued that babies would be "subjected to the implanting of jazz emotions by such enforced proximity to a theatre and jazz palace."[8]

In 1921 the National Music Chairman of the General Federation of Women's Clubs wrote an article in which she expressed all the current feeling against the new music. It was barbaric, she said, and that "it has a demoralizing effect upon the human brain has been demonstrated by many scientists." Jazz was "the expression of protest against law and order, that bolshevik element of license striving for expression in music."[9] The National Association of Teachers of Speech, in a similar vein, in 1931 included "jazz" among a list of the ten most unpleasant words in English."[9]

Among the Negroes, too, there were some leaders who opposed jazz as debasing the Negro community and preventing its advance along the line of acceptance of the white standards in all realms. Negroes associated with jazz music as players, singers, dancers, promoters and managers make relatively high incomes for Negroes. The class hierarchy among Negroes, as Davis and Gardner show, is largely determined by qualifications other than those of income and occupation, since white society excludes Negroes from the "better" types of work and thus limits their occupational range. The result is that upper-class Negroes cannot segregate themselves from other classes of Negroes to the extent that they would like. As Davis and Gardner state: "They feel that it is lamentable at dances, at church—or even in college fraternities, of all places—with porters, waitresses, and jazz-band musicians."[1 1]

Leaders of Negro communities have spoken out against the influence of jazz. This is to be expected of those "race leaders" who believe that Negroes can improve their status mainly by acceptance of the standards of the white community, which clearly disapproved of jazz as barbaric and sensual—characterizations which Negroes have tried to dissociate from themselves.

The chief pastor of the First Emmanuel Church, Independent Christian, in Harlem, commended the city's announced policy of restricting "disreputable" dance halls in 1926. Commenting on this policy, the editor of the Negro paper, the *New York Age,* said that Negroes wanted to maintain a "high class of respectability" in their neighborhoods, and he attacked the immorality at Harlem rent-parties, in which a particular style of piano jazz was being developed that is now associated with the names of James P. Johnson, "Fats" Waller and Willie "The Lion" Smith. At the same time, Negro residents of a particular block on West 113th Street protested against granting dance-hall privileges to a building run by the Independent Order of Saint Luke.[1 2]

During the revival of jazz and "swing" in 1935-1940, similar objections were voiced by Negro spokesmen. In 1939 the *Pittsburgh Courier,* a Negro paper, received many letters protesting the "swinging" of Negro spirituals. The secretary of the Antioch Missionary Baptist Association wrote from Natchez, Mississippi: "We . . . protest this insidious evil. Music as it is now sung, in gin shops, dance halls, on records, by orchestras, black and white, is truly a disgrace to the entire race." A music teacher in an Alabama high school for Negroes wrote: "The sacrilegious desecration of our 'spirituals' . . . is entirely wrong and out of place."[1 3] This defense of the spiritual against jazz treatment is especially significant since, as will be shown later, spirituals constitute the main Negro contribution in art that has been considered wholesome and worthy of imitation by the most conservative levels of white society.

The treatment of jazz by Negro writers reveals that it is not considered the kind of cultural achievement of the race that ought to be mentioned or recommended. Thus *The Journal of Negro History* from its inception in 1916 through the issues of 1946 did not publish a single article on jazz or a single review of a book on jazz. Of five articles dealing with Negro music, which appeared in 1919, 1932, 1935, 1939 and 1942, only one refers to jazz even briefly. This was an article on "Negro Musicians and Their Music," which mentioned jazz in a way that could not be recognized by persons who are not very familiar with the music. At the end of a paragraph on Negro composers, the writer mentioned "Clarence Williams, native of Louisiana, who has produced and published over one thousand compositions."[14] No indication was given that Williams grew up with jazz in New Orleans, played it, wrote down many of its tunes and later became a music publisher.

The most prominent chroniclers of Negro achievement in America, Benjamin Brawley, W. E. B. DuBois and Edwin R. Embree, scarcely mention jazz in their books. In a book called *The Negro in Literature and Art,* published in 1918, Brawley did not mention jazz in a chapter on music.[15] In the next year he published a revised edition of his 1913 volume, *Short History of the American Negro,*[16] but again made no mention of jazz even in a chapter entitled "Literature and Art." In 1937 Brawley's *Negro Builders and Heroes*[17] appeared, but in 292 pages on the Negro's contribution to American life no discussion of jazz was included. In *Black Folk Then and Now,*[18] published in 1939, DuBois ignored jazz in his one-paragraph discussion of American Negro music. Only Edwin R. Embree appears to have been influenced to some extent by the white music critics and historians who have written extensively since 1935 about New Orleans jazz. In his *Brown America*[19] published in 1937, he gave two pages to the Negro in jazz.

16 MORROE BERGER

Although such direct and implied unfavorable views of jazz have declined in the last decade, occasionally there is still some prejudice expressed against it, and even implemented as well. In June of 1945 the director of the Hollywood Bowl refused to rent the stadium for a jazz concert, stating that he did not like the word "jazz" to be associated with it.[20] In February 1946 the managing director of Constitution Hall in Washington, D. C., refused to rent the auditorium to a jazz band leader who had given concerts in Carnegie Hall and Town Hall in New York. In rejecting the musician's request, the director of Constitution Hall stated that this action was taken "not because of the attraction itself but rather because of the type of audience which attends. . . ."[21]

The writers of "Topics of the Times" in the *New York Times* have represented intelligent, conservative opinion in America. The treatment of jazz in this column reveals the early rejection of jazz and the eventual resigned and good-humored toleration of it during the revival of jazz in the form of "swing" in 1935-1940.

During 1924 "Topics of the Times" compared jazz to the new types of poetry: "Jazz is to real music exactly what most of the 'new poetry,' so-called, is to real poetry. Both are without the structure and form essential to music and poetry alike, and both are the products, not of innovators, but of incompetents."[22]

A few weeks later the columnist suggested that the "merits of jazz" could be determined by comparing "the intelligence of those who like it with that of those whom it wearies and offends."[23] A month after this and twice during 1925 there appeared in "Topics of the Times" remarks extremely derogatory of jazz bands,[24] of the music itself,[25] and of its effect.[26] By 1926, however, the writer of "Topics of the Times" found jazz somewhat subdued: ". . . in general, the very tones of jazz have softened, and its days of hilarity are behind it."[27] This judgement turned out to be not quite correct, but at the time of the "swing craze" of the late 1930s, a *Times* editorial looked upon the phenomenon with more good humor. Commenting on the conduct of jitterbugs at the Carnival of Swing held on Randall's Island in New York in 1938, the editorial stated: "But there was not a mite of harm in them. They were of all races, all colors, all walks—or rather all swings and shags—of life."[28]

MUSIC PROFESSION AND BUSINESS

The reception of jazz among *nonjazz* musicians and persons on the periphery of the profession, such as dancing masters, music dealers, critics and dance hall owners, according to news items in the *New York Times,* was more mixed than among the leaders of church, business and community and the educators.

Between 1919 and 1944 there were 14 items in which the musical group attacked jazz, and nine in which they defended it. In addition, there were five items in which musicians usually associated with jazz spoke against certain trends within jazz which, they said, ought to be eliminated. These items will be considered separately.

Of the 14 items unfavorable to jazz, six reported the views of music performers, four the views of dance teachers, two of music critics, one of a group of dance hall owners, and one of a music dealer. The objections of the performers, composers and critics are closely related, and usually were directed at jazz musicians as a group, the effects of jazz, and its alleged base qualities. As late as 1941, the pianist-conductor José Iturbi refused to perform at a Robin Hood Dell concert with jazz clarinetist Benny Goodman, who was scheduled to play a Mozart concerto. Iturbi stated: ". . . it would be detrimental to me to appear with a jazz-band leader."[29] (A few years later he apparently took a different view of what constituted dignity for a classical musician, for he appeared in a comedy role and as a pianist with the comic Jimmy Durante in a Hollywood movie called "Music for Millions.") In 1928 the conductor, Walter Damrosch, addressing a conference of music teachers, said of jazz: "It is rhythm without music and without soul. . . . Undoubtedly it stifles the true musical instinct."[30] In 1924 a concert pianist in New York said that jazz was permissible in the cabaret and dance hall, "but it should not be permitted to invade the sacred precincts of our concert halls."[31]

The close association of jazz with certain styles of dancing brought dancing teachers into the controversy over jazz. With the rise of one-step dances between 1914 and 1918, community and church leaders attacked them as vulgar. The steps were prohibited by church groups, and dance halls in large cities, especially New York and Chicago, were charged with harboring immoral dancing and serving as rendezvous for prostitutes and their customers. This campaign against dancing threatened the livelihood of traditional "dancing masters," who strove to dissociate their own work from the kind of dancing that drew the heated objections. Thus in 1919 the National Association of Dancing Masters, at their New York convention, launched a campaign against jazz dancing and other extreme steps, especially the shimmy.[32]

Performers' and composers' views constitute a very large portion of the statements favorable to jazz. Of ten *New York Times* items in favor of jazz between 1919 and 1944, eight reported the opinions of performers and composers of nonjazz music, and two reported the remarks of critics. These statements, in general, dealt with the purely musical aspects of jazz, and pointed to its vitality or its possibilities in "art music." Leopold Godowsky announced in 1924 that he would use a jazz theme in a new work, adding: "Jazz music is a revelation in rhythm."[33] Leopold Stokowski in the same year claimed that jazz held out "wonderful possibilities for the future."[34] Twenty years later, defending jazz against an attack by Artur Rodzinski, Stokowski said that jazz is being absorbed into "art music."[35]

As was mentioned above, five items in the *Times* reported unfavorable views on certain aspects of jazz by performers and composers who were associated with jazz. The views expressed in these items correspond to the dancing masters' attempt to purge dancing of steps that provoked widespread complaint. Thus these performers and composers were using the jazz idiom, to some degree, but were trying to eliminate objections to jazz by eschewing the features objected to. In 1927 a committee of the National Association of Orchestra Directors was formed to investigate improper dancing and "bad jazz," in an effort to raise the standards of jazz.[36] In 1935 Irving Berlin stated: "Jazz music, and mind you I don't like that word jazz, but for want of a better expression we'll call it that, is American folk music. It began with the old southern songs of Stephen Foster and the negro spirituals, but it isn't purely negro in its characteristics. . . ." Obviously referring not to New Orleans jazz but to the music of Tin Pan Alley, Berlin clearly tried to give jazz a more respectable pedigree—Stephen Foster and the spirituals and non-Negro elements, rather than Negro work songs, blues and the music played in bawdy-houses.

A different perspective on the music profession's attitude toward jazz is offered by the treatment of jazz in three magazines devoted to older music: *The Etude, The Musician* and *The Musical Quarterly*. Between 1922 and 1941 there appeared in all three periodicals a total of 21 articles rejecting all kinds of jazz; seven articles rejecting all jazz except the "advanced," highly orchestrated jazz of the large bands such as Paul Whiteman's; seven articles granting jazz a limited, minor place in music and two articles treating jazz unapologetically as worthwhile music in itself.

The years 1922-41 may be divided into four periods, roughly coinciding with certain jazz trends. 1922-25 was a period in which New Orleans Negroes were enjoying relative popularity in Chicago, and in which young white musicians were learning to play their style. 1926-29 were years in which Negroes and white jazz players became more popular in larger bands than formerly, especially in New York. From 1930 through 1934 jazz was in an eclipse, with many players

MORROE BERGER

dropping out of music and others joining nonjazz bands playing popular dance music. During 1935-41 jazz enjoyed a revival of popularity both in a form closely related to the original and as "swing."

The music magazines gave jazz different treatment in each of these four periods. It was not until 1935 that an article[37] appeared which accepted jazz as music worthwhile in itself, without qualifying this acceptance in any way. Even this article, however, did not discuss the place or merits of jazz, but rather its influence on French music. The first genuine acceptance of jazz did not come until 1941, in an article in *The Musical Quarterly*.[38] This article is significant in three aspects: (1) it is the only one published in all three magazines from 1922 through June 1945 which showed the writer's awareness that there was a kind of music called hot jazz whose devotees have as much or more contempt for popular commercial jazz and swing as the most serious advocates of classical music; (2) it is the only article in all three magazines during the same period in which the author fully accepted jazz without qualification as a genuine artistic achievement; (3) the author is not a traditionalist in music or other realms, for he has written frequently on the arts in publications that proclaim their adherence to Marxism, namely, *Science and Society*, *New Masses* and *The Daily Worker*.

Although no other writer for these three music periodicals went so far, the growing popularity of jazz had some effect upon musical discussion. During 1922-25 seven out of a total of eight articles rejected all of jazz; during 1926-29 six out of nine took this position; during 1930-34, four out of five; and during the recent revival of 1935-40, only four out of 15. To complement this diminishing proportion of articles rejecting jazz without qualification, a growing proportion of articles on jazz saw something commendable in it. The proportions, for the same periods, of the articles praising "advanced" jazz or giving jazz in general a limited place in music, are: one out of eight for 1922-25; three out of nine for 1926-29; one out of five for 1930-34; and nine out of 13 for 1935-41. If we include in the last period the two articles fully accepting jazz, the proportion then becomes 11 out of 15.

A comparison of the first and last periods shows the growing toleration of jazz, and the recognition of it as having some worth. It must still be recalled, however, that of all the articles on jazz in all three of the magazines for the entire period 1919 through June 1945, only one showed an understanding of hot jazz as opposed to its imitators, and an unqualified acceptance of this kind of popular music.

Music teachers in public and private schools are the upholders and transmitters of classical musical orthodoxy in the United States. The magazine which is edited with the special purpose of appealing to this group is *The Etude*. Hence a more detailed consideration of its treatment of jazz should reveal more of the nature of the opposition to jazz from this source.

In general *The Etude* has been unfavorable to jazz since 1923, when it began to discuss this music extensively in editorials and signed articles. As jazz continued to grow in popularity in various forms, writers in *The Etude* began to find certain of its qualities to be acceptable as "good music," although jazz as a whole was still deplored. Towards the end of the 1920s and in the early 1930s apparently the editors felt pressure of a different sort, for they began to publish material advising music teachers to yield to youth's inclinations toward jazz but to use this seeming retreat in order to conquer their pupils' interest in jazz. At the same time they also published material instructing readers in the technical mastery of jazz forms.

As a magazine edited for persons concerned with musical education, *The Etude's* treatment of jazz shows some ambivalent tendencies. While presenting its readers with articles and editorials praising certain kinds of jazz it also offered material rejecting jazz as a whole. As will become evident from quotations from this material, *The Etude* was

MORROE BERGER

caught between a desire to reject jazz as "unlearned" music, vulgar and of immoral origin and effect, and desire to keep its readers in touch with music students' tastes and inclinations, as well as with the public taste in music, so that those readers who were also performers might know what audiences wanted.

From 1923 (the year in which the *Readers' Guide* lists *The Etude's* first discussion of jazz) until June 1945, *The Etude* printed 13 articles and editorials the main point of which was that all jazz is to be rejected (the last item of this group appeared in 1940). The keynote to *The Etude's* approach to jazz is expressed in its first editorial on the subject in January 1924: "First, Jazz, at its worst, is an unforgivable orgy of noise, a riot of discord, usually perpetrated by players of scant musical training . . . . Second, Jazz, at its worst, is often associated with vile surroundings, filthy words, unmentionable dances. . . . Yet, in the music itself there is often much that is charming and genuinely fascinating when written and played effectively. There is no more harm in well-written jazz than there is in a Liszt Rhapsody. . . . Good Jazz can be a wholesome tonic; bad Jazz is always a dangerous drug."[3 9]

A few months later[4 0] *The Etude* conducted a symposium on jazz, presenting the views of six composers, four performers and three writers. Eight of the statements were favorable to "advanced" or "refined" jazz as clever or amusing or as an "expression" of the era. Five contributors rejected jazz without qualification. None of the 13 showed awareness of the existence of hot jazz as distinguished from the more popular kind played by large bands. In announcing the symposium, *The Etude* stated: "We . . . do most emphatically *not endorse* Jazz, merely by *discussing* it." The same editorial reiterated the magazine's "stand": "Jazz, like much of the thematic material glorified by the great masters of the past, has come largely from the humblest origin.

"In its original form it has no place in musical education and deserves none. It will have to be transmogrified many times before it can present its credentials for the Valhalla of music." Again it praised the work and "skilled hands of such orchestral leaders of high-class jazz orchestras conducted by Paul Whiteman, Isham Jones, Waring and others . . . ."[41]

In the very next issue[42] *The Etude* continued the symposium by presenting the views of three composers, two performers and two writers. Four of the statements rejected all jazz as vulgar, two saw acceptable qualities in highly orchestrated jazz, and one (the conductor, Stokowski, again) considered jazz worthy in its own right.

Four months later, in the January 1925 issue,[43] the editors reported that in the four months since the symposium they had received many letters and articles on jazz from readers. Twenty-five percent of these contributions, the editors stated, approved of the "better kind of jazz," while 75 percent opposed all jazz. The editors gave some evidence of the opposition to jazz expressed by the readers, as well as of their own viewpoint, in a report of a drawing that had been received:

"On one side was a desolate old back yard, filled with rubbish, tin cans and weeds, representing Jazz, with a beautiful flower growing out of the heap representing 'the better kind of Jazz.' On the other side was a glorious garden representing good music, beautiful music.

"We must admit that the comparison was a powerful and fairly accurate one. . . ."

The first popular period of jazz in white society was the early 1920s. *The Etude's* reaction to this trend has just been reviewed. When jazz reached another period of upsurge beginning in 1935, *The Etude's* reaction was somewhat different. In the first period, as has been shown, it stressed the unacceptable features of jazz and only briefly mentioned "the better kind of jazz." Thus between 1923 and 1926 it printed seven articles and editorials critical of all jazz, and none which dealt *mainly* with "the better type." But between 1935 and 1940, *The Etude* published only two

MORROE BERGER

articles critical of all jazz, and nine articles devoted *mainly* to pointing out that *some* jazz was acceptable.

As it had done during the 1920s *The Etude* again in the 1930s praised the kind of jazz that required considerable musical training, and the musicians and bandleaders who had such training. This was the only criterion that the editors and writers seemed to apply in their distinction between good and bad jazz. Good jazz was highly orchestrated and required training. Bad jazz was not scored and was played by untrained men. This is not surprising in view of the fact that "unlearned" music leaves no place for the musical educator, or reduces his role in the musical world.

Between 1938 and 1943, *The Etude* published extensive interviews with four popular bandleaders, always stressing the training of jazz musicians. Bandleader Phil Spitalny in 1938 pointed out that jazz players need musical education.[44] The following year Paul Whiteman revealed in an interview that untrained musicians and unscored jazz are disdained.[45] In 1940 a writer interviewing Fred Waring mentioned only "rhythm work" and "rhythm players," not jazz.[46] The editors in announcing an interview with Raymond Scott in 1943 said of him: "A seriously trained musician, he has brought to jazz a sound musical background. . . ."[47] A year later *The Etude* published an article signed by Paul Whiteman and introduced him in these terms: "Most people think of Mr. Whiteman as a jazz musician. Actually, he is a musician who has chosen to devote himself to jazz. . . . He is first of all a serious and thoughtful musician. He has had thorough musical schooling. His father was at one time supervisor of music in the public schools of Denver. . . ."[48] Thus the editors placed Whiteman in a familiar, acceptable context for readers of *The Etude*.

Another expression of *The Etude's* ambivalent attitude toward jazz is revealed in two further types of treatment: articles suggesting ways in which music teachers can remove or diminish their pupils' interest in jazz, and technical discussions explaining how jazz techniques may be mastered.

The first of the articles suggesting how youth might be weaned from jazz was written by a music teacher in 1928.[49] Using the title, "Yes, I Teach 'Em Jazz," the writer said that she used jazz as "bait" to get her pupils interested in "good" music. In 1934 another teacher wrote on "Conquering the Jazz Craze of Young Pianists."[50] This teacher's technique was to "dose" pupils with "light jazz pieces" to such an extent that "a dislike would be created for it." When they became tired of jazz, the teacher kept requiring them to play it until they could no longer stand it and were happy to concentrate only on classical music. The writer stated: "I felt that I had accomplished a real service for classical music and for the pupils themselves."

As late as 1944, a regular columnist for *The Etude,* conducting "The Teacher's Round Table," offered similar advice to teachers.[51] Two readers had written asking for suggestions for dealing with boogie-woogie music. One wrote: "Will you please discuss the matter of Boogie Woogie. In my teaching I run up against this constantly, and I permit it. . . . Will you tell me frankly if I am wrong in doing this—for I can take it!" The second reader asked: "Please tell me what to do with a boy, fifteen years old, who wants to play only Boogie Woogie? . . ." *The Etude's* advice to the second reader was to follow the first reader's practice and permit the boy to play boogie-woogie, since the chances were "ten to one" that he would eventually return to his love of good music. "But be sure to make your boy *slave* at his B.W. while the craze lasts. . . . If you follow this task I'm sure your 'Boogieman' will soon fade into the limbo of unremembered adolescent problems."

The role of jazz as a preliminary to appreciation of classical music is stressed in other articles in *The Etude*. In an aforementioned article[52] Paul Whiteman stated of jazz: "It is not a substitute for Beethoven. . . . But it can help lead one to Beethoven! . . ." In an editorial in 1938[53] *The Etude*

MORROE BERGER

pointed out that jazz music "supports" radio and thus permits listeners to hear classical music too. Though jazz is not good music, the editorial continued, it is often the first step toward the appreciation of good music. "Many a beautiful flower has blossomed where there was once a dung hill."

Along with unfavorable statements about all jazz and favorable statements about "advanced" jazz, The Etude printed two articles designed to help its readers acquire jazz techniques. One in 1931 discussed "The Right and the Wrong Way to Interpret Syncopation,"[54] in a largely nonevaluative vein, with the implication, then, that this technique was a legitimate one. In 1942, a similar article appeared, entitled "Swing Music in Accordion Playing."[55] Without taking a stand on whether the accordion player should or should not "swing," the author explained how swing music could be played on the instrument by already accomplished technicians.

JAZZ IN THE SOUTH AND THE NORTH

One of the implications of the fact that jazz has been associated with the Negro is that it would not be accepted so readily where the Negro is more depressed and would flow to those areas among whites where the Negro is treated with a greater degree of equality. Thus jazz would be expected to find more imitators and listeners among northern than among southern whites. There are four types of evidence that bear out this expectation: the place of birth and upbringing of the white imitators of Negro New Orleans jazz; the geographical distribution of Negro musicians in 1930; the geographical distribution of the sale of hot jazz records for the periods for which such data are available; and the geographical distribution of sales of magazines devoted exclusively to hot jazz music of Negroes and whites.

1) Various sources[56] give the place of birth and upbringing of 41 white musicians who imitated Negro New Orleans jazz.

New Orleans and its environs are excluded from this computation, because New Orleans whites were at the very scene of the emergence of jazz, and New Orleans has a tradition of Negro-white relations much different from that of the rest of the South. Of these 41 white musicians who imitated jazz, only two were born in the South, one in Texas and one in Tennessee. In one sense this trend was to be expected in view of the evidence, given in the next paragraph, that a large proportion of all Negro musicians and music teachers lived in the North in 1930. Besides, as is shown in another section, the migration of New Orleans Negro jazz players was to the North, rather than to other parts of the South.

2) The geographical distribution of Negro musicians is not so good an index of the relative popularity of jazz in the North and the South as the others discussed in this section. Nevertheless the data on this point have some relevance if we make two reasonable assumptions: that a substantial proportion of the Census classification of Negro "musicians and music teachers" was made up of jazz players; that Negro jazz players would tend to move to those parts of the country where they could expect to be paid reasonably well, that is, to where jazz was accepted, rather than where it was not accepted.

The only data here are for 1930. Reid made some relevant computations from a table in the Bureau of the Census volume on *Negroes in the United States, 1920-1932.*[57] In 1930 the North had 20.3 percent of the total United States Negro population, but 58 percent of all Negro musicians and music teachers were living in the North. In the same year the South had 78.7 percent of the Negro population, but only 36.2 percent of the Negro musicians and music teachers. Thus the North was higher both absolutely and relatively. This greater number and proportion in the North may be interpreted merely as an indication of the generally broader opportunities for Negroes in the North. Yet the data mean more than this in the light of the fact that of all the Negroes in the principal professions, only 22.1 percent were living in the North in 1930, while 76.4 percent were living in the South. Thus the greater number and proportion of Negro musicians and music teachers in the North is not merely an indication of the general wider opportunities for Negroes there, but show that Negro musicians are very strikingly attracted to the North or are born there. In either case, these data suggest, however obliquely, that Negro music, of which jazz has been the most widespread form, was in 1930 far more accepted in the North than in the South.[58]

3) In 1946 there were two magazines devoted to hot jazz: *The Record Changer*, published in Washington, D. C., and *The Jazz Record*, in New York City. Subscriptions and retail sales of both magazines totalled 3,557 in December of 1946. Of this number, 76.3 percent were in the following states: California, Illinois, Mississippi, Michigan, New Jersey, New York, Ohio, Pennsylvania and the District of Columbia. The 16 states included in the Census Bureau's classifications, South Atlantic, East South Central, West South Central, had only 11 percent of the total copies distributed. If we omit Virginia and Maryland, most of whose sales are to persons from various states who work for the federal government in the District of Columbia, then the remaining 14 southern states have only 6.5 percent of the total sales. These 14 states, however, comprised 27.7 percent of the total population in the continental United States in 1940.[59]

4) Data on the sales of records in the United States are not compiled for all labels and for geographical divisions. An estimate, however, has been made for this study by Milton Gabler, president of Commodore Records, the leading company in the hot jazz field, and executive of Decca Records, one of the three largest commercial recording companies. After consultation with representatives of other companies, and an examination of shipping forms for the two companies with which he is associated, Gabler was able to make

confident estimates of the geographical distribution of sales of the three types of nonclassical music, for 1935, 1940 and 1946. The nature of the recording business necessitated the use of regions different from those used by the Bureau of the Census. As used in the following discussion, the *Northeast* includes the following states: Maine, New Hampshire, Vermont, Massachusetts, Rhode Island, Connecticut, New York, New Jersey, Pennsylvania, Delaware, Maryland, District of Columbia. The *Southeast* includes Virginia, West Virginia, North Carolina, South Carolina, Georgia, Florida. The *North Central and Mountain* states include Ohio, Indiana, Illinois, Michigan, Wisconsin, Minnesota, Iowa, Missouri, North Dakota, South Dakota, Nebraska, Kansas, Montana, Wyoming, Idaho, Colorado, New Mexico, Arizona, Utah, Nevada. The *South Central* states include Kentucky, Tennessee, Alabama, Mississippi, Arkansas, Louisiana, Oklahoma, Texas. The *Pacific* states include Washington, Oregon, California.

From 1935 to 1946 the Northeastern and North Central (including the Mountain) states accounted for about three-fourths of all the United States sales of hot jazz records; there has been a slight decline in this proportion since about 1939. The Southeastern and South Central states, however, in the same period, together accounted for only about a tenth of the total sales of records of this kind of popular music; this proportion has also declined slightly, since about 1940. Meanwhile during this 11-year span the proportion of hot jazz records sold in the Pacific states (mainly California) rose from about a tenth of the total sales in the United States to about a third.

While the sale of jazz records to the two southern regions in 1946 comprised only about a tenth of the total sales in the United States, the proportion of popular, commercial records of songs (heard most often in the movies and on the radio) sold to the South was about a fifth in 1946. What are called "popular dance" records are made mainly by white bands, such as those led by Glen Gray, Ted Weems, Kay Kyser,

　　　　　　　　　　　　　　　　　　MORROE BERGER

Sammy Kaye and Guy Lombardo. Of all the kinds of American popular music derived in any degree from Negro jazz, this kind is *farthest* removed from the hot jazz developed largely by Negroes in New Orleans around 1900. The South, then, buys about a fifth of all records of this kind of music, whereas it buys only about a tenth of the total number of hot jazz records sold. Hot jazz is the class of popular music that is closest in form and spirit (and even performers) to New Orleans jazz.

Before 1935 the distinction between hot jazz and popular dance music was quite sharp, from the standpoint of the songs played and the musicians who played them, as well as the form and spirit of the two types of music. Since 1935, however, the distinction, while still unmistakable, has become less sharp. The rise of "swing" music offered an opportunity for many hot jazz musicians to make more money by playing in the popular name bands of Benny Goodman, Tommy Dorsey, Artie Shaw and others. At the same time swing music was closer to the form and spirit of Negro hot jazz than popular dance music was or is. Two of the leading swing bands featured Negro players. Benny Goodman's famous quartet included the Negroes Lionel Hampton and Teddy Wilson. During another period, Goodman used the Negro "Cootie" Williams as trumpet soloist outside the trumpet section in the band. Artie Shaw used the Negro trumpeter "Hot Lips" Page. Many Negro orchestras became very popular among swing fans after 1935, for example, those of Jimmy Lunceford, Count Basie, Cab Calloway, and later Lucky Millinder and Lionel Hampton.

Thus swing music, while not so closely associated with the Negro as is hot jazz, nevertheless is connected with him more than is popular dance music. It may be revealing, then, to examine the data on the geographical distribution of swing records. In 1946 the two southern regions accounted for about a tenth of the total sales of swing records, compared with a similar proportion for jazz records and a fifth for popular dance records. The proportion of the national total of swing records sold in the South was almost negligible in 1935 (at the start of the "swing craze"), and rose to a little more than a tenth in 1940, after which it declined.

By an examination of the data on place of birth and upbringing of white musicians, who imitated Negro jazz players, on the geographical distribution of Negro musicians in 1930, on the geographical distribution of sales of two magazines devoted to hot jazz, and on the geographical distribution of the sales of hot jazz, swing and popular dance records, it has been shown that hot jazz music, most associated with the Negro, is accepted by the Northern white community more than by the Southern white community.

ACCEPTANCE OF NEGRO SPIRITUALS

The two broad types of music most closely associated with the Negro in America are jazz and spirituals. To white Americans each type has a different kind of appeal and each attracts different levels of the community. In addition, each type presents to the white a different stereotype of the Negro. We have already seen in this section something of the stereotype of the Negro as the originators and audience of jazz. Now we consider the Negro stereotype constructed by the white who thinks of the Negro in connection with the spiritual.

The fourth implication listed, early in this discussion, as following from the fact of the Negro's low status is that whites who reject jazz partly because of its "immoral" associations are more likely to accept Negro spirituals as worthy of imitation. The reason for this is that the spiritual is, to the white, more consonant with the Negro's social status. The jazz Negro stereotype shows him as happy, but not clownish in the old minstrel style; dangerous because he does not accept the highest white standards of sexual behavior and "law and order"; independent of the bounty of

32   MORROE BERGER

his superiors—in this case, in a form of entertainment. In none of these ways does the Negro conform to his traditional role as an ex-slave and at present an inferior being. Spirituals, on the other hand, present the Negro to the white in a perfectly "safe" mood. Here the Negro is submissive, religious, superstitious, deeply faithful and not given to singing words that the whites fear they cannot understand. As the evidence is offered, these points will not only be validly established but will also become clearer.

Before analyzing the data, two assumptions made in this section must be examined explicitly since they have recently been brought into question. The first is that the spirituals are Negro; the second is that they express submission and only a religious spirit.

During the 1920s a great deal of research was done on the origin of the spiritual, and a group of investigators slowly formed which insisted that this kind of music was first developed by whites and later imitated by Negroes. Individual members of this group attached varying degrees of originality to the Negroes in their use of this white tradition. Guy B. Johnson, however, expressed the general approach: ". . . it is certain that a few white songs have grown out of negro songs, but on the whole it appears that the general pattern and many of the details of the religious music which the negro developed during slavery were borrowed from white music."[60] Two points must be made concerning the relevance of this claim to the thesis of this section. First, whatever the source of original material out of which spirituals developed, the change in that material was, as is implied in Johnson's statement, effected by Negroes. Second, whatever the degree of originality we ought to grant the Negro in the development of spirituals, there is little question but that the white community considers them Negro contributions. This is revealed in the very attempt by Johnson and others to offer some "correction" of this impression by presenting evidence on the origin of the spirituals. Thus, spirituals are still Negro "phenomena" for the purposes of this paper.

On a few occasions writers have attempted to show that the spirituals are not expressions of submissiveness, and that they are more than religious songs. The most recent of these attempts was by Lovell in *The Journal of Negro Education*.[61] In the Negro spiritual, he says, "religion is chiefly an arsenal of pointed darts, a storehouse of images, a means of making shrewd observations." More than religious, they were "the key" to the Negro's "revolutionary sentiments and to his desire to flee the territory." Lovell sees the spirituals as allegories expressing revolt and the longing to escape the South. Over two decades before Lovell's attempt, Hiram K. Moderwell, a writer on drama and music, made a similar attempt in *The New Republic*.[62] He saw the words of spirituals as covert symbols for freedom, and the music itself took a seemingly religious form, he asserted, because "the Negro's longing for freedom was precisely the one emotion to which he dared not give open expression, under pain of the lash." Combining psychoanalysis and functional analysis, then, a plausible case can be made for this point of view. Yet for the purpose of this section, the spiritual may be taken as a submissive, religious phenomenon, since that is how it appears to the white community with whose reception of it we are now concerned. The very attempts of Lovell and Moderwell, to show the spiritual as something else, again shows how strongly this older view of the spiritual is held not only among whites but also among Negroes.

Three types of evidence will be presented to show that the leaders of the white community and the guardians of its values have accepted spirituals, whereas, as we have seen, they have rejected jazz: the extent to which jazz and spirituals are taught in the public grammar and secondary schools of the North and South; the treatment of spirituals in two music magazines; and the treatment of spirituals in the general magazine press.

34   MORROE BERGER

1) A mail survey was conducted in November-December 1946, among the music departments of schools in various northern and southern cities to discover the songbooks used for music instruction in the upper elementary grades and in secondary schools. The results revealed that at least one Negro spiritual, listed as such, appears in at least one of the song books used in the following states and cities:

Southern: North Carolina; Alabama; Louisiana; Nashville and Memphis, Tennessee; Savannah, Atlanta and Columbus, Georgia; Clarksdale, Mississippi. (No returns were received from South Carolina, the only remaining southern state included in the survey.)

Nonsouthern: California; Fort Wayne, Indiana; Newark, New Jersey; Worcester, Massachusetts; Chicago and Springfield, Illinois; Cedar Rapids, Iowa; New York and Rochester, New York; Scranton, Pennsylvania. (No returns were received from Maine, the only remaining nonsouthern state included in the survey.)

The cities and states reporting used five different series of books for the upper elementary grades and the secondary schools. (Books for the lower grades were not used in this computation because spirituals are technically too advanced for them in the opinion of most songbook editors.) Each of the series included at least one Negro song, and in all five there appeared a total of 55 such songs. Most were listed as "Negro Spiritual," a few each as "Negro Melody," "Spiritual," "American Negro Air" or "Southern Melody."

Apart from these five series of books, the cities and states reported eight single texts in use. Of these, only one did not contain a single Negro song. The other seven had a total of 25, designated in the same ways as those in the five series.

Thus in both the five series of texts and the eight single texts there were a total of 80 songs of Negro origin. Of these 80, 55 were listed as "Negro Spiritual" and the other 25 as "Negro Melody," "Spiritual," "American Negro Air" and "Southern Melody."

In all these school songbooks, of course, no jazz songs

were found. In one of them, however, edited in 1941 for high school music instruction, there is a section called "Popular Composers of Modern America."[63] In this section, edited by Sigmund Spaeth, a music critic who has at various times vigorously opposed the influence of jazz, there are eight songs, one each by Jerome Kern, Richard Rodgers, George Gershwin, Arthur Schwartz, Cole Porter, Ferde Grofe, Vincent Youmans and Irving Berlin. Among the popular music writers of Tin Pan Alley and Hollywood, these eight are farthest removed from the influence of Negro jazz. The eight songs reprinted, too, are not even "popular dance" tunes; rather, they are in the tradition of musical comedy tunes derived not so much from jazz as from older types of popular "ballad" music of America.

2) In the discussion of the treatment of jazz in music magazines it was reported that *The Etude, The Musician* and *The Musical Quarterly* printed, between 1922 and 1941, 21 articles rejecting jazz in its entirety, seven rejecting all but "advanced" jazz, seven granting jazz a limited, minor place in music, and two treating jazz as music worthwhile in itself. This presents a sharp contrast to the treatment of spirituals in *The Etude* and *The Musician*. Between 1890 and June 1945, the *Reader's Guide* lists 15 articles on spirituals in these two publications. Every one was favorable to this kind of Negro music. Only two of the 15 (appearing in 1936 and 1942) diverged from the accepted interpretation of the spiritual as an expression of deeply religious feeling, submissiveness, and the desire for religious "escape" from the sufferings imposed by slavery.

Evidence of the acceptance of the spiritual and the rejection of jazz by musical orthodoxy is revealed in three surveys of Negro music published in *The Etude*. In 1924 a Negro violinist and composer, writing on "The Musical Genius of the American Negro," discussed all kinds of Negro music. His one reference to jazz came when he deplored the lack of opportunities for Negro musicians, some of whom, he said, were forced to join jazz bands to earn a living.[64] In 1935 the writer who conducted *The Etude's* "Question and Answer Department" was asked to review "the progress of the Negro in music from the appearance of the spirituals" to the present.[65] In giving what he called a brief summary of the most important events of the present century," the writer made no mention of jazz. In 1936 a Negro composer and music teacher surveyed Negro music from "Spirituals to Symphonies."[66] Though exhibiting considerable pride in Negro musical achievement, the writer did not mention jazz.

3) The general periodical press listed in *Reader's Guide* published 130 articles on jazz between 1917 and June 1945. Of these 130 articles, 28 rejected all jazz, 49 gave jazz a limited, minor place in music, 49 accepted jazz as worthwhile music in itself (the *kind* of magazines which accepted jazz in this way is significant) and four did not evaluate jazz but treated it as just another subject for a magazine article (this is in itself an evaluation, of course). Contrasted with this *divided* reception of jazz is the general periodical press's *unanimous* acceptance of Negro spirituals. Of 32 articles on this subject between 1890 and June 1945, every one was favorable. Four of these 32 articles also dealt with jazz in some detail, rejecting it while accepting the spirituals. Only two · of these 32 articles, however, deviated from the traditional interpretation of the spiritual as an expression of submissiveness to God or fate, the religious "escape" from suffering.

The opposition to jazz and the acceptance of the spiritual was characteristically expressed in 1927 by one writer: "With reference to jazz music. I do not feel that it deserves to have attached to it the same importance as the music already mentioned." Describing jazz as worldly and not favored by religious Negroes, the writer added: "Jazz music is more or less incidental, and is not an index to the negro's soul, as are the spirituals."[67] This intimation by whites that the Negro "spirit" is not "really" represented by jazz occurs frequently.

An editorial in *The Etude* in 1934 expressed the same sentiment after remarking that Negro bands are among the worst of those that play "vulgarized music" (jazz): "When we recollect the lovely things that R. Nathaniel Dett and other Negro composers have produced, many of the monotonous, raucous Negro jazz bands seem like a libel on the race."[6][8] In 1926 the governor of South Carolina, in an interview in New York, said of the Charleston step then sweeping the white North: "When I was a boy all negroes did it, but nowadays they are too respectable."[6][9] This point of view is most extremely represented in an article, published in 1903, by a white southern woman with a reputation as a Negro folklorist.[70] She attacked the writing and spread of "coon songs," which she called "false, flippant." Negroes, she said, should be taught the spirituals, for as they moved into cities they were forgetting this great "slave music." She added: "They should be taught that slavery, with its occasional abuses, was simply a valuable training in their evolution from savagery."

The evidence reviewed in this chapter was intended to show the validity of the four implications said to follow from the hypothesis that in diffusion the prestige of the donors has considerable bearing on the reception given to certain cultural traits by a borrowing group, and the fact that Negroes are a low-status group in this country. These four implications, now established by the evidence, are:

1) Leaders of the white community, especially those concerned with "public morality" and education, opposed jazz music and jazz dances because jazz was considered licentious and was associated with vice and "primitive" conduct. Certain kinds of Negro community leaders were shown to share this attitude.

2) Musicians and persons on the periphery of the profession opposed jazz because it was a new kind of music competing with the old, and it was played by persons who were not educated in the traditional way

and who did not conform to the rules of public conduct evolved by the long history of the concert stage.

3) The white South, holding the Negro in a lower status position than the white North, was less favorable to jazz, since that music showed the Negro in a light more incompatible with his status and treatment in the South than with his status and treatment in the North.

4) Jazz was not so readily accepted as spirituals among white community leaders, educators and musicians because the Negro as jazz player or listener did not conform so much as the Negro as spiritual singer to the role white society reserves for him.

This examination of the reception of jazz raises four main questions for future research.

1) Why did the spread of jazz evoke such intense, emotional opposition? The answer to this question may illuminate the way in which groups react to the introduction of certain practices and arts which *in themselves* do not challenge values, but which imply or connote a challenge to beliefs in a realm different from the practice of the art in question. Thus jazz was rejected largely from nonmusical considerations (although some of the objections were stated in musical terms); it carried with it an image and an interpretation of the Negro that were not compatible with the image and the attitude in the minds of the leaders of white society in America. Further analysis of the precise mechanisms involved in this rejection of jazz might bring to light some hypotheses concerning intergroup relations of dominance and subordination.

2) Why did jazz continue to spread despite the strongly unfavorable reactions of community and religious leaders? The answer to this question may illuminate the particular psychological "needs" of white America, and perhaps yield some suggestions about the role of a folk art like jazz in an urban society. A consideration of the appeal of jazz for white America may also reveal with some degree of exactness just

what white and Negro Americans have in common in cultural tastes and psychological drives.

3) What is the actual process of diffusion of jazz from Negroes to whites? The answer to this question involves a study of the exact way in which jazz spread from group to group in American society until it reached urban middle-class intellectual whites, a group far removed in point of education, income, life experiences and life chances from the group in which jazz originally developed. Other questions are raised in this context: What kind of jazz diffused? What changes did jazz undergo in its diffusion? What are the new associations with jazz since its diffusion? A full study of this problem might also yield some new notions about the nature of the diffusion process itself, since the diffusion of jazz is a case that is quite different from most cases of diffusion thus far studied in anthropology and sociology. Most discussions have stressed: (1) The borrowing of subordinate from super-ordinate cultures; jazz is an opposite case. (2) The borrowing of techniques and artifacts; jazz is an art form, entailing many values outside the realm of art. (3) The borrowing by one culture from a widely differing culture—e.g., American Indian from American, or "primitives" from Europeans; jazz is a case of borrowing within a single broad cultural whole.

4) Of what significance is it that jazz brings together Negroes and whites in a relationship of social equality? The answer to this question involves a consideration of the effect of a white person's acceptance of jazz upon his conception of himself and upon his image of and attitude toward the Negro. It also involves a study of the effect upon both the Negro jazz player and the Negro jazz follower of the fact that each is accepted as the social equal of the whites interested in the same music. There is perhaps no other area of Negro-white contact, except possibly in radical political parties, where the Negro is accepted so fully as an equal (and so often admired as a superior) without condescension. This fact has considerable significance for Negro-white relations and group hostility in general.

MORROE BERGER

NOTES

1. *New York Times,* 8 February 1924, p. 4.

2. *Ibid.,* 12 November 1924, p. 14.

3. *Ibid.,* 6 December 1927, p. 29.

4. *Ibid.,* 7 May 1926, p. 10.

5. *Ibid.,* 30 January 1922, p. 11.

6. *Ibid.,* 15 February 1925, p. 17.

7. *Ibid.,* 12 July 1925, Section II, p. 2.

8. *Ibid.,* 4 February 1926, p. 4.

9. Anne Shaw Faulkner, "Does Jazz Put the Sin in Syncopation?" *The Ladies' Home Journal* (Vol. 38, No. 8), August 1921, pp. 16, 34.

10. *New York Times,* Magazine, 18 August 1946, p. 41.

11. Allison Davis, Burleigh Gardner and Mary R. Gardner, *Deep South,* University of Chicago Press, 1941, p. 241.

12. *New York Times,* 21 June 1926, p. 5.

13. *Current History* (Vol. 50, No. 5), July 1939, p. 52.

14. Lucy Harth Smith, "Negro Musicians and Their Music," *The Journal of Negro History,* 1935, Vol. XX, p. 430.

15. Duffield and Company, N.Y.

16. Macmillan, N. Y.

17. University of North Carolina Press, Chapel Hill.

18. Holt, N.Y.

19. Viking, N.Y.

20. *Esquire's 1946 Jazz Book,* ed. by P. E. Miller, Smith and Durrell, N.Y., 1945, pp. 187-88.

21. *New York Times,* 21 February 1946, p. 23.

22. *Ibid.,* 8 October 1924, p. 18.

23. *Ibid.,* 13 November 1924, p. 20.

24. *Ibid.,* 12 December 1924, p. 20.

25. *Ibid.,* 12 January 1925, p. 14.

26. *Ibid.*, 28 January 1925, p. 16.

27. *Ibid.*, 13 April 1926, p. 24.

28. *Ibid.*, 31 May 1938, p. 18.

29. *Ibid.*, 27 June 1941, p. 15.

30. *Ibid.*, 17 April 1928, p. 26.

31. *Ibid.*, 14 November 1924, p. 16.

32. *Ibid.*, 31 August 1919, p. 13.

33. *Ibid.*, 10 October 1924, p. 22.

34. *Ibid.*, 16 May 1924, p. 22.

35. *Ibid.*, 23 January 1944, p. 239.

36. *Ibid.*, 6 April 1927, p. 20.

37. M. Robert Rogers, "Jazz Influence on French Music," *The Musical Quarterly*, 1935, Vol. 21, pp. 53-68.

38. Louis Harap, "The Case for Hot Jazz," *The Musical Quarterly*, 1941, Vol. 27, pp. 47-61

39. "What's the Matter with Jazz?" *The Etude*, Vol. 41, January 1924, p. 6.

40. "Where Is Jazz Leading America?" *The Etude*, Vol. 42, August 1924, pp. 517-520.

41. "Where the Etude Stands on Jazz," *ibid.*, p. 515.

42. September 1924, pp. 595-96.

43. January 1925, pp. 5-6.

44. Rose Heylbut, "The Hour of Charm," *The Etude*, Vol. 56, October 1938, p. 40.

45. "New Concepts in Present Day Music," *ibid.*, Vol. 57, April 1939, p. 227.

46. Rose Heylbut, "The Requirements of Rhythm Playing," *ibid.*, September 1940, p. 583.

47. David Ewen, "The Artistic Possibilities of Good Jazz," *ibid.*, Vol. 61. July 1943, pp. 431-32.

48. Paul Whiteman, "Keep Jazz Within Its Limits," *ibid.*, Vol. 62, August 1944, p. 437.

49. Isabel Wister, "Yes, I Teach 'Em Jazz," *ibid.*, Vol. 46, August 1928, p. 588.

50. R. M. Goodbrod, *ibid.*, Vol. 52, February 1934, p. 82.

51. Guy Maier, *ibid.*, Vol, 62, December 1944, p. 686.

52. See note 48.

53. "A Symphony a Day," *The Etude*, Vol. 56, November 1938, pp. 705, 751.

54. Edwin H. Pierce, *ibid.*, Vol. 49, July 1931, p. 472.

55. Pietro Deiro, *ibid.*, Vol. 60, July 1942, p. 491.

56. *Esquire's Jazz Book*, 1944, 1945, 1946, Chicago. Frederic Ramsey, and Charles Edward Smith, eds., *Jazzmen*, Harcourt, Brace, N. Y., 1939. Paul Edward Miller, *Yearbook of Swing*, Downbeat Pub. Co., Chicago, 1939.

57. Ira de A. Reid, "The Negro in the American Economic System," 3 Vols., 1940, prepared for Myrdal study of the Negro, ms. in Schomburg Collection, New York Public Library. See Vol. 2, p. 372.

58. Data for *The Record Changer* were supplied by the publisher. Data for *The Jazz Record* were obtained by the writer from the magazine's subscription list.

59. *Statistical Abstract of the United States, 1944-45*, Bureau of the Census, Government Printing Office, Wash., D. C., 1945, table 6, p. 6.

60. Guy B. Johnson, "The Negro Spiritual," *American Anthropologist*, 1931, Vol. 33, p. 170.

61. John Lovell, Jr., "The Social Implications of the Negro Spiritual," *The Journal of Negro Education*, 1939, Vol. 8, pp. 634-42.

62. Hiram K. Moderwell, "The Epic of the Negro," *The New Republic*, 8 September 1917, Vol. 12, pp. 154-55.

63. Osbourne McConathy, Russell V. Morgan, George L. Lindsay, *Music, the Universal Language*, Silver Burdett, N. Y., 1941.

64. C. C. White, "Musical Genius of the American Negro," *The Etude*, Vol. 42, May 1924, pp. 305-06.

65. *The Etude*, Vol. 53, June 1935, p. 375.

66. Shirley Graham, "Spirituals to Symphonies," *The Etude*, Vol. 54, November 1936, pp. 691-92.

67. Cleveland G. Allen, "The Negro's Contribution to American Music," *Current History*, May 1927, Vol. xxvi, p. 249.

68. "Musical Slang," *The Etude*, Vol. 52, July 1934, pp. 393-94.

69. *New York Times*, 19 January 1926, p. 8.

70. Jeannette R. Murphy, "The True Negro Music and Its Decline," *The Independent*, 23 July 1903, Vol. 55, pp. 1723-30.

The Impact of Mechanization

NEIL LEONARD

Before 1917 Americans heard jazz "live," that is, played directly to them, in dance halls, saloons, barrel houses, brothels, lumber and turpentine camps, riverboats and at minstrel and vaudeville shows, carnivals, parades and funerals. After the war people still heard it "live," but more and more it reached them "canned," that is, through mechanical sound-reproducing devices: the player piano, the phonograph, the radio and the film sound track. Conceived at the end of the nineteenth century, these devices were developed and widely marketed in the first part of the twentieth. They grew up with jazz and strongly influenced its diffusion and evolution.

The first instrument to reproduce canned music for a large audience was the player piano (or pianola). Shortly after 1900 its manufacturers marketed piano rolls which played a variety of music from Chopin to ragtime. At first the sound was poor. As one listener wrote: "The notes were shot out like bullets. . . . In the overwhelming solos there was no recognition of the principles which underlie playing; no important or unimportant sounds, no increase or decrease in volume. Such crudeness soon gave place to machine-like imitation of light and shade, to sound emphasis of the melodic line, and variations of speed."[1] By World War I improved pianolas had become fashionable and sounded fragments of Beethoven's *Moonlight Sonata* or, more often, "Alexander's Ragtime Band," in many places of entertainment and in thousands of homes.

In the early 1900s the phonograph was no commercial rival to the pianola. The music of early records was often scarcely discernible from the surface scratch, squeaks and snorts that came out of the horn. Before long, however, several improvements, notably the replacement of cylindrical records with flat disks, made the phonograph more marketable. Gradually, recordings of academic singers, instrumentalists, and eventually full orchestras helped the "victrola" to become more profitable than the player piano. So-called popular records sold well also, particularly after the onset of the dance rage. By the twenties popular musicians received as much for their records as did their academic counterparts, and from then on the biggest profits came from popular music.

In 1921 over 100 million records were manufactured, and Americans spent more money for them than for any other form of recreation.[2] The depression of 1922 and the arrival of radio hit the phonograph industry hard. In the mid-twenties, when acoustical recording was abandoned in favor of electrical recording, business improved; but when the economy collapsed in 1929, the recording industry suffered, along with the rest of the country. In 1933 only 2,500,000 records were made. Gradually, the record business revived with the help of the juke box, which found its way into almost every restaurant and bar across the country. There were 350,000 juke boxes at work by 1940 and 44 percent of the records sold went into them. By 1942 sales figures for records reached an unprecedented 127 million. The vast majority of these were popular records (mostly jazz and commercial jazz). In 1939 Americans bought 45 million "popular" records and only 5 million "classical," a ratio of nine to one.[3]

Following Marconi's experiments in the nineties, radio developed rapidly, particularly after De Forrest invented the vacuum tube in 1906. During World War I the government controlled the radio industry, but after 1918 it was thrown open to commercial exploitation and quickly attracted wide public interest. In 1922 the "radio boom" was well under-way; over 200 stations and 3 million sets were in operation. By 1926 there were 694 stations. The number of receivers in use grew to an estimated 15 million in 1931 and reached 51 million by the end of the decade.[4]

During the twenties music constituted three-fourths of the material heard on the radio.[5] At first braodcasters pro-grammed only a small amount of academic music because they believed it did not appeal to a mass audience and because many academic musicians were reluctant to broad-cast. Some of them considered a radio performance—distorted by static and other disturbance, which they dubbed "De Forrest's prime evil"—below their dignity.[6] In the twenties commercial jazz dominated radio. An editorial in *Etude* declared in 1924, "Listen in on the radio any night. Tap America anywhere in the air and nine times out of ten Jazz will burst forth."[7] Four years later Charles Merz sampled for one week the content of radio programs from stations throughout the country. Of 357 hours broadcast by ten typical large stations, Merz found 259 devoted to popular "harmony and rhythm" and 42 to "serious music." Of 294 hours broadcast by ten typical smaller stations, 189 were given over to "syncopation" and 77 to "serious or partway serious" music.[8] The predominance of time alloted to "jazz" entertainers such as the Cliquot Club Eskimos, Ipana Trouba-dors, and A&P Gypsies was more imposing than the figures indicated. Merz pointed out that the policy of large stations was to broadcast the serious part of the daily program, lectures on the Dawes Plan and academic music, early, and to leave the evenings, when the largest number of people tuned in, free for popular entertainment, mostly commercial jazz.[9]

In the thirties new types of programs were taking up some of the hours formerly devoted to music, but commercial jazz still dominated broadcasting by a wide margin. During 1933, "dance and light music" filled 43 percent of the broadcasting time on the NBC and CBS networks combined, while "classical and semi-classical" took up 18 percent. In 1939 the figures were 37 percent for "dance and light" and 10 percent for "classical and semiclassical."[10]

The development of motion pictures was also extra-ordinarily rapid. By the end of World War I they had come a long way from the peep show and nickelodeon. Flickering images had changed to distinct pictures, and multi-reel narratives were being shown in comfortable theaters. An estimated 35 million Americans went to the movies at least once a week in 1920. At first the film shared the bill with vaudeville acts, but the arrival of talking pictures in 1927 gradually forced live entertainment out of the theater. By this time weekly movie attendance had jumped to 110 million, or four-fifths of the American population. The Depression reduced the film audience as it had the number of phonograph and radio listeners. Weekly attendance climbed to 77 million by 1935, however, and once again approached 100 million in 1939.[11]

Music played an important part in the movie industry. From the first, a piano or small orchestra accompanied the film intensifying the stereotyped dramatic situations with stereotyped dilutions of jazz or academic music. With the arrival of "talkies" a mixture of academic and popular music blared from the sound track. Hundreds of commercial jazz songs were written for film musicals, like the first of the "talkies," *The Jazz Singer*. Both in musicals and nonmusicals syncopated *crescendi* and blue-toned *sforzandi* of symphonic and refined jazz helped to create atmosphere, to suggest unspoken thoughts or other implications, to provide continuity, and to build up or round off dramatic episodes.

Probably it is impossible to explain adequately the effect of the relentless projection of canned music, mostly commercial jazz, into American ears. Yet one result is clear: reproducing devices made music available cheaply and easily and consequently greatly speeded its diffusion. A leading radio performer reached more people in the course of a single program than a vaudeville headliner played before in an entire year. In little more than a week reproducing devices could make a song a hit across the nation.[12] On the other hand, their use exhausted material rapidly. Before the arrival of canned music, the commercial life of a song lasted months, sometimes a year or longer. Reproducing devices repeated a tune so often that the public tended to tire of it in 60 days. The market demanded more and more songs, and the public heard so many jazz tunes that, as music publisher Edward Marks pointed out, it had trouble in distinguishing between them.[13] The radio in particular saturated the public's sensibility with jazz sounds. Charles Merz declared:

There are literally hundreds of bands, jazz orchestras and syncopated entertainers whose fame the radio has broadcast into millions of homes reaching all the way from city flats to the loneliest farms in the wheat country. . . . We tune in—on a mighty rhythm to which millions of people are marking time, the pulse beat of a nation. All over the country the trombones blare and the banjos whang and the clarinets pipe the rhythm. All over the country the same new tunes that will be generations old before the week is out are hammered home to the same vast audience from a hundred different places. . . . If it is true that from 20 to 30 million Americans are listening in on the radio every evening, then for a large part of that evening they are listening in on the greatest single sweep of synchronized and syncopated rhythm that human ingenuity has yet conceived.[14]

NEIL LEONARD

By the end of the twenties reproducing devices had made jazz sounds exceedingly familiar to most people. No longer did syncopation, polyrhythm, *glissandi,* blue notes, and antiphonal effects sound completely barbarous, and indignant complaints about them grew scarce after 1928.

While commercial dilutions dominated the musical output of the phonograph, the radio and the movies, real jazz remained on the fringes of the business. Jazzmen seldom played on the radio or in films, and made relatively few recordings. Yet despite their comparatively small number, jazz records affected the growth of jazz significantly.

At first, most of the jazz diffused mechanically was on so-called race records, which were directed to Negroes. All of the King Oliver, Bessie Smith, early Duke Ellington, and Louis Armstrong, and even some of the Bix Beiderbecke disks came out as race records. Far from considering their contents to be art music, issuing companies regarded them as popular music and advertised them as "red hot," "guaranteed to put you in that dancing mood," or as "the latest hot stuff to tickle your toes." Race records were cheap to make. They required from one to ten musicians, who frequently earned no more than five dollars a side, ten dollars for the leader. Often the performers composed their own material inexpensively in the recording studio, and if there were any royalties, they were small.[15] And race records were as easy to market as they were cheap to make. They required no expensive, nationwide promotion or distrubition since they could be sold readily in Negro areas.

Even though race and the few other real jazz records were but a trickle in the enormous tide of disks that came from the recording industry, they immeasurably speeded the acceptance of jazz. The phonograph, the first device to preserve the music of improvising bands, permitted a single performance to be heard simultaneously and repeatedly at different places throughout the country. The first few sides made by the Original Dixieland Band, selling as they did in the millions,[16] did more to facilitate the acceptance of jazz than hundreds of jazz bands playing "live" could have done. Furthermore, records served as devices of self-instruction. In 1916, when the Victor Talking Machine Company approached Freddie Keppard and his Original Creole Band with a recording offer, he is reported to have said to his musicians, "Nothin' doin', boys. We won't put our stuff on records for everybody to steal."[17] A few months later the recorded music of the Original Dixieland Jazz Band provided a model for aspiring jazzmen everywhere to imitate. In such widely separated places as Boston, Chicago and Spokane young musicians copied or learned to accompany their favorite performers on records.

The experience of cornetist Jimmy McPartland and his high school friends illustrates how young jazzmen learned from records. One day in a local soda parlor they found a record of the New Orleans Rhythm Kings. "Boy, when we heard that—I'll tell you we went out of our minds," McPartland recalls. "Everybody flipped. It was wonderful." They replayed the record during the course of several days and "we decided we would get a band and play like these guys." In one way or another they obtained instruments and tried to accompany the record. "What we used to do was put the record on . . . play a few bars, and then all get our notes. We'd have to tune our instruments up to the record machine, to the pitch, and go ahead with a few notes. Then stop! A few more bars of the record, each guy would pick out his notes and boom! We would go on and play it. . . . It was a funny way to learn, but in three or four weeks we could finally play one tune all the way through."[18] Records permitted aspiring jazzmen to learn music without bothering with the formalism, discipline, technique and expense of traditional training. Mechanical reproducing devices hastened the acceptance of jazz not only by familiarizing both listeners and musicians with nontraditional characteristics of the new music but also by helping to bring it into closer alignment with traditional values.

NEIL LEONARD

The widespread diffusion of canned music had an all-important part in bringing to a head traditional opposition to jazz. Live performances of jazz before lower-class audiences in unsavory locations had caused traditionalists concern enough but when reproducing devices brought the music with astonishing frequency to the ears of the general public, traditionalists became alarmed. It was one thing to know about jazz played in brothels and other disreputable places patronized by supposedly disreputable people, yet it was quite another thing to hear sound tracks and records bring it to middle- and upper-class places of amusement and to find radios and phonographs blaring it into "respectable" homes. Sound-reproducing devices translated traditionalists' concern about jazz into demands to suppress it. One of the most powerful suppressive measures was the pressure on the music business to purify or eradicate jazz.

The popular music industry has long sought to produce the lowest common denominator in its material: that music which will please as many and offend as few potential customers as possible. After 1917 the industry ignored complaints about jazz as long as they did not threaten profits. By the late twenties, however, creators and distributors of popular music had grown sensitive to traditionalist criticism about jazz, and many of them became concerned to clean it up for both business and ethical reasons.

As early as 1921 a group of Tin Pan Alley publishers organized the Music Publishers' Protective Association to censor popular songs. Citing the increasing use of mechanical, sound-reproducing devices, the chairman of the Executive Board, E. C. Mills, explained: "The publishers do not want to be sponsors of indecent material. These songs go into the homes of the country." Accordingly, the association began a "vigilant watch for such sentiments and expressions which are common to the suggestive." It adopted as its motto, "Just keep the words clean and the music will take care of itself," and proceeded to weed out any material which was indecent or which made fun of any law, sect or race. Member publishers had to register all songs with the association and post a bond as a pledge of obedience to the regulations. Mills, who was also chairman of the Administrative Committee of ASCAP (American Society of Composers, Authors and Publishers), claimed the co-operation of certain vaudeville producers, sheet-music jobbers, phonograph and piano-roll companies and interested laymen.[19]

By 1927 the demands to clean up popular songs had reached the proportions of an organized movement. A convention of fifty member-firms of the New York Piano Merchants' Association resolved not to sell any sheet music, records or piano rolls with "lewd, lascivious, salacious, or suggestive" titles or lyrics. They sent a copy of their resolution to publishers and record companies.[20] Three months later the National Association of Orchestra Directors appointed a "czar" and a committee to investigate hotels, night clubs and dance halls to determine "the kind of jazz that tends to create indecent dancing" and to instruct band leaders on "the correct rendition."[21] In June of the same year, the National Association of Music Merchants passed a resolution declaring that American music had been lowered by "smut words" and pledged to do nothing to make music unfit for American homes. They called on Congress to permit censorship of songs in order to maintain "a high standard of decency, morality, and fitness."[22]

Nor were the radio, film and eventually the phonograph industries deaf to traditionalist objections about jazz. Radio broadcasters were particularly sensitive to any complaints. In 1925 Carl Dreher wrote: "They are in a constant stew about 'adverse publicity.' A few letters from irate listeners give them the horrors. They run their stations for advertising or good will, and as soon as any one looks at them cross-eyed their knees shake. When in doubt, they wield the blue pencil, and any one who tries to please the whole world is in doubt most of the time."[23] Two years later the federal government

NEIL LEONARD

began to encourage broadcasters' squeamishness about questionable material. In 1927 Congress passed the Radio Act creating a commission to allocate wave length, license stations and generally oversee broadcasting. Section 26 of the Act declared that the commission had no powers of censorship, but added that "no person within the jurisdiction of the United States shall utter any obscene, indecent or profane language by means of radio communication." This section was written (as section 326) into the Federal Communications Act of 1934.[24]

The commissions created by both acts were bound to license only those broadcasters deemed to be "operating in the public interest, convenience, and necessity" and since licenses were granted for only a short time, censorship resulted in practice if not in theory. "Fear of disapproval," explained David Sarnoff, the head of RKO (Radio-Keith-Orpheum), can blue-pencil a dozen programs for every one that an official censor might object to.... Few realize that post-program discipline by the government can be a form of censorship that is all the more severe because it is undefined."[25] Government vagueness obliged every station master to act as a censor in self-defense. The big networks developed internal censorship, euphemistically called "Continuity Acceptance" at NBC and "Continuity Editing" at CBS.[26] In 1929 the National Association of Broadcasters adopted a code of ethics which proscribed broadcasting material that would be banned from the mails as "obscene or offensive."[27]

As a result of government and private regulation, anything that seemed in the slightest degree "objectionable" was ruled off the air. Real jazz and certain lyrics associated with it were frequently unacceptable. By 1942 NBC had blacklisted the words of 290 songs. Of these, 217 could not be sung at all, while the remainder could be performed only with cleaned-up lyrics.[28] The first known instance of radio censorship of any type occurred when Station WFFA banned the song

"Little Red Riding Hood" because of the line "How could Little Red Riding Hood have been so very good and still keep the wolf from the door?"[29] Later NBC changed the words "Silk stockings thrown aside" to "Gloves thrown aside."[30] Offensive musical elements were also deleted or refined before they reached the microphone. During the twenties, one New York Station disallowed "jazz" between certain hours while another, WRNY, dropped it altogether.[31] The FCC did not rule directly on jazz until 1938, when Chairman Frank McNinch answered a complaint of the Bach Society of New Jersey by urging station masters to use "a high degree of discrimination" in broadcasting the music.[32]

Long before McNinch's statement, broadcasters recognized the need for discretion in transmitting jazz, yet most were reluctant to stop broadcasting a major attraction. Audience response assured them that support for the music outweighed opposition to it. For instance, when an organization called the "Keep-the-Air-Clean-on-Sunday-Society" tried to make WMCA, New York, stop broadcasting jazz on Sunday, letters from listeners favoring the music prevented its being dropped.[33] Broadcasters also knew that the general approval applied only to refined jazz. In 1927 Kingsley Welles stressed this point in his column, "The Listeners' Point of View," in *Radio Broadcast*. He quoted from a letter from a "typical listener" who had written that "the universal condemnation of jazz is contrary to the true feeling of a majority of radio listeners. . . . Would these objectors want to stop the broadcasting of such organizations as those of Paul Whiteman, Vincent Lopez, Jean Goldkette and many others?" "Decidedly not," answered Welles.[34]

Arguments of the proponents of symphonic jazz provided further reasons for broadcasters to support or tolerate the transmission of refined jazz. As the manager of musical programs for one western station declared in 1925, "Personally I feel that jazz is not all bad. . . . Lately, jazz has gathered to itself some notable defenders among the musically correct. Serious minded musicians have perceived under the battered and tattered appearance of jazz, evidence of a new vitality in music, a struggle after a new form of expression, crude as the hieroglyphics of Cubism, but genuine art, nevertheless. The moans, shrieks, cat-calls and sobs of jazz will eventually disappear, but the vibrancy of its stimulating rhythms will remain to be caught some time by a master composer."[35]

Movie producers were sensitive to traditionalist criticism also. After the Armistice a series of suggestive films and Hollywood scandals aroused complaints from traditionalists; indignant clergymen, church organizations, women's clubs and other guardians against vice demanded reform. By 1922 six states had passed legislation to censor films. To prevent further censorship from outside, the film industry appointed Will Hays head of the Motion Picture Producers and Distributors Association of America and overseer of Hollywood morals both on and off the screen. Among other steps, the association, better known as the Hays office, developed and enforced a production code. In general the code stipulated that no film could sympathetically portray manners and morals too contrary to those founded on traditional values. For example, the sanctity of the home and marriage was to be upheld and the treatment of sex was to be handled delicately. Obscenity in words, gesture, reference, song, joke or suggestion was forbidden.[36]

The Hays office set a moral tone which helped keep real jazz out of films. There was always the danger that a movie offering the new music as a special attraction would not be acceptable. In 1929 when the uninhibited "Empress of the Blues," Bessie Smith, made a two-reel short, *St. Louis Blues,* it was condemned for its bad taste and suppressed.[37] Other films starring jazzmen were more fortunate, but generally real jazz found little favor in Hollywood until the thirties.

Although the radio and film industries tended to exclude real jazz, the phonograph companies were less obliged to do so. Like other producers of canned music, record-makers sought material that would please as many and offend as few people as possible. At the same time, however, because of the nature of records and the ways in which they were distributed, record-makers could still cater profitably to minority tastes. Records did not necessarily reach the general public; more often than not, individuals bought them to play for a limited audience. In any event, the sounds of distasteful records were easily kept out of public places and off the public air.

Race records, which covered most of the real jazz recordings of the twenties, seldom found their way into white neighborhoods, and therefore no formal organization like the FCC or the Hays office emerged to censor their content. Still, record-makers could not completely ignore traditionalist rules of decency. In 1927, for example, Louis Armstrong made "S.O.L. Blues" (Okeh 8496), which the Okeh Company considered too offensive to market. Armstrong had to return to the studio the following day to remake the number ("Gully Low Blues" Okeh 8474) using a "clean" title and more appropriate lyrics.[38]

Growing centralization of the entertainment business had an important role in bringing jazz closer to traditional values. As technical improvements permitted increased commercial exploitation of sound-producing devices, show business became, more than ever, big business. By the twenties Wall Street had invested heavily in commercial entertainment and at the end of the decade radio and films were among the nation's leading industries. While the process of centralization may be said to have begun before World War I, not until the twenties and thirties did the entertainment business fall under the control of a handful of corporations. In 1926 NBC marked the beginning of network broadcasting by linking 19 stations. In 1937 it had 138. The Columbia Broadcasting System, which had started in 1927 with 16 stations, was sending its programs to 110 in 1938.[39] As radio became

NEIL LEONARD

centralized, it swallowed up the leading phonograph companies. In January, 1929, the Victor Talking Machine Company merged with RCA (Radio Corporation of America). Nine years later CBS bought the American Record Company, whose catalogue included Columbia, Okeh, Vocalion, Brunswick and some minor labels. The arrival of the talking picture brought about further concentration. RCA took over the Keith-Albee-Orpheum vaudeville circuit and the Pathé film company, and formed RKO (Radio-Keith-Orpheum). Warner Brothers merged with the Stanley Corporation of America and First National Pictures.

To satisfy their unending need for songs, film companies purchased the leading New York music-publishing firms or created their own musical affiliates. Warner Brothers bought the Tin Pan Alley houses of Harms, Witmark, Remick and that of DeSylva, Brown and Henderson. RKO controlled the firms of Leo Feist and Carl Fischer. Robbins became a subsidiary of Metro-Goldwyn-Mayer. Paramount owned the Famous Music Company and Twentieth-Century-Fox incorporated the Red Star Publishing Company.[40]

This process of centralization gave a progressively smaller number of executives more and more control over the choice of material to be distributed. Owning or controlling affiliates in almost every phase of the entertainment business, the men in charge sought above all a standardized product which they could sell through every medium to as many people in as many places as possible. To be fully exploitable, music now had to be suitable not only for dance halls, the stage and phonograph records (all of which could cater to minority tastes) but also for radio and films, which reached the general, nationwide audience. Although the collectively improvised jazz of Louis Armstrong's Hot Five or the blues sung by Bessie Smith sounded less strange than they had a few years earlier, they still had little market appeal for the general audience. Furthermore, the suggestive lyrics, which shocked traditionalists, met with the disapproval of the Radio

Commission and the Hays office. The words of "It's Tight Like That" (VO 1216) by "George Tom" and "Tampa Red" offer a good example.

Now the girl I love is long and slim,
When she gets it it's too bad, Jim.
It's tight light that, beedle um bum,
It's tight like that, beedle um bum.
Hear me talkin' to you, it's tight like that.

Record companies continued to sell such material to the Negro audience,[41] but they knew that lyrics like these and the music associated with them could never be sold for use on radio or in films. Thus, centralization of the entertainment business helped to prevent the spread of collectively improvised jazz and certain blues.

In addition, the interlocking directorates fostered by centralization facilitated the suppression of jazz. Take for example, the power possessed by one company to implement its antijazz policy. The Radio Music Company was founded in 1929 primarily as a publishing affiliate of NBC. E. C. Mills, whom we encountered earlier as the head of the Music Publishers' Protective Association and of ASCAP, was the president of the Radio Music Company. He proclaimed that its employees intended to make "an active and intelligent use" of the NBC facilities in order to improve American music, and he added: "The new firm will have its influence in putting jazz in the background of the American musical picture. We have had perhaps too much jazz, and there is no denying the influence of music on peoples' inclinations, it seems about time for someone to assume leadership in the movement away from jazz. I think we should go back to the melody and let it serve instead of noise to give us the inspiration we expect from music."[42] The following list of members of the board of directors of the Radio Music Company indicates the vast influence within the music business of the makers of this antijazz policy. The chairman of the board was the president of NBC, M. H. Aylesworth.

NEIL LEONARD

Other board members were the executive vice-president of RCA, David Sarnoff; the president of the Radio Victor Corporation, E. E. Schumaker; the president of RKO, Hiram S. Brown; the president of Leo Feist, Inc., Leo Feist; the president of Westinghouse Electric and Manufacturing Company, H. P. Davis; the director of the Roxy Theater and a power in the music business, S. L. Rothafel; and the president of Carl Fischer, Walter J. Fischer. Other publishers and leading songwriters also cooperated. In 1921, when a leading figure in the business like Mills had tried to curtail jazz, he could count on only the help of several publishers and a few others in connected industries. By 1929, however, concentration of control of commercial entertainment had helped to pyramid his power so that he could expect the cooperation of many of the most prominent policy-makers in the music business.

In their attempts to control every production process and outlet, the large corporations in the entertainment business set up headquarters in New York or Hollywood and sought to divide the country into trade areas serviced by provincial cities.[43] New York was the center for the music industry. Here bands were booked for personal appearances, record dates and radio jobs. Here talents were assayed, the largest salaries paid and the biggest reputations made. For gifted jazzmen in the late twenties earning $22.50 a week in Chicago, Kansas City or Dallas, the glitter of Manhattan and the prospect of $100-$200 a week was hard to withstand.[44] "Most of the Chicago gang had gone to New York around 1928," wrote pianist Joe Sullivan, "and plenty more musicians were streaming into Manhattan to get their kicks and grab their share of the fantastically high salaries which were being paid at that time."[45]

Most of the jazzmen who came to New York found their hopes of playing jazz for high salaries to be false. People who hired musicians had little use for jazz. Only a few clubs and ballrooms in New York or elsewhere employed collectively improvising jazzmen. And the anti- or non-jazz policy of many producers of canned music made jazz musicians' jobs for record, radio and film companies increasingly scarce as the entertainment business became progressively centralized.

In addition, the growing use of sound-reproducing devices directly affected the market for musicians in a manner that provided further hardship for jazzmen. Whether or not mechanical sound devices destroyed more jobs than they ultimately created is a moot question. Yet, it is clear that their introduction resulted in at least temporary displacement for musicians of all types. Radio, to take one medium, sharply cut down the demand for live performances. A striking illustration of this obsolescence occurred in Boston in 1924. Three thousand seats had been sold for a Fritz Kreisler concert, but, when the news got out that the performance would also be broadcast, over half the ticket-holders returned their tickets and presumably listened to the concert over the radio.[46] After 1929 the Depression cut deeper into the opportunities of all musicians.

These circumstances forced many jazzmen to abandon collectively improvised jazz for a living at least. The relatively few jobs calling for live performance were usually with refined jazz bands. And without an occasional job with one of the organizations that produced canned music it was difficult to make much money or a reputation that would lead to other jobs. Even before the centralization of the entertainment business, jazzmen had recognized the importance of being heard on records and had sometimes paid record companies for the privilege of recording in the hope that the result would prove marketable. After centralization, however, the importance of canned performances to a musician's career became more obvious than ever before. Consequently, the temptation to yield to the demands of the entertainment industry grew. Many jazzmen succumbed quickly to the temptation. Those who resisted it usually found that before long they had to submit if they wanted to

NEIL LEONARD

continue to be musicians. Submissions obliged jazzmen to replace the most "offensive" characteristics of jazz with elements of traditional popular music. Too often the results were musical trash and jazzmen gave in to them with varying degrees of willingness. Some performers, such as Benny Goodman and Louis Armstrong resigned themselves without complaint. In 1954, defending himself against charges that he had wasted his talents on bad popular songs, Armstrong said, "They put a piece of music up in front of you—you ain't supposed to tell the leader 'I don't want to play this.' And I was brought up that way." In discussing this quotation, Chadwick Hansen has pointed out that since Armstrong has almost always led his own band, he is not the leader here, and thus his statement is a metaphor for the entertainment business.[47] Other jazzmen resigned themselves more reluctantly to Tin Pan Alley material. "I never knew one of them," wrote clarinetist Artie Shaw, "who didn't feel exactly the same as I did about what we were doing. Which could be put into the following words: "Sure it stinks, but it pays good dough so the hell with it."[48] Still other jazzmen could not give in to the dictates of the industry because they lacked sufficient traditional training or would not comply because they disdained refined jazz. They generally retired from music, at least temporarily, sometimes for good.

In yielding to the demands of the market many jazzmen surrendered outright to refined jazz. Others, men like Louis Armstrong, Duke Ellington and Benny Goodman, found ways to mix their music with traditional popular music and yet retain the essential elements of jazz. The results of their efforts prepared the way for a new kind of jazz called "swing."

From Neil Leonard, *Jazz and the White Americans,* Chapter 5. Copyright © 1962, the University of Chicago Press. Reprinted by permission.

THE IMPACT OF MECHANIZATION   61

NOTES

1. Arthur Whiting, "The Mechanical Player," *Yale Review,* VIII (July, 1919), 830.

2. Roland Gelatt, *The Fabulous Phonograph* (Philadelphia, 1954), pp. 83-171, 189, 212-13, 308; U.S. Bureau of Census, *Biennial Census of Manufacturers,* 1923, 0. 1012; Edward B. Marks and Abbott J. Liebling, *They All Sang* (New York, 1934), pp. 104-5; Julius Weinberger, "Economic Aspects of Recreation," *Harvard Business Review,* XV (Summer, 1937), 452.

3. David Ewen, *Music Comes to America* (New York, 1942), pp. 200, 202; Weinberger, "Economic Aspects of Recreation," p. 452; Gelatt, *Fabulous Phonograph,* p. 213; *Biennial Census of Manufacturers,* p. 1012; Abel Green and Joe Laurie, Jr., *Show Biz: From Vaude to Video* (New York, 1951), p. 234; Francis Chase, *Sound and Fury* (New York, 1942), pp. 265-67.

4. Green and Laurie, *Show Biz,* p. 231; Barry Ulanov, *A History of Jazz in America* (New York, 1952), p. 114; Gelatt, *Fabulous Phonograph,* p. 216; Ewen, *Music Comes to America,* p. 208.

5. Foster R. Dulles, *America Learns To Play: A History of Popular Recreation, 1607-1940* (New York, 1940), p. 327.

6. Ewen, *Music Comes to America,* p. 210.

7. *Etude,* IV (January, 1924), 5.

8. Charles Merz, *The Great American Bandwagon* (New York, 1928), pp. 47-48. Other evidence may be found in G. A. Lundberg, "The Content of Radio Programs," *Social Forces,* VII (1928), 59. Checking New York City radio stations during February, 1927, Lundberg found only 22 percent of their time given to what he called "dance music" and 48 percent given to "other music." The apparent inconsistency between these and Merz's figures seems to result from geographical differences in taste and, more important, from the vague terminology of both reports. Merz speaks of all music with a jazz sound, whereas Lundberg apparently refers to music listed in newspaper program-schedules as dance music. Probably much of the "other music" Lundberg speaks of sounded like jazz even though newspapers did not list it as "dance music."

9. Merz, *Great American Bandwagon,* pp. 48-49.

10. Llewellyn White, *The American Radio* (Chicago, 1947), p. 16.

11. Dulles, *America Learns to Play,* pp. 287-97, 301-2; Jesse P. Steiner,

NEIL LEONARD

"Recreation and Leisure Time Activities," in *Recent Social Trends,* II (New York, 1933), 940-41; David Ewen, *Panorama of American Popular Music* (Englewood Cliffs, N. J., 1957), pp. 280-82; Green and Laurie, *Show Biz,* pp. 247, 251, 270.

12. See Isaac Goldberg, *Tin Pan Alley* (New York, 1930), pp. 308-09.

13. Marks, and Liebling, *They All Sang,* pp. 207-8.

14. Merz, *Great American Bandwagon,* pp. 46-50.

15. George Avakian, "The History of Columbia Is the Saga of Jazz," *Down Beat,* XXIII (December 12, 1956), 14.

16. H. O. Brunn, *The Original Dixieland Jazz Band* (Baton Rouge, La., 1960), p. 22.

17. William Russell and Stephen W. Smith, "New Orleans Music" in Frederick Ramsey, Jr., and Charles Edward Smith (eds.), *Jazzmen* (New York, 1939), p. 22.

18. Nat Shapiro and Nat Hentoff (eds.), *Hear Me Talkin' To Ya* (New York, 1955), pp. 119-20.

19. *New York Times,* July 6, 1924, Section VIII, p. 14.

20. *Ibid.,* February 3, 1927, p. 3.

21. *Ibid.,* April 6, 1927, p. 30.

22. *Ibid.,* June 10, 1927, p. 23.

23. Carl Dreher, "In Defense of Broadcasting," *Radio Broadcast,* VIII (December, 1925), 192.

24. Ruth Brindze, *Not To Be Broadcast* (New York, 1937), p. 143; Chase, *Sound and Fury* pp. 233, 236.

25. Robert West, *The Rape of Radio* (New York, 1941), p. 460.

26. *Ibid.,* p. 461.

27. White, *American Radio,* p. 70.

28. Chase, *Sound and Fury,* pp. 226-27; West, *Rape of Radio,* p. 462.

29. Green and Laurie, *Show Biz,* p. 292.

30. Chase, *Sound and Fury,* pp. 227-67.

31. *New York Times,* May 31, 1929, p. 26.

32. *Ibid.,* November 3, 1938, p. 25.

33. *Ibid.,* March 14, 1927, p. 19; and March 15, 1927, p. 28.

34. Kingsley Welles, "The Listeners' Point of View: Is the Popularity of

Jazz Music Waning?" *Radio Broadcast,* VIII (December, 1925), 177-78.

35. *Ibid.,* p. 178.

36. Maurice Bardèche and Robert Brasillach, *The History of Motion Pictures,* trans. Iris Barry (New York, 1938), pp. 205-9; Green and Laurie, *Show Biz,* pp. 253-55; Dulles, *America Learns To Play,* pp. 299-300.

37. George Hoefer, "Bessie Smith," in Nat Shapiro and Nat Hentoff (eds.), *Jazz Makers* (New York, 1957, p. 137.

38. George Avakian, liner notes of Vol. II of "The Louis Armstrong Story," Columbia Record CL 852.

39. White, *American Radio,* p. 35.

40. Gelatt, *Fabulous Phonograph,* pp. 247, 251, 273; Green and Laurie, *Show Biz,* pp. 247, 266; Goldberg, *Tin Pan Alley,* pp. 312-14.

41. For discussion of this subject see Samuel Charters, *The Country Blues* (New York, 1959), *passim.*

42. *Musical Courier,* XCIX (December 14, 1929), p. 49.

43. See Paul S. Carpenter, *Music: An Art and a Business* (Norman, Okla., 1950), pp. 3-5.

44. Otis Ferguson, "The Five Pennies," in Ramsey and Smith, *Jazzmen,* p. 240.

45. Shapiro and Hentoff, *Hear Me Talkin' to Ya,* p. 269.

46. Green and Laurie, *Show Biz,* p. 243.

47. Chadwick Hansen, "Social Influences on Jazz Style: Chicago 1920-30," *American Quarterly,* XII (Winter, 1960), p. 505.

48. Artie Shaw, *The Trouble with Cinderella,* (New York, 1952), p. 259.

The Culture
and Career of
the Dance Musician

HOWARD S. BECKER

The dance musician, to whose culture or subculture this chapter is devoted, may be defined simply as someone who plays popular music for money. He is a member of a service occupation and the culture he participates in gets its character from the problems common to service occupations. The service occupations are, in general, distinguished by the fact that the worker in them comes into more or less direct and personal contact with the ultimate consumer of the product of his work, the client for whom he performs the service. Consequently, the client is able to direct or attempt to direct the worker at his task and to apply sanctions of various kinds, ranging from informal pressure to the withdrawal of his patronage and the conferring of it on some others of the many people who perform the service.

Service occupations bring together a person whose full-time activity is centered around the occupation and whose self is to some degree deeply involved in it, and another person whose relation to it is much more casual. It may be inevitable that the two should have widely varying pictures of the way the occupational service should be performed.

Members of service occupations characteristically consider the client unable to judge the proper worth of the service and bitterly resent attempts on his part to exercise control over the work. Conflict and hostility arise as a result, methods of defense against outside interference become a preoccupation of the members and a subculture grows around this set of problems.

Musicians feel that the only music worth playing is what they call "jazz," a term which can be partially defined as that music which is produced without reference to the demands of outsiders. Yet they must endure unceasing interference with their playing by employers and audience. The most distressing problem in the career of the average musician, as we shall see later, is the necessity of choosing between conventional success and his artistic standards. In order to achieve success he finds it necessary to "go commercial," that is, to play in accord with the wishes of the nonmusicians for whom he works; in doing so he sacrifices the respect of other musicians and thus, in most cases, his self-respect. If he remains true to his standards, he is usually doomed to failure in the larger society. Musicians classify themselves according to the degree to which they give in to outsiders; the continuum ranges from the extreme "jazz" musician to the "commercial" musician.

Below I will focus on the following points: the conceptions that musicians have of themselves and of the non-musicians for whom they work and the conflict they feel to be inherent in this relation; the basic consensus underlying the reactions of both commercial and jazz musicians to this conflict; and the feelings of isolation musicians have from the larger society and the way they segregate themselves from audience and community. The problems arising out of the difference between the musician's definition of his work and that of the people he works for may be taken as a prototype for the problems deviants have in dealing with outsiders who take a different view of their deviant activities.[1]

HOWARD S. BECKER

THE RESEARCH

I gathered the material for this study by participant observation, by participating with musicians in the variety of situations that made up their work and leisure lives. At the time I made the study I had played the piano professionally for several years and was active in musical circles in Chicago. This was in 1948 and 1949, a period when many musicians were taking advantage of their benefits under the G.I. Bill, so the fact that I was going to college did not differentiate me from others in the music business. I worked with many different orchestras and many different kinds of orchestras during that period and kept extensive notes on the events that occurred while I was with other musicians. Most of the people I observed did not know that I was making a study of musicians. I seldom did any formal interviewing, but concentrated rather on listening to and recording the ordinary kinds of conversation that occurred among musicians. Most of my observation was carried out on the job, and even on the stand as we played. Conversations useful for my purposes often took place also at the customary "job markets" in the local union offices where musicians looking for work and band leaders looking for men to hire gathered on Monday and Saturday afternoons.

The world of the dance musician is a highly differentiated one. Some men work mostly in bars and taverns, either in outlying neighborhoods or in the downtown area. Some play with larger bands in ballrooms and night clubs. Others do not work steadily in one place, but work with orchestras that play for private dances and parties in hotels and country clubs. Still other men play with nationally known "name" bands or work in radio and television studios. Men who work in each kind of job setting have problems and attitudes that are in part characteristic of that setting. I worked mostly in bars, taverns and occasionally with various kinds of "jobbing" bands. But I had enough contact with members of other groups, through meetings on occasional dance jobs and at the union hall, to be able to get evidence on their attitudes and activities as well.

Since completing the research, I have worked as a musician in two other locations, a small university town (Champaign-Urbana, Illinois) and a large city, though not so large as Chicago (Kansas City, Missouri). There are differences in the organization of the music business associated with the differences in size of these cities. In Chicago, it is much more possible for a musician to specialize. He may be a ballroom musician, or work only in taverns and night clubs (as I did). In the smaller towns, there is not as much work for any one kind and, furthermore, there are fewer musicians in proportion to the population. Therefore, one musician may be called on to perform in any of the several settings I have described, either because he has little choice of where to play or because the leader looking for someone to work for him has little choice among the available musicians. Although I have not kept formal notes on my experiences in these other settings, none of them furnished data that would require changes in the conclusions I reached on the basis of the Chicago materials.

MUSICIAN AND "SQUARE"

The system of beliefs about what musicians are and what audiences are is summed up in a word used by musicians to refer to outsiders—"square." It is used as a noun and as an adjective, denoting both a kind of person and a quality of behavior and objects. The term refers to the kind of person who is the opposite of all the musician is, or should be, and a way of thinking, feeling and behaving (with its expression in material objects) which is the opposite of that valued by musicians.

The musician is conceived of as an artist who possesses a mysterious artistic gift setting him apart from all other people. Possessing this gift, he should be free from control by outsiders who lack it. The gift is something which cannot be

HOWARD S. BECKER

acquired through education; the outsider, therefore, can never become a member of the group. A trombone player said, "You can't teach a guy to have a beat. Either he's got one or he hasn't. If he hasn't got it, you can't teach it to him."

The musician feels that under no circumstances should any outsider be allowed to tell him what to play or how to play it. In fact, the strongest element in the colleague code is the prohibition against criticizing or in any other way trying to put pressure on another musician in the actual playing situation "on the job." Where not even a colleague is permitted to influence the work, it is unthinkable that an outsider should be allowed to do so.

This attitude is generalized into a feeling that the musicians are different from and better than other kinds of people and accordingly ought not to be subject to the control of outsiders in any branch of life, particularly in their artistic activity. The feeling of being a different kind of person who leads a different kind of life is deep-seated, as the following remarks indicate:

> I'm telling you, musicians are different than other people. They talk different, they act different, they look different. They're just not like other people, that's all. . . . You know it's hard to get out of the music business because you feel so different from others.

> Musicians live an exotic life, like in a jungle or something. They start out, they're just ordinary kids from small towns—but once they get into that life they change. It's like a jungle, except that their jungle is a hot, crowded bus. You live that kind of life long enough, you just get to be completely different.

> Being a musician was great, I'll never regret it. I'll understand things that squares never will.

An extreme of this view is the belief that only musicians are sensitive and unconventional enough to be able to give real sexual satisfaction to a woman.

Feeling their difference strongly, musicians likewise believe they are under no obligation to imitate the conventional behavior of squares. From the idea that no one can tell a musician how to play it follows logically that no one can tell a musician how to do anything. Accordingly, behavior which flouts conventional social norms is greatly admired. Stories reveal this admiration for highly individual, spontaneous, devil-may-care activities; many of the most noted jazzmen are renowned as "characters," and their exploits are widely recounted. For example, one well-known jazzman is noted for having jumped on a policeman's horse standing in front of the night club in which he worked and ridden it away. The ordinary musician likes to tell stories of unconventional things he has done:

> We played the dance and after the job was over we packed up to get back in this old bus and make it back to Detroit. A little way out of town the car just refused to go. There was plenty of gas; it just wouldn't run. These guys all climbed out and stood around griping. All of a sudden, somebody said, "Let's set it on fire!" So someone got some gas out of the tanks and sprinkled it around, touching a match to it and woosh, it just went up in smoke. What an experience! The car burning up and all these guys standing around hollering and clapping their hands. It was really something.

This is more than idiosyncrasy; it is a primary occupational value, as indicated by the following observation of a young musician: "You know, the biggest heroes in the music business are the biggest characters. The crazier a guy acts, the greater he is, the more everyone likes him."

As they do not wish to be forced to live in terms of social conventions, so musicians do not attempt to force these conventions on others. For example, a musician declared that ethnic discrimination is wrong, since every person is entitled to act and believe as he wants to:

> Shit, I don't believe in any discrimination like that. People are people, whether they're Dagos or Jews or

HOWARD S. BECKER

Irishmen or Polacks or what. Only big squares care what religion they are. It don't mean a fucking thing to me. Every person's entitled to believe his own way, that's the way I feel about it. Of course, I never go to church myself, but I don't hold it against anybody who does. It's all right if you like that sort of thing.

The same musician classified a friend's sex behavior as wrong, yet defended the individual's right to decide what is right and wrong for himself: "Eddie fucks around too much; he's gonna kill himself or else get killed by some broad. And he's got a nice wife too. He shouldn't treat her like that. But what the fuck, that's his business. If that's the way he wants to live, if he's happy that way, then that's the way he oughta do." Musicians will tolerate extraordinary behavior in a fellow musician without making any attempt to punish or restrain him. In the following incident the uncontrolled behavior of a drummer loses a job for an orchestra; yet, angry as they are, they lend him money and refrain from punishing him in any way. It would be a breach of custom were anyone to reprimand him.

Jerry: When we got up there, the first thing that happened was that all his drums didn't show up. So the owner drives all around trying to find some drums for him and then the owner smashes a fender while he was doing it. So I knew right away that we were off to a good start. And Jack! Man, the boss is an old Dago, you know, no bullshit about him, he runs a gambling joint; he don't take any shit from anyone. So he says to Jack, "What are you gonna do without drums?" Jack says, "Be cool, daddio, everything'll be real gone, you know." I thought the old guy would blow his top. What a way to talk to the boss. Boy, he turned around, there was fire in his eye. I knew we wouldn't last after that. He says to me, "Is that drummer all there?" I said, "I don't know, I never saw him before today." And we just got finished telling him we'd been playing together six months. So that helped, too. Of course, when Jack started playing, that was the end. So loud! and he don't play a beat at all. All he uses the bass drum for is accents. What kind of drumming is that? Otherwise, it was a good little outfit. . . . It was a good job. We could have been there forever. . . . Well, after we played a couple of sets, the boss told us we were through.

Becker: What happened after you got fired?

Jerry: The boss gave us 20 apiece and told us to go home. So it cost us 17 dollars for transportation up and back, we made three bucks on the job. Of course, we saw plenty of trees. Three bucks, hell, we didn't even make that. We loaned Jack seven or eight.

The musician thus views himself and his colleagues as people with a special gift which makes them different from nonmusicians and not subject to their control, either in musical performance or in ordinary social behavior.

The square, on the other hand, lacks this special gift and any understanding of the music or way of life of those who possess it. The square is thought of as an ignorant, intolerant person who is to be feared, since he produces the pressures forcing the musician to play inartistically. The musician's difficulty lies in the fact that the square is in a position to get his way: if he does not like the kind of music played, he does not pay to hear it a second time.

Not understanding music, the square judges music by standards foreign to musicians and not respected by them. A commercial saxophonist observed sarcastically:

It doesn't make any difference what we play, the way we do it. It's so simple that anyone who's been playing longer than a month could handle it. Jack plays a chorus on piano or something, then saxes or something, all unison. It's very easy. But the people don't care. As long as they can hear the drum they're all right. They hear the drum, then they know to put their right foot in front of their left foot and their left foot in front of their right foot. Then if they can hear the melody to whistle to, they're happy. What more could they want?

The following conversation illustrates the same attitude:

Joe: You'd get off the stand and walk down the aisle, somebody'd say, "Young man, I like your orchestra very much." Just because you played soft and the tenorman doubled fiddle or something like that, the squares liked it. . . .

Dick: It was like that when I worked at the M———— Club. All the kids that I went to high school with used to come out and dig the band. . . . That was one of the worst bands I ever worked on and they all thought it was wonderful.

Joe: Oh, well, they're just a bunch of squares anyhow.

"Squareness" is felt to penetrate every aspect of the square's behavior just as its opposite, "hipness," is evident in everything the musician does. The square seems to do everything wrong and is laughable and ludicrous. Musicians derive a good deal of amusement from sitting and watching squares. Everyone has stories to tell about the laughable antics of squares. One man went so far as to suggest that the musicians should change places with the people sitting at the bar of the tavern he worked in; he claimed they were funnier and more entertaining than he could possible be. Every item of dress, speech and behavior which differs from that of the musician is taken as new evidence of the inherent insensitivity and ignorance of the square. Since musicians have an esoteric culture these evidences are many and serve only to fortify their conviction that musicians and squares are two different kinds of people.

But the square is feared as well, since he is thought of as the ultimate source of commercial pressure. It is the square's ignorance of music that compels the musician to play what he considers bad music in order to be successful.

Becker: How do you feel about the people you play for, the audience?

Dave: They're a drag.

Becker: Why do you say that?

Dave: Well, if you're working on a commercial band, they like it and so you have to play more corn. If you're working on a good band, then they don't like it, and that's a drag. If you're working on a good band and they like it, then that's a drag, too. You hate them anyway, because you know that they don't know what it's all about. They're just a big drag.

This last statement reveals that even those who attempt to avoid being square are still considered so, because they still lack the proper understanding, which only a musician can have—"they don't know what it's all about." The jazz fan is thus respected no more than other squares. His liking for jazz is without understanding and he acts just like the other squares; he will request songs and try to influence the musician's playing, just as other squares do.

The musician thus sees himself as a creative artist who should be free from outside control, a person different from and better than those outsiders he calls squares who understand neither his music nor his way of life and yet because of whom he must perform in a manner contrary to his professional ideals.

REACTIONS TO THE CONFLICT

Jazz and commercial musicians agree in essentials on their attitude toward the audience, although they vary in the way they phrase this basic consensus. Two conflicting themes constitute the basis of agreement: the desire for free self-expression in accord with the beliefs of the musician group, and the recognition that outside pressures may force the musician to forego satisfying that desire. The jazzman tends to emphasize the first, the commercial musician the second; but both recognize and feel the force of each of these guiding influences. Common to the attitudes of both kinds of musician is an intense contempt for and dislike of the square audience whose fault it is that musicians must "go commercial" in order to succeed.

HOWARD S. BECKER

The commercial musician, though he conceives of the audience as square, chooses to sacrifice self-respect and the respect of other musicians (the rewards of artistic behavior) for the more substantial rewards of steady work, higher income and the prestige enjoyed by the man who goes commercial. One commercial musician commented:

They've got a nice class of people out here, too. Of course, they're squares, I'm not trying to deny that. Sure, they're a bunch of fucking squares, but who the fuck pays the bills? They pay 'em, so you gotta play what they want. I mean, what the shit, you can't make a living if you don't play for the squares. How many fucking people you think aren't squares? Out of a hundred people you'd be lucky if 15 percent weren't squares. I mean, maybe professional people—doctors, lawyers, like that: they might not be square, but the average person is just a big fucking square. Of course, show people aren't like that. But outside of show people and professional people, everybody's a fucking square.[2] They don't know anything.

I'll tell you. This is something I learned about three years ago. If you want to make any money you gotta please the squares. They're the ones that pay the bills, and you gotta play for them. A good musician can't get a fucking job. You gotta play a bunch of shit. But what the fuck, let's face it. I want to live good. I want to make some money; I want a car, you know. How long can you fight it? . . .

Don't get me wrong. If you can make money playing jazz, great, But how many guys can do it? . . . If you can play jazz, great, like I said. But if you're on a bad fucking job, there's no sense fighting it, you gotta be commercial. I mean, the squares are paying your salary, so you might as well get used to it, they're the ones you gotta please.

Note that the speaker admits it is more "respectable" to be

independent of the squares, and expresses contempt for the audience, whose squareness is made responsible for the whole situation.

These men phrase the problem primarily in economic terms: "I mean, shit if you're playing for a bunch of squares you're playing for a bunch of squares. What the fuck are you gonna do? You can't push it down their throats. Well, I suppose you can make 'em eat it, but after all, they *are* paying you."

The jazzman feels the need to satisfy the audience just as strongly, although maintaining that one should not give in to it. Jazzmen, like others, appreciate steady jobs and good jobs and know they must satisfy the audience to get them, as the following conversation between two young jazzmen illustrates:

Charlie: There aren't any jobs where you can blow jazz. You have to play rumbas and pops [popular songs] and everything. You can't get anywhere blowing jazz. Man, I don't want to scuffle all my life.

Eddie: Well, you want to enjoy yourself, don't you? You won't be happy playing commercial. You know that.

Charlie: I guess there's just no way for a cat to be happy. 'Cause it sure is a drag blowing commercial, but it's an awful drag not ever doing anything and playing jazz.

Eddie: Jesus, why can't you be successful playing jazz? . . . I mean, you could have a great little outfit and still play arrangements, but good ones, you know.

Charlie: You could never get a job for a band like that.

Eddie: Well, you could have a sexy little bitch to stand up in front and sing and shake her ass at the bears [squares]. Then you could get a job. And you could still play great when she wasn't singing.

Charlie: Well, wasn't that what Q—————'s band was

HOWARD S. BECKER

like? Did you enjoy that? Did you like the way she sang?

Eddie: No, man, but we played jazz, you know.

Charlie: Did you like the kind of jazz you were playing? It was kind of commercial, wasn't it?

Eddie: Yeah, but it could have been great.

Charlie: Yeah, if it had been great, you wouldn't have kept on working. I guess we'll always just be unhappy. It's just the way things are. You'll always be drug with yourself. . . . There'll never be any kind of a really great job for a musician.

In addition to the pressure to please the audience which emanates from the musician's desire to maximize salary and income, there are more immediate pressures. It is often difficult to maintain an independent attitude. For example:

I worked an Italian wedding on the Southwest Side last night with Johnny Ponzi. We played about half an hour, doing the special arrangements they use, which are pretty uncommercial. Then an old Italian fellow (the father-in-law of the groom, as we later found out) began hollering, "Play some polkas, play some Italian music. Ah, you stink, you're lousy." Johnny always tries to avoid the inevitable on these wedding jobs, putting off playing the folk music as long as he can. I said, "Man, why don't we play some of that stuff now and get it over with?" Tom said, "I'm afraid if we start doing that we'll be doing it all night." Johnny says, "Look, Howard, the groom is a real nice guy. He told us to play anything we want and not to pay any attention to what the people say, so don't worry about it. . . ."

The old fellow kept hollering and pretty soon the groom came up and said, "Listen, fellows. I know you don't want to play any of that shit and I don't want to embarrass my wife for him, so play some Dago music to keep him quiet, will yuh?" Johnny looked around at us and made a gesture of resignation.

He said, "All right, let's play the *Beer Barrel Polka.*"
Tom said, "Oh shit! Here we go." We played it and then
we played an Italian dance, the *Tarentelle.*

Sometimes the employer applies pressure which makes even
an uncompromising jazzman give in, at least for the duration
of the job:

> I was playing solo for one night over at the Y—————
> on —————rd St. What a drag! The second set, I was
> playing *Sunny Side,* I played the melody for one chorus,
> then I played a little jazz. All of a sudden the boss
> leaned over the side of the bar and hollered, "I'll kiss
> your ass if anybody in this place knows what tune
> you're playing!" And everybody in the place heard him,
> too. What a big square! What could I do? I didn't say
> anything, just kept playing. Sure was a drag.

Somewhat inconsistently, the musician wants to feel that
he is reaching the audience and that they are getting some
enjoyment from his work, and this also leads him to give in
to audience demands. One man said:

> I enjoy playing more when there's someone to play
> for. You kind of feel like there isn't much purpose in
> playing if there's nobody there to hear you. I mean,
> after all, that's what music's for—for people to hear and
> get enjoyment from. That's why I don't mind playing
> corny too much. If anyone enjoys it, then I kind of get
> a kick out of it. I guess I'm kind of a ham. But I like to
> make people happy that way.

This statement is somewhat extreme; but most musicians feel
it strongly enough to want to avoid the active dislike of the
audience: "That's why I like to work with Tommy. At least
when you get off the stand, everybody in the place doesn't
hate you. It's a drag to work under conditions like that,
where everybody in the place just hates the whole band."

ISOLATION AND SELF-SEGREGATION

Musicians are hostile to their audiences, afraid that they
must sacrifice their artistic standards to the squares. They

HOWARD S. BECKER

exhibit certain patterns of behavior and belief which may be viewed as adjustments to this situation. These patterns of isolation and self-segregation are expressed in the actual playing situation and in participation in the social intercourse of the larger community. The primary function of this behavior is to protect the musician from the interference of the square audience and, by extension, of the conventional society. Its primary consequence is to intensify the musician's status as an outsider, through the operation of a cycle of increasing deviance. Difficulties with squares lead to increasing isolation which in turn increase the possibilities of further difficulties.

As a rule, the musician is spatially isolated from the audience. He works on a platform, which provides a physical barrier that prevents direct interaction. This isolation is welcomed because the audience, being made up of squares, is felt to be potentially dangerous. The musicians fear that direct contact with the audience can lead only to interference with the musical performance. Therefore, it is safer to be isolated and have nothing to do with them. Once, where such physical isolation was not provided, a player commented:

> Another thing about weddings, man. You're right down on the floor, right in the middle of the people. You can't get away from them. It's different if you're playing a dance or in a bar. In a dancehall you're up on a stage where they can't get at you. The same thing in a cocktail lounge, you're up behind the bar. But a wedding—man, you're right in the middle of them.

Musicians, lacking the usually provided physical barriers, often improvise their own and effectively segregate themselves from their audience.

> I had a Jewish wedding job for Sunday night. . . . When I arrived, the rest of the boys were already there. The wedding had taken place late, so that the people were just beginning to eat. We decided, after I had conferred with the groom, to play during dinner. We set up in a far corner of the hall. Jerry pulled the piano

around so that it blocked off a small space, which was thus separated from the rest of the people. Tony set up his drums in this space, and Jerry and Johnny stood there while we played. I wanted to move the piano so that the boys could stand out in front of it and be next to the audience, but Jerry said, half-jokingly, "No, man. I have to have some protection from the squares." So we left things as they were. . . .

Jerry had moved around in front of the piano but, again half-humorously, had put two chairs in front of him, which separated him from the audience. When a couple took the chairs to sit on, Jerry set two more in their place. Johnny said, "Man, why don't we sit on those chairs?" Jerry said, "No, man. Just leave them there. That's my barricade to protect me from the squares."

Many musicians almost reflexively avoid establishing contact with members of the audience. When walking among them, they habitually avoid meeting the eyes of squares for fear this will establish some relationship on the basis of which the square will then request songs or in some other way attempt to influence the musical performance. Some extend the behavior to their ordinary social activity, outside of professional situations. A certain amount of this is inevitable, since the conditions of work—late hours, great geographic mobility and so on—make social participation outside of the professional group difficult. If one works while others sleep, it is difficult to have ordinary social intercourse with them. This was cited by a musician who had left the profession, in partial explanation of his action: "And it's great to work regular hours, too, where you can see people instead of having to go work every night." Some younger musicians complain that the hours of work make it hard for them to establish contacts with "nice" girls, since they preclude the conventional date.

But much self-segregation develops out of the hostility toward squares. The attitude is seen in its extreme among the

HOWARD S. BECKER

"X————— Avenue Boys," a clique of extreme jazzmen who reject the American culture *in toto*. The quality of their feeling toward the outside world is indicated by one man's private title for his theme song: "If You Don't Like My Queer Ways You Can Kiss My Fucking Ass." The ethnic makeup of the group indicated further that their adoption of extreme artistic and social attitudes was part of a total rejection of conventional American society. With few exceptions the men came from older, more fully assimilated national groups: Irish, Scandinavian, German and English. Further, many of them were reputed to come from wealthy families and the higher social classes. In short, their rejection of commercialism in music and squares in social life was part of the casting aside of the total American culture by men who enjoyed a privileged position, but were unable to achieve a satisfactory personal adjustment within it.

Every interest of this group emphasized their isolation from the standards and interests of conventional society. They associated almost exclusively with other musicians and girls who sang or danced in night clubs in the North Clark Street area of Chicago and had little or no contact with the conventional world. They were described politically thus: "They hate this form of government anyway and think it's real bad." They were unremittingly critical of both business and labor, disillusioned with the economic structure, and cynical about the political process and contemporary political parties. Religion and marriage were rejected completely, as were American popular and serious culture, and their reading was confined solely to the more esoteric *avant garde* writers and philosophers. In art and symphonic music they were interested in only the most esoteric developments. In every case they were quick to point out that their interests were not those of the conventional society and that they were thereby diffentiated from it. It is reasonable to assume that the primary function of these interests was to make this differentiation unmistakably clear.

Although isolation and self-segregation found their most

extreme development among the "X———— Avenue Boys," they were manifested by less deviant musicians as well. The feeling of being isolated from the rest of the society was often quite strong; the following conversation, which took place between two young jazzmen, illustrates two reactions to the sense of isolation.

Eddie: You know, man, I hate people. I can't stand to be around squares. They drag me so much I just can't stand them.

Charlie: You shouldn't be like that, man. Don't let them drag you. Just laugh at them. That's what I do. Just laugh at everything they do. That's the only way you'll be able to stand it.

A young Jewish musician, who definitely identified himself with the Jewish community, nevertheless felt this professional isolation strongly enough to make the following statements.

You know, a little knowledge is a dangerous thing. That's what happened to me when I first started playing. I just felt like I knew too much. I sort of saw, or felt, that all my friends from the neighborhood were real square and stupid. . . .

You know, it's funny. When you sit on that stand up there, you feel so different from others. Like I can even understand how Gentiles feel toward Jews. You see these people come up and they look Jewish, or they have a bit of an accent or something, and they ask for a rumba or some damn thing like that, and I just feel, "What damn squares, these Jews," just like I was a *goy* myself. That's what I mean when I say you learn too much being a musician. I mean, you see so many things and get such a broad outlook on life that the average person just doesn't have.

On another occasion the same man remarked:

You know, since I've been out of work I've actually gotten so that I can talk to some of these guys in the neighborhood.

[You mean you had trouble talking to them before?]
Well, I'd just stand around and not know what to say.
It still sobers me up to talk to those guys. Everything
they say seems real silly and uninteresting.

The process of self-segregation is evident in certain
symbolic expressions, particularly in the use of an occupational slang which readily identifies the man who can use it
properly as someone who is not square and as quickly reveals
as an outsider the person who uses it incorrectly or not at all.
Some words have grown up to refer to unique professional
problems and attitudes of musicians, typical of them being
the term "square." Such words enable musicians to discuss
problems and activities for which ordinary language provides
no adequate terminology. There are, however, many words
which are merely substitutes for more common expressions
without adding any new meaning. For example, the following
are synonyms for money: "loot," "gold," "geetz," and
"bread." Jobs are referred to as "gigs." There are innumerable synonyms for marijuana, the most common being
"gage," "pot," "charge," "tea," and "shit."

The function of such behavior is pointed out by a young
musician who was quitting the business:

I'm glad I'm getting out of the business, though. I'm
getting sick of being around musicians. There's so much
ritual and ceremony junk. They have to talk a special
language, dress different, and wear a different kind of
glasses. And it just doesn't mean a damn thing except
"we're different."

CLIQUES AND SUCCESS

The musician conceives of success as movement through a
hierarchy of available jobs. Unlike the industrial or white
collar worker, he does not identify his career with one
employer; he expects to change jobs frequently. An informally recognized ranking of these jobs—taking account of the
income involved, the hours of work and the degree of
community recognition of achievement felt—constitutes the

scale by which a musician measures his success according to the kind of job he usually holds.

At the bottom of this scale is the man who plays irregularly for small dances, wedding receptions and similar affairs, and is lucky to make union wages. At the next level are those men who have steady jobs in "joints"—lower class taverns and night clubs, small "strip joints," etc.—where pay is low and community recognition lower. The next level is comprised of those men who have steady jobs with local bands in neighborhood ballrooms and small, "respectable" night clubs and cocktail lounges in better areas of the city. These jobs pay more than joint jobs and the man working them can expect to be recognized as successful in his community. Approximately equivalent to these are men who work in so-called "class B name" orchestras, the second rank of nationally known dance orchestras. The next level consists of men who work in "class A name" bands, and in local orchestras that play the best night clubs and hotels, large conventions, etc. Salaries are good, hours are easy and the men can expect to be recognized as successful within and outside of the profession. The top positions in this scale are occupied by men who hold staff positions in radio and television stations and legitimate theaters. Salaries are high, hours short and these jobs are recognized as the epitome of achievement in the local music world, and as jobs of high-ranking respectability by outsiders.

A network of informal, interlocking cliques allocates the jobs available at a given time. In securing work at any one level, or in moving up to jobs at a new level, one's position in the network is of great importance. Cliques are bound together by ties of mutual obligation, the members sponsoring each other for jobs, either hiring one another when they have the power or recommending one another to those who do the hiring for an orchestra. The recommendation is of great importance, since it is by this means that available individuals become known to those who hire; the person who

HOWARD S. BECKER

is unknown will not be hired, and membership in cliques insures that one has many friends who will recommend one to the right people.

Clique membership thus provides the individual with steady employment. One man explained:

> See, it works like this. My right hand here, that's five musicians. My left hand, that's five more. Now one of these guys over here gets a job. He picks the men for it from just these guys in this group. Whenever one of them gets a job, naturally he hires this guy. So you see how it works. They never hire anybody that isn't in the clique. If one of them works, they all work.

The musician builds and cements these relationships by getting jobs for other men and so obligating them to return the favor:

> There were a couple of guys on this band that I've got good jobs for, and they've had them ever since. Like one of those trombone players. I got him on a good band. One of the trumpet players, too. . . . You know the way that works. A leader asks you for a man. If he likes the guy you give him, why every time he needs a man he'll ask you. That way you can get all your friends on.

Security comes from the number and quality of relationships so established. To have a career one must work; to enjoy the security of steady work one must have many "connections":

> You have to make connections like that all over town, until it gets so that when anybody wants a man they call you. Then you're never out of work.

A certain similarity to the informal organization of medical practice should be noted. Musicians cooperate by recommending each other for jobs in much the same way that members of the medical "inner fraternity" cooperate by furnishing each other with patients.[3] The two institutional complexes differ, however, in that medical practice (in all except the largest cities) tends to revolve around a few large hospitals which one, or a few, such fraternities can control. In music, the number of possible foci is much greater, with a correspondingly greater proliferation of organization and, consequently, there are more opportunities for the individual to establish the right connections for himself and a lessening of the power of any particular clique.

In addition to providing a measure of job security for their members, cliques also provide routes by which one can move up through the levels of jobs. In several cliques observed, membership was drawn from more than one level of the hierarchy; thus men of lower position were able to associate with men from a higher level. When a job becomes available higher in the scale, a man of the lower level may be sponsored by a higher-ranking man who recommends him, or hires him and takes the responsibility for the quality of his performance. A radio staff musician described the process in these terms:

Now the other way to be a success is to have a lot of friends. You have to play good, but you have to have friends on different bands and when someone leaves a band, why they're plugging to get you on. It takes a long time to work yourself up that way. Like I've been 10 years getting the job I have now.

If the man so sponsored performs successfully he can build up more informal relationships at the new level and thus get more jobs at that level. Successful performance on the job is necessary if he is to establish himself fully at the new level, and sponsors exhibit a great deal of anxiety over the performance of their protégés. The multiple sponsorship described in this incident from my field notes illustrates this anxiety and its sources in the obligations of colleagues:

A friend of mine asked me if I was working that night. When I told him no, he led me over to another guy who, in turn, led me to an old fellow with a strong Italian accent. This man said, "You play piano, huh?" I said, "Yes." He said, "You play good, huh?" I said, "Yes." He said, "You play good? Read pretty good?" I said, "Not bad. What kind of deal is this?" He said, "It's at a club here in the Loop. It's nine to four-thirty, pays two-fifty an hour. You're sure you can handle it?" I said, "Sure!" He touched my shoulder and said, "OK. I just have to ask you all these questions. I mean, I don't know you, I don't know how you play, I just have to ask, you see?" I said, "Sure." He said, "You know, I have to make sure, it's a spot downtown. Well, here. You call this number and tell them Mantuno told you to call—Mantuno. See, I have to make sure you're gonna do good or else I'm gonna catch hell. Go on, call 'em now. Remember, Mantuno told you to call."

He gave me the number. I called and got the job. When I came out of the booth my friend who had originated the deal came up and said, "Everything all right? Did you get the job, huh?" I said, "Yeah, thanks an awful lot." He said, "That's all right. Listen, do a good job. I mean, if it's commercial, play commercial. What the hell! I mean, if you don't then it's my ass, you know. It isn't even only my ass, it's Tony's and that other guy's, it's about four different asses, you know."

In short, to get these top job positions requires both ability and the formation of informal relationships of mutual obligation with men who can sponsor one for the jobs. Without the necessary minimum of ability one cannot perform successfully at the new level, but this ability will command the appropriate kind of work only if a man has made the proper connections. For sponsors, as the above quotation indicates, the system operates to bring available men to the attention of those who have jobs to fill and to provide them with recruits who can be trusted to perform adequately.

The successful career may be viewed as a series of such steps, each one a sequence of sponsorship, successful performance, and the building up of relationships at each new level.

I have noted a similarity between the musician's career and

careers in medicine and industry, shown in the fact that successful functioning and professional mobility are functions of the individual's relation to a network of informal organizations composed of his colleagues. I turn now to the variation in this typical social form created by the strong emphasis of musicians on maintaining their freedom to play without interference from nonmusicians, who are felt to lack understanding and appreciation of the musician's mysterious, artistic gifts. Since it is difficult (if not impossible) to attain this desired freedom, most men find it necessary to sacrifice the standards of their profession to some degree in order to meet the demands of audiences and of those who control employment opportunities. This creates another dimension of professional prestige, based on the degree to which one refuses to modify one's performance in deference to outside demands—from the one extreme of "playing what you feel" to the other of "playing what the people want to hear." The jazzman plays what he feels while the commercial musician caters to public taste; the commercial viewpoint is best summarized in a statement attributed to a very successful commercial musician: "I'll do anything for a dollar."

As I pointed out earlier, musicians feel that there is a conflict inherent in this situation, that one cannot please the audience and at the same time maintain one's artistic integrity. The following quotation, from an interview with a radio staff musician, illustrates the kind of pressures in the top jobs that produce such conflict:

> The big thing down at the studio is not to make any mistakes. You see, they don't care whether you play a thing well or not, as long as you play all the notes and don't make any mistakes. Of course, you care if it doesn't sound good, but they're not interested in that. . . . They don't care what you sound like when you go through that mike, all they care about is the commercial. I mean, you might have some personal pride about it, but they don't care. . . . That's what you have to do. Give him what you know he likes already.

HOWARD S. BECKER

The job with most prestige is thus one in which the musician must sacrifice his artistic independence and the concomitant prestige in professional terms. A very successful commercial musician paid deference to artistic independence while stressing its negative effect on career development:

> I know, you probably like to play jazz. Sure I understand. I used to be interested in jazz, but I found out that didn't pay, people didn't like jazz. They like rumbas. After all, this is a business, ain't that right? You're in it to make a living or you're not, that's all. And if you want to make a living you can't throw jazz at the people all the time, they won't take it. So you have to play what they want, they're the ones that are paying the bills. I mean, don't get me wrong. Any guy that can make a living playing jazz, fine. But I'd like to see the guy that can do it. If you want to get anywhere you gotta be commercial.

Jazzmen, on the other hand, complain of the low position of the jobs available to them in terms of income and things other than artistic prestige.

Thus the cliques to which one must gain access if one is to achieve job success and security are made up of men who are definitely commercial in their orientation. The greatest rewards of the profession are controlled by men who have sacrificed some of the most basic professional standards, and one must make a similar sacrifice in order to have any chance of moving into the desirable positions:

> See, if you play commercial like that, you can get in with these cliques that have all the good jobs and you can really do well. I've played some of the best jobs in town—the Q————— Club and places like that—and that's the way you have to do. Play that way and get in with these guys, then you never have to worry. You can count on making that gold every week and that's what counts.

Cliques made up of jazzmen offer their members nothing but the prestige of maintaining artistic integrity; commercial cliques offer security, mobility, income and general social prestige.

This conflict is a major problem in the career of the individual musician, and the development of his career is contingent on his reaction to it. Although I gathered no data on the point, it seems reasonable to assume that most men enter music with a great respect for jazz and artistic freedom. At a certain point in the development of the career (which varies from individual to individual), the conflict becomes apparent and the musician realizes that it is impossible to achieve the kind of success he desires and maintain independence of musical performance. When the incompatibility of these goals becomes obvious, some sort of choice must be made, if only by default, thus determining the further course of his career.

One response to the dilemma is to avoid it, by leaving the profession. Unable to find a satisfactory resolution of the problem, the individual cuts his career off. The rationale of such a move is disclosed in the following statement by one who had made it:

> It's better to take a job you know you're going to be dragged [depressed] with, where you expect to be dragged, than one in music, where it could be great but isn't. Like you go into business, you don't know anything about it. So you figure it's going to be a drag and you expect it. But music can be so great that it's a big drag when it isn't. So it's better to have some other kind of job that won't drag you that way.

We have seen the range of responses to this dilemma on the part of those who remain in the profession. The jazzman ignores audience demands for artistic standards while the commercial musician does the opposite, both feeling the pressure of these two forces. My concern here will be to discuss the relation of these responses to career fates.

The man who chooses to ignore commercial pressures finds himself effectively barred from moving up to jobs of greater prestige and income, and from membership in those cliques which would provide him with security and the opportunity for such mobility. Few men are willing or able to take such an extreme position; most compromise to some degree. The pattern of movement involved in this compromise is a common career phenomenon, well known among musicians and assumed to be practically inevitable:

I saw K————— E—————. I said, "Get me a few jobbing dates, will you?" He said, imitating one of the "old guys,"[4] "Now son, when you get wise and commercial, I'll be able to help you out, but not now." In his normal voice he continued, "Why don't you get with it? Gosh, I'm leading the trend over to commercialism, I guess. I certainly have gone in for it in a big way, haven't I?"

At this crucial point in his career the individual finds it necessary to make a radical change in his self-conception; he must learn to think of himself in a new way, to regard himself as a different kind of person:

This commercial business has really gotten me, I guess. You know, even when I go on a job where you're supposed to blow jazz, where you can just let yourself go and play anything, I think about being commercial, about playing what the people out there might want to hear. I used to go on a job with the idea to play the best I could, that's all, just play the best I know how. And now I go on a job and I just automatically think, "What will these people want to hear? Do they want to hear Kenton style, or like Dizzy Gillespie [jazz orchestras], or like Guy Lombardo [a commercial orchestra], or what?" I can't help thinking that to myself. They've really gotten it into me, I guess they've broken my spirit.

A more drastic change of self-conception related to this career dilemma is found in this statement:

I'll tell you, I've decided the only thing to do is really

go commercial—play what the people want to hear. I think there's a good place for the guy that'll give them just what they want. The melody, that's all. No improvising, no technical stuff—just the plain melody. I'll tell you, why shouldn't I play that way? After all, let's quit kidding ourselves. Most of us aren't really musicians, we're just instrumentalists. I mean, I think of myself as something like a common laborer, you know. No sense trying to fool myself. Most of those guys are just instrumentalists, they're not real musicians at all, they should stop trying to kid themselves they are.

Making such a decision and undergoing such a change in self-conception open the way for movement into the upper levels of the job hierarchy and create the conditions in which complete success is possible, if one can follow up the opportunity by making and maintaining the proper connections.

One way of adjusting to the realities of the job without sacrificing self-respect is to adopt the orientation of the craftsman. The musician who does this no longer concerns himself with the *kind* of music he plays. Instead, he is interested only in whether it is played *correctly,* in whether he has the skills necessary to do the job the way it ought to be done. He finds his pride and self-respect in being able to "cut" any kind of music, in always giving an adequate performance.

The skills necessary to maintain this orientation vary with the setting in which the musician performs. The man who works in bars with small groups will pride himself on knowing hundreds (or even thousands) of songs and being able to play them in any key. The man who works with a big band will pride himself on his intonation and technical virtuosity. The man who works in a night club or radio studio boasts of his ability to read any kind of music accurately and precisely at sight. This kind of orientation, since it is likely to produce just what the employer wants and at a superior level of quality, is likely to lead to occupational success.

HOWARD S. BECKER

The craftsman orientation is easier to sustain in the major musical centers of the country: Chicago, New York, Los Angeles. In these cities, the volume of available work is great enough to support specialization, and a man can devote himself single-mindedly to improving one set of skills. One finds musicians of astounding virtuosity in these centers. In smaller cities, in contrast, there is not enough work of any one kind for a man to specialize, and musicians are called on to do a little of everything. Although the necessary skills overlap—intonation, for instance, is always important—every man has areas in which he is just barely competent. A trumpet player may play excellent jazz and do well on small jazz jobs but read poorly and much less well when he works with a big band. It is difficult to maintain pride as a craftsman when one is continually faced with jobs for which he has only minimal skills.

To sum up, the emphasis of musicians on freedom from the interference inevitable in their work creates a new dimension of professional prestige which conflicts with the previously discussed job prestige in such a way that one cannot rank high in both. The greatest rewards are in the hands of those who have sacrificed their artistic independence, and who demand a similar sacrifice from those they recruit for these higher positions. This creates a dilemma for the individual musician, and his response determines the future course of his career. Refusing to submit means that all hope of achieving jobs of high prestige and income must be abandoned, while giving in to commercial pressures opens the way to success for them. (Studies of other occupations might devote attention to those career contingencies which are, likewise, a function of the occupation's basic work problems vis-à-vis clients or customers.)

PARENTS AND WIVES

I have noted that musicians extend their desire for freedom from outside interference in their work to a generalized feeling that they should not be bound by the ordinary conventions of their society. The ethos of the profession fosters an admiration for spontaneous and individualistic behavior and a disregard for the rules of society in general. We may expect that members of an occupation with such an ethos will have problems of conflict when they come into close contact with that society. One point of contact is on the job, where the audience is the source of trouble. The effect of this area of problems on the career has been described above.

Another area of contact between profession and society is the family. Membership in families binds the musician to people who are squares, outsiders who abide by social conventions whose authority the musician does not acknowledge. Such relationships bear seeds of conflict which can break out with disastrous consequences for the career and/or the family tie. This section will spell out the nature of these conflicts and their effect on the career.

The individual's family has a great influence on his occupational choice through its power to sponsor and aid the neophyte in his chosen career. Hall, in his discussion of the early stages of the medical career, notes that:

> In most cases family or friends played a significant role by envisaging the career line and reinforcing the efforts of the recruit. They accomplished the latter by giving encouragement, helping establish the appropriate routines, arranging the necessary privacy, discouraging anomalous behavior, and defining the day-to-day rewards.[5]

The musician's parents ordinarily do not aid the development of his career in this way. On the contrary, as one man observed, "My God, most guys have had a terrific hassle with their parents about going into the music business." The reason is clear: regardless of the social class from which he comes, it is usually obvious to the prospective musician's family that he is entering a profession which encourages his breaking with the conventional behavior patterns of his family's social milieu. Lower-class families seem to have been most distressed over the irregularity of musical employment, although there is evidence that some families encouraged such a career, seeing it as a possible mobility route. In the middle-class family, choice of dance music as an occupation is viewed as a movement into Bohemianism, involving a possible loss of prestige for both individual and family, and is vigorously opposed. Considerable pressure is applied to the person to give up his choice:

> You know, everybody thought it was pretty terrible when I decided to be a musician. . . . I remember I graduated from high school on a Thursday and left town on Monday for a job. Here my parents were arguing with me and all my relatives, too, they were really giving me a hard time. . . . This one uncle of mine came on so strong about how it wasn't a regular life and how could I ever get married and all that stuff.

The conflict has two typical effects on the career. First, the prospective musician may, in the face of family pressure, give up music as a profession. Such an adjustment is fairly common at an early stage of the career. On the other hand, the young musician may ignore his family's desires and continue his career, in which case he is often deprived of his family's support at an earlier age than would otherwise be the case and must begin to "go it alone," making his way without the family sponsorship and financial aid that might otherwise be forthcoming. In music, then, the career is ordinarily begun, if at all, without the family aid and encouragement typical of careers in many other occupations.

Once he has married and established his own family, the musician has entered a relationship in which the conventions of society are presented to him in an immediate and forceful way. As a husband he is expected by his wife, typically a nonmusician, to be a companion and provider. In some occupations there is no conflict between the demands of work and of the family. In others there is conflict, but socially-sanctioned resolutions of it exist which are accepted by both partners as, for example, in medical practice. In deviant occupations, such as the music business, professional expectations do not mesh at all with lay expectations, with consequent difficulties for the musician.

Musicians feel that the imperatives of their work must take precedence over those of their families, and they act accordingly:

> Man, my wife's a great chick, but there's no way for us to stay together, not as long as I'm in the music business. No way, no way at all. When we first got married it was great. I was working in town, making good gold, everybody was happy. But when that job was through, I didn't have anything. Then I got an offer to go on the road. Well, hell, I needed the money, I took it. Sally said, "No, I want you here in town, with me." She'd sooner have had me go to work in a factory! Well, that's a bunch of crap. So I just left with the band. Hell, I like the business too much, I'm not gonna put it down for her or any woman.

Marriage is likely to turn into a continuing struggle over this issue; the outcome of the struggle determines whether the man's musical career will be cut short or will continue, as the following incident from my field notes illustrates:

> The boys down at the Z————— Club are trying to get Jay Marlowe to go back to work there full time. He's splitting the week with someone now. He's got a day job in the same office in which his wife works, doing bookkeeping or some minor clerical job. The boys are trying to talk him into quitting. Apparently his wife is bitterly opposed to this.
>
> Jay's been a musician all his life, as far as I know; probably the first time he ever had a day job. Gene, the drummer at the Z————— Club, said to me, "It's foolish for him to have a day job. How much can he make down there? Probably doesn't clear more than 30, 35 a week. He makes that much in three nights here. Course,

HOWARD S. BECKER

his wife wanted him to get out of the business. She didn't like the idea of all those late hours and the chicks that hang around bars, that kind of stuff. But after all, when a guy can do something and make more money, why should he take a sad job and work for peanuts? It don't make sense. Besides, why should he drag himself? He'd rather be playing and it's a drag to him to have that fucking day job, so why should he hold on to it?" Johnny, the saxophone player, said, "You know why, because his wife makes him hold on to it." Gene said, "He shouldn't let her boss him around like that. For Christ sake, my old lady don't tell me what to do. He shouldn't put up with that crap."

They've started to do something about it. They've been inviting Jay to go out to the race track with them on week days and he's been skipping work to do so. Gene, after one of these occasions, said, "Boy was his wife mad! She doesn't want him to goof off and lose that job, and she knows what we're up to. She thinks we're bad influences. Well, I guess we are, from her way of thinking."

[A few weeks later Marlowe quit his day job and returned to music.]

For other men who feel their family responsibilities more strongly the situation is not so simple. The economic insecurity of the music business makes it difficult to be a good provider, and may force the individual to leave the profession, one of the typical patterns of response to this situation:

No, I haven't been working too much. I think I'm going to get a goddamn day job. You know, when you're married it's a little different. Before it was different. I worked, I didn't work, all the same thing. If I needed money I'd borrow five from my mother. Now those bills just won't wait. When you're married you got to keep working or else you just can't make it.

Even if the career is not cut off in this fashion, the

demands of marriage exert a very strong pressure that pushes the musican toward going commercial:

> If you want to keep on working, you have to put up with some crap once in a while. . . . I don't care. I've got a wife and I want to keep working. If some square comes up and asks me to play the "Beer Barrel Polka" I just smile and play it.

Marriage can thus speed the achievement of success by forcing a decision which affords, although it does not guarantee, the opportunity for movement into those cliques which, being commercially oriented, are best able to keep their members in steady work.

The family then, as an institution that demands that the musician behave conventionally, creates problems for him of conflicting pressures, loyalties and self-conceptions. His response to these problems has a decisive effect on the duration and direction of his career.

Reproduced by the permission of the Society for Applied Anthropology from Vol. 12, No. 1, 1953, *Human Organization*.

NOTES

1. For other studies of the jazz musician, see: Carlo L. Lastrucci, "The Professional Dance Musician," *Journal of Musicology*, III (Winter, 1941), 168-172; William Bruce Cameron, "Sociological Notes on the Jam Session," *Social Forces*, XXXIII (December, 1954), 177-182; and Alan P. Merriam and Raymond W. Mack, "The Jazz Community," *Social Forces*, XXXVIII (March, 1960), 211-222.

2. Most musicians would not admit these exceptions.

3. Oswald Hall, "The Stages of a Medical Career," *American Journal of Sociology*, LIII (March 1948), 332.

4. "Old guys" was the term generally used by younger men to refer to the cliques controlling the most desirable jobs.

5. Hall, *op. cit.*, p. 328. See also Becker, "The Implications of Research on Occupational Careers. . . ," *op. cit.;* and James W. Caper and Howard S. Becker, "Adjustments to Conflicting Expectations in the Development of Identification with an Occupation," *Social Forces*, 36 (October, 1957), 11-16.

HOWARD S. BECKER

Paying Dues:
Changes in the
Jazz Life

NAT HENTOFF

"Paying dues" is the jazz musician's term for the years of learning and searching for an individual sound and style while the pay is small and irregular. Sometimes there isn't enough work in jazz to live on, and the apprentice is forced into paying the hardest dues of all—the taking of a day job.

In the earliest years of jazz, however, few of the players took the music that seriously. The "musicianers" of the South and Southwest at the beginning of the century regarded the need to work at another trade during the day as a matter of course. In the country, many were sharecroppers or independent farmers who taught themselves whatever instruments were available and played for their own amusement or at local dances and picnics in their spare time. They formed raw unorthodox brass bands and string groups, but hardly regarded themselves as "artists." For them, music was self-expression and also served a community purpose that brought them added status and income.

Later, in the cities, men who played in brass bands for parades and worked dances at night were often also barbers, cigar makers, longshoremen, bricklayers, carpenters or roof-

99

ers. Some—particularly the wandering blues pianists and singers—worked on the periphery of the law, supporting themselves partly by gambling, pimping or becoming professional pool sharks. The majority of the early jazzmen, however, were relatively responsible citizens who, in their roles as musicians, were playing a thoroughly functional music.

Jazz (or "ragtime" as the music was loosely called in the South) was played for dances, parades, intermissions at brothels and to complement the joy, rage or sorrow of whiskey in the blood. The music worked if it made its listeners feel better. The early jazz musician measured his success by how far ahead he was hired. The only critics were the dancers and the drinkers.

Gradually, in the second decade of the century, it became possible for more players to make the music a full-time career. But none of the early travelers was ever allowed to forget that he was primarily an "entertainer." The first waves of jazz professionals worked carnivals and tent shows; made the vaudeville circuit; and accompanied blues singers and comedians, sometimes taking part in the latter's sketches.

The jazzmen who gained their basic experience in the 1920s and 1930s operated under the same contract. Many still doubled in vaudeville, and when they did play at dance halls or in small combos at bars, they worried if the audience remained motionless. Usually they had to include enough "novelty songs" and even some visual comedy to keep the drinkers amused.

It was worst for Negro musicians playing to white audiences, particularly, of course, in the South. Texas pianist Sam Price recalls: "If a man hired you to work someplace, you had to act a fool in order to hold a job. The drummer had to do all these stick deals, and put the stick in his mouth. If you were a pianist, it helped to be able to Charleston at the same time." In playing for Negro audiences and in some white rooms in the North and Midwest, there were occasionally musical kicks on the job, to be sure, but the major pleasure and challenges of the music-making itself were often reserved for the after-hours sessions where musicians were the only audience.

When British bandleader-critic Humphrey Lyttelton defended Louis Armstrong's commercialism a few years ago, his main argument was that Louis had known no other possibilities in the formative years of his career. Lyttelton cited the mid-twenties, during the period when the Hot Five recordings were made, which contained some of Armstrong's most brilliantly daring work. But outside the recording studio, conditions were different. Lyttelton asked how present-day critics of Armstrong would "react to the Reverend Satchelmouth, to the 'boy and girl' dance routine which he used to do with Zutty Singleton or to the version of *Heebie Jeebies* in which, according to an eye-witness, he sang not words but 'a guttural mouthing of incoherent nonsense, supplemented with unearthly grimaces'?"

"They might go even back further," Lyttelton continued, "to the Good Old Days in New Orleans, 1918, when, with Kid Ory's band, he worked out 'a little jive routine with dancing and fooling around between numbers to get laughs.' And if they want to know who taught him such deplorable goings-on, they needn't look to publicity men or agents or commercial bigshots. Let them ask Kid Ory, himself a master of New Orleans hokum; or Joe Oliver, who specialized in. . . muted 'effects' like the horse-laugh, the baby-cry and the talking cornet, using glasses, bottles, tin mugs and anything else that came to hand."

Inexorably, however, the standards of musicianship rose, because jazz *had* become a profession, if not yet an acknowledged "art." One sign of the departure from the folk practices of jazz's infancy was the fact that by the 1920s nearly all apprentices learned their trade from the beginning on regular instruments. Two decades before, it was still not uncommon for a youngster to begin on makeshifts of his own invention. Kid Ory's first instrument was a home-made banjo; Jelly Roll Morton put together his own percussion set from two chair-rounds and a tin pan; clarinetist Johnny Dodds first developed an embouchure on a penny whistle while his brother, Baby Dodds, accompanied him on a pile of tin cans. Many of the early jazzmen then graduated to instruments of varying and vulnerable condition that an older member of the family had discarded or that could be bought cheaply in a pawn shop. Some of the first jazzmen waited a long time before they had a really adequate instrument. The next generation, however, usually started on a higher grade of instrument, and quickly became conscious of brand names. Today, most young players will ration their food rather than compromise on the quality of their horns. Some jazzmen, once they achieve renown, insist that companies make up new instruments to their specifications.

There was soon less and less room for semi-amateurs in jazz. For all the romance that has been interwoven with the early history of jazz, criteria of intonation and technique were spotty at first. Old New Orleans musicians insist, for example, that many bands had only one or two superior soloists. The other musicians were relatively competent, but often were better cigar makers than trombonists or drummers. Vaudeville performers and night club singers were more demanding, however, in their requirements of musicians than were picnic-goers or neighborhood dancers. A jazz professional had to be at ease in more than just a few keys, and especially as the big bands developed, he had to be able to read if he wanted steady work. Lester Young was fired from his own father's band—which played carnivals and tent shows—because he had learned his horn entirely by ear. His father wouldn't let Lester back until he had learned to read. "That hurt me real bad," Young remembered, "I practiced every day and was back in the band in about six months."

Among the musicians, a hierarchy of excellence had been established long before there were music magazines and polls.

NAT HENTOFF

Buddy Bolden and later, King Oliver had enjoyed acknowledged pre-eminence in New Orleans; Louis Armstrong dominated Chicago and New York in the 1920s and well into the 1930s; pianists "Luckey" Roberts, James P. Johnson and Willie "the Lion" Smith were the criteria for such younger pianists in New York in the 1920s as Duke Ellington, Count Basie and Fats Waller. In every city along the seaboard and throughout the South, Southwest and Midwest, there were local style-setters. Some never recorded, or weren't recorded in the right context, but they are still referred to with awe by musicians who learned from them.

The increased traveling of jazz musicians soon made the hierarchies of jazz less localized. Coleman Hawkins and Louis Armstrong were demonstrating in each town they played that jazz was evolving into a virtuoso discipline, and they usually replaced the local experts as models for the apprentices. Moreover, through the popularization of phonograph records, the beginning player in Wisconsin or Florida had, by the end of the 1920s, a wide selection of major influences to study. As the challenges increased from within the music, new jazzmen were driven to achieve greater command of their instruments and to be able to play more than a dance date or vaudeville engagement required.

Before the first critic wrote that a jazzman was developing a "significant contribution" to the language, the players held their own seminars at after-hour sessions where the musicians themselves were faculty, student body and critics. New ideas were exchanged and tested; new players were pitted against the established stylists.

"We used to call them cuttin' contests," Coleman Hawkins, the patriarch of the jazz tenor saxophone, recalls. "Like you'd hear about a very good tenor in some night spot, and I'd have to go down there and cut him." "We weren't out to change the world musically," Duke Ellington adds. "We wanted to make a living and get as much self-satisfaction out of our work as we could."

Another stimulus to self-consciousness arrived with the specialist magazines. The historians and discographers of the "new art" already existed in Europe in the 1920s, but only those relatively few jazzmen who traveled abroad in those years were aware of them. The jazz cult began to grow on native grounds in the early 1930s. First were the collectors who began to analyze recordings that had been originally made, for the most part, to entertain and had often been released by companies primarily for the Negro market. As trade magazines such as *Down Beat* began to grow in the middle and late 1930s, musicians were able to read acidulous debates about their styles. They also followed the popularity polls that *Down Beat* and similar journals instituted.

For all the clamor in the jazz press, however, the musicians knew that the large majority of the audience they faced each night was merrily ignorant of the aesthetics of jazz. They still came to hear music that made them feel good, music that was usually accompaniment for dancing and drinking. The true jazz public was still small in the 1930s, and its representatives could be easily identified as those few customers who listened intently over a night-long beer in preoccupied contrast to the happy imbibers all around. At dances, the *aficionados* stood immovable in front of the bandstand and tried to draw the musicians into discographical discussions at intermission.

Not only was the majority of the audience that came to listen indifferent to jazz as "art," but throughout the 1930s, sections of the general populace were actively opposed to the music and regarded its players darkly. There were whites who recoiled from jazz because it had been created by Negroes or had been associated with places where inhibitions were quickly lost.

As recently as 1960, Sol Hurok thundered in a British TV debate, "I know cases, murder cases, committed after a wild jazz session and a couple of drinks. . . . Jazz fans lose their sentiment for the parents, for the people, for the community.

There's no morality exists any more after this terrible jazz."

There were also many middle-class and upper-middle-class Negroes who objected furiously to jazz because the music reminded them of the past, of the South and slavery. They also feared that the emotional freedom and passion of jazz would reinforce the caricature of the "natural" Negro drawn by the white majority. Ragtime pianist Luckey Roberts recalls that by the early 1900s, the blues were not allowed to be played in the parlors of many "decent" Negro homes. Ralph Ellison, growing up in Oklahoma City in the 1920s, remembers that "jazz was regarded by most of the respectable Negroes of the town as a backward, low-class form of expression, and there was a marked difference between those who accepted and lived close to their folk experience and those whose status strivings led them to reject and deny it." Ellison himself was later forbidden to play jazz at Tuskegee under threat of expulsion.

Sterling Brown, a professor at Howard University, struggled for years to introduce a knowledge and appreciation of jazz to the "official" precincts of the campus. "I did get to the point," he once said drily, "of being able to play a Mihaud recording in the library and point out that the composition had been influenced by jazz. I think though that I'm still suspect among some of my colleagues because I like and write about the blues."

Pianist Billy Taylor, whose interest in jazz was regarded coldly by the faculty at Virginia State College, wrote in an article for the now defunct Negro magazine, *Duke,* titled "Don't Know Anything About Jazz": "Classes in jazz appreciation and jazz technique have long been conducted in many major United States colleges and universities, but I haven't heard of any such courses being even mentioned in our Negro institutions of higher learning. Negro high schools and colleges which could do much to make promising young jazz musicians aware of their potential aren't doing it and haven't even tried! They could show these budding players the achievements of their predecessors in the field and offer them encouragement and guidance instead of, as in too many instances, treating such students as offbeat characters and putting them on the defensive by frustrating their attempts to practice and perform for their fellow students. . . . Where are the Negro priests and ministers who could take an active part in showing the good that jazz has done?"

As recently as 1960, a group of young Negro intellectuals was deciding on the policies of a new weekly Harlem paper. The editor, who enjoyed jazz, suggested that the paper give the music and musicians wide coverage in contrast to the avoidance of jazz by most of the Negro press. "It was one of the hardest battles I had," he said later. "Nearly all the other staff members opposed giving jazz more than a little space even though every one of them spent at least one night a week in a jazz club and collected records. They didn't think jazz was 'respectable' enough for a paper as important as we wanted ours to become."

Whatever their reasons for rejecting jazz, few opponents of the music in the 1920s and 1930s, Negro or white, could claim it was particularly difficult to understand. While there was increasing subtlety in the way the rhythms were shaped by the soloists, the rhythmic base of a jazz group's performance was infectiously pulsating and sturdily regular. While the harmonies of the music had grown more complex, the improvised variations remained reasonably easy to follow in the case of most musicians. And the players continued to classify themselves as entertainers. What happened after hours was, they felt, of interest only to themselves.

It was the modern jazz of Charlie Parker, Thelonious Monk, Bud Powell and Dizzy Gillespie that accomplished the major shift in the attitude of the jazzman toward his music and his public. Parker and Gillespie had both grown up in big bands and were all too aware of the relationship between jazz and show business. (Gillespie still is; but his clowning, although it disturbs some of the more austere of the younger musicians and critics, is considerably more sophisticated and

NAT HENTOFF

"inside" than the more openly vaudevillian turns of an older generation of jazzmen such as Louis Armstrong.) The young modernists of the early 1940s were also heirs of the pride that jazzmen had been taking in their expanding capacities. They felt, however, that jazz up to that point no longer sufficiently challenged them. Accordingly, they evolved a musical language that required closer attention than the jazz that preceded them. It could be danced to only by resiliently creative improvisers, such as the regulars at the Savoy Ballroom in Harlem. The pulse of the music remained constant but it was persistently overlayed by the drummer's complex polyrhythms which involved multiple subtle accents and displacements of the beat. ("Dropping bombs" became a graphic term for the disturbing new drumming.)

Harmonically, the modernists became so intrigued by the challenging, expanded chordal possibilities of improvisation advanced by Charlie Parker and his colleagues that until recently, most players "ran changes" (improvised on the chords of a tune) instead of developing melodic variations on the theme. The modernists often played new lines that were based on the chords—but not the melody—of a standard tune. The casual listeners groped for the tantalizing, implied melody and many gave up jazz itself as well as the search in frustration.

By the 1950s, however, the concept of jazz as an object in itself, a nonfunctional music in the sense that it is no longer designed for dancing or background listening, had attracted a sizable new audience for the music. The listeners, or most of them, accepted the music on the players' terms and went to Birdland as if it were Town Hall. Older musicians who have occasionally played modern jazz clubs in recent years are often made nervous by the seeming passivity and stern concentration of contemporary "serious" listeners. Anita O'Day, who is temperamentally of the jazz-as-entertainment tradition, speaks for most of the premodernists in insisting: "I feel better when the audience is balling it up a little; then I can relax too." Several of the modernists agree with her, but most expect silence and sustained attention from the customers.

A large part of the contemporary jazz audience, however, is apt to be more "serious" in its mien than in its comprehension of the music. Much of the audience, as has been true in every jazz generation so far, is young and more compulsive about being "hip" to the newest innovations in the music than it is concerned with the content of those innovations. Most of the more febrile enthusiasts, however, abandon the music in their twenties. They may play the recordings of their adolescent years in brief bouts of nostalgia; but like those of their parents who waited in line to see a Benny Goodman stage show, they gradually lose touch with jazz. They are youngsters who find in jazz a surface corollary of their own safely transitory "rebellion" of adolescence. They become attracted to jazz partly because their parents and teachers generally don't "dig" the music. In the early 1950s they were titillated by the bombastic dissonances of Stan Kenton's otherwise largely empty music, but found Thelonious Monk too "far out." In the late 1930s, their predecessors bought all the new records of Artie Shaw, but had barely heard of Lester Young.

An increasing percentage of listeners are staying, however, through their twenties, thirties and beyond. To the musicians, the turnover is still unsettlingly huge in each generation, and any knowledgeable jazzman who has been around for more than a few years knows that he can decline in popularity precipitously. Yet he also knows that there are more listeners in the clubs and at concerts who are eager to invest the same amount of care and time in understanding his work as their equally committed counterparts in classical music. Jazz, in short, is slowly beginning to acquire a durable audience. Included are listeners who have overcome the initial difficulties of modern jazz and are now willing to cope with the further challenges of John Coltrane and Ornette

NAT HENTOFF

Coleman. Through study and listening, more of them know and enjoy the entire scope of jazz history—the Afro-American folk base; early blues and ragtime; the raw collective improvisation of the New Orleans marching-and-dance bands; the tangy, preswing era, riff-build drive of the southwestern and midwestern territory units; and such of the first waves of solo virtuosi as Louis Armstrong, Earl Hines, Roy Eldrige, Coleman Hawkins, Art Tatum and Duke Ellington. They recognize that jazz had a complex, strongly expressive tradition before Charlie Parker; and that as of 1961, it is beginning what should be its most unpredictable, daringly exploratory decade.

The contemporary jazz audience, both its majority of instantly intoxicated adolescents and its smaller but significantly growing "serious" segment, is in any case radically different from the customers that jazz musicians had to please for the first 40 years of the music's history. Except for ragged remnants of parade bands in New Orleans, the music hasn't been played for funerals or store openings for a long time—although it is still occasionally enlisted for political rallies. As for contemporary brothels, the preference there, I expect, would be for Mantovani. Jazz is now seldom even played for dancing, except for occasional dates by such big bands as Basie's and Ellington's.

Jazz concert opportunities have accordingly expanded, but the music is still most often heard in night clubs where many jazzmen are more comfortable despite the obligato of drinks being served and consumed.

"How," asks Miles Davis, "are you going to feel free at a jazz *concert?* And feeling free, after all, is the whole act of jazz. There ain't but two things you can do at a concert—go there and play or go there and sit down. You can't drink; you can't move around." When a friend insisted that the future of jazz was on the concert circuit, Miles snorted. "All right. You listen to what the musicians say *after* a concert. Every time, backstage, someone will say, 'Now, where are you gonna *blow?*' You can't stretch out and really play at a concert and you can't make everybody sit still and feel the same way."

The modern jazzman, as truculently aloof as he may sometimes appear, still wants to reach and move his listeners. Miles Davis retreats into gloomy reappraisal of his work if a room is cold. Thelonious Monk, though he will not dilute his music for more widespread approval, is delighted if the audience is large and enthusiastic. What have been altered are the *terms* on which the jazz musician communicates with his listeners.

The jazzman, no matter how commercially inclined—and not all modern jazzmen are paragons of musical integrity—has inevitably become self-consicous about his work. The modern jazz combo, for example, is much more carefully integrated than the average small group of the 1930s and tries for as distinctively identifiable a repertory and group style as the musicians' imaginations allow.

In more and more clubs, the audience expects the experimenting and "stretching" out to be done during working hours for *them,* and not later for musicians only. As Miles Davis, Thelonious Monk and Ornette Coleman have proved, it has become "commercial" (in the denotative sense of that word) to be as uncompromising in public as one wants to be.

Not all contemporary jazz leaders are interested in further searching, publicly or privately. Some, such as Erroll Garner, have found and stay with a safe formula, but even these formulas are based on a more substantial jazz content than previous "commercial" (using the term connotatively) routines such as George Shearing's emascualted modern jazz or Lionel Hampton's sweaty show-boating.

It is still far from easy for an unknown player with a strikingly original approach to win acceptance in contemporary jazz; but he is now more apt to find the stiffest initial resistance from the established jazz musicians rather than from the audience. A constricting side-effect of many

NAT HENTOFF

modern jazzmen's increased self-consciousness has been a fear of anything too disruptively "new." Having won attention for their music, they are suspicious of any developments that may suddenly make them sound dated. Thelonious Monk waited for years for large-scale acceptance among musicians, partly because most of the latter were afraid they couldn't play his music. In 1960, Ornette Coleman found more support from nonprofessionals than he did at first from all but a few musicians.

An irony of the current jazz scene, then, is that much of the audience is more open to the unexpected than many of the musicians. As noted, part of that audience may be receptive mainly for superficial reasons based on a desire to belong to the innermost circle of hipsters. At least, however, it *is* much more attuned to experimentation than the jazz public of any preceding generation.

If the established modern jazz musician is not always fully aware of how much the jazz public is now willing to try to understand, the older jazzman—with his longterm, fiercely pragmatic experience of jazz as a subdividsion of popular show business—finds it hard to realize that a basic change has taken place. An example is Duke Ellington. Now in his sixties, Ellington remains the most original composer in jazz, but he is unable to abandon his fragmentized view of the jazz public. For a time he tried to but his optimism was premature. From 1943 to 1950, Ellington prepared an annual Carnegie Hall program of new and at least hopefully major works. He usually repeated the concert at Boston's Symphony Hall and similar locations. The initial reaction was encouraging—though not from the critics—but Ellington eventually became discouraged and decided that there was not a large enough "serious" jazz audience to support such ventures.

Ellington continues to compose, but his musicians complain that they get to perform only a small percentage of his new material. In fact, most of Ellington's more remarkable early originals are no longer played by him. The band concentrates on the more familiar Ellington standards and on those of his new recordings that appear to have the most commercial potential. Ellington hires mediocre singers to appeal to what he expects will be the square element in any audience. Even in his concert programs, he invariably mixes only a small amount of provocative new material with medleys of "old favorites" and slight pieces aimed primarily at the type of nonjazz night club-goers to whom he still occasionally plays in such locations as Las Vegas.

In the summer of 1956, Ellington was presented in two concerts as part of the jazz series of the Stratford, Ontario, Shakespeare Festival. He selected a characteristic program that included a few challenging numbers, a lengthy, banal drum exhibition and several flimsy vocal novelties. The audience, which had come both for the plays and to learn more about jazz, was visibly disappointed. Ellington admitted after the first night that he had underestimated the listeners, but his ingrained habit of "entertaining" the broadest possible audience to keep his band and himself solvent led him to repeat exactly the same program for his second Stratford concert.

Three years later, in Europe, Ellington disappointed audiences in Britain and on the continent by seldom changing his programs and by scheduling only a few of his more challenging works. When the tour's promoter, Norman Granz, criticized him bitterly one evening for his conservatism, Ellington answered with equal heat that he knew what the audiences had come for and he intended to give them what they wanted. Ellington was wrong. European jazz audiences, in fact, have generally been more demanding musically than those in America for some time.

From the 1920s on, the European public for jazz, as Francis Newton has noted in his book, *The Jazz Scene*, has been markedly middle-class and intellectual. . . . On the Continent, jazz had the advantage of fitting smoothly into the ordinary pattern of *avant-garde* intellectualism." In

NAT HENTOFF

America, until comparatively recently, most American intellectuals ignored jazz or excoriated it along with nearly all popular culture. Most of those comparatively few intellectuals who adopted jazz did so because they viewed it with bellicose romanticism as one of the last vestiges of a folk-rooted "purer" popular art. As the music, no longer a functional folk expression, inevitably became more sophisticated, many of the intellectuals left it in anger, keening that jazz had become corrupted by European influences and by the very fact that it had turned professional.

James Agee mourned that it used to be possible to hear "true lyric jazz at the point when the deep-country and the town have first fertilized each other, and before imitation, ambition and the possibility of earning much of anything . . . destroyed it." More recently, Nelson Algren complained that jazz was losing its vitality and "should be kept in the kitchen." Ralph Ellison, who has been a musician and has written excellent appreciations of Charlie Christian and Jimmy Rushing for the *Saturday Review,* also looks back at the older, less technically complicated players as having been among the last extensions of John Henry. "The older jazzmen," he says, "were even bigger in size. They *looked* as if they had more to say."

Yet by the late 1950s, more of the younger American intellectuals, even including some Negro writers and educators, had become intrigued by jazz and joined the small but multiplying adult section of the jazz audience. The quarterlies are still largely ignorant of jazz and its subculture, but the music now has its own "serious" journals in America as well as abroad. Among the critics for these magazines are several of the musicians themselves, another index of the changing intellectual climate of jazz.

Most of the younger players now approach jazz as a career with as much seriousness as apprentices in classical music. More are coming from middle- and upper-class homes. Jazz has always had some children of skilled workers, businessmen, and professionals; and the percentage rose during the 1920s as more Negro children of solid bourgeois families (Coleman Hawkins, Don Redman, Duke Ellington, Fletcher Henderson) began to find in jazz an expanding area for their ambitions. Particularly in the past decade, however, many white and Negro children, whose families have the resources to support schooling for more conventional careers, are choosing jazz as a life's work.

The young jazzman today often does attend an established music school because of the increasingly demanding requirements of jazz; but once he is trained, he still must—as has been true throughout jazz history—find his own way.

When Sahib Shihab, a reedman, told Thelonious Monk a few years ago that he was returning to Julliard for additional courses, Monk cautioned him: "Well, I hope you don't come out any worse than you sound now." "I know what he meant," said Shihab. "He was referring to what has happened to several jazz musicians who go to school, and then, when they get out, are scared to play certain things that don't fit with what they've been taught. They lose that urgency of personal discovery that's jazz."

For all the changes that have taken place in the nature of the music, the musicians and the audience for jazz, the goal of the jazz musician still remains that proclaimed by Charles Mingus, a bristlingly serious modern jazzman: "I play or write *me,* the way I feel, through jazz, or whatever, whether it's hip or not. Music is a language of the emotions. If someone has been escaping reality, I don't expect him to dig my music . . . my music is alive and it's about the living and the dead, about good and evil. It's angry, and it's real because it *knows* it's angry."

NAT HENTOFF

A Theory of the Jazz Community

ROBERT A. STEBBINS

One of the ubiquitous trends in social behavior is the formation of comprehensive systems of interaction known as communities. Everywhere in the world and throughout man's existence on earth, the formation of communities has been evident, from the primitive tribe to the contemporary nation-state.

Among the exciting developments within the more complex communities of mankind, such as cities and nations, is the emergence of subcommunity forms which both complement and contest the arrangements of the larger society. Status communities and ethnic communities of many sorts belong among the contemporary subcommunities. It is instructive to apply this concept of subcommunity formation to areas of behavior such as the worlds of art and jazz, when that behavior can be shown to approach closure and completeness with respect to a distinctive way of life.

This chapter deals with two major tasks: 1) the development of a special theory of the jazz community as a unique form of status community and 2) a judgement as to the validity of referring to the social world of the jazz musician as a community. It should be mentioned that while this formulation is conceived in terms of the jazz subculture, it also has widespread application elsewhere in the area of social deviance. Since the concept of status group has its roots in the general theory of community, we shall briefly outline that concept.

THE GENERAL THEORY OF COMMUNITY[1]

A fully constituted community is taken to be a complete system of social interaction; that is, a set of social groups sufficient to solve for a plurality of individuals all the problems of collective life falling in the compass of a normal year and in the compass of a normal life. Community formation has been explained by the three general principles or processes of institutional stabilization, interinstitutional consistency and institutional completeness.

Stabilization refers to man's capacity to learn from experience and remember superior solutions to the basic problems confronting him during his life. Institutions may be defined as "standardized solutions to the problems of collective life," and it must be added that these solutions often become embedded in the habits of the individual and the customs of the group.

Stabilization processes in one area of life eventually intersect with those of other institutional areas creating the possibility of inconsistencies and conflict. People attempt to avoid these clashes by engineering schemes of behavior consonant with both sets of institutions; they strive for interinstitutional consistency. The family may be adjusted to economic requirements, economic to religious, religious to political.

Completeness refers to the degree to which the basic institutions are developed for carrying on the "fundamental functions" of the community. The modification of institutions of socialization, mastery of nature, and social control has a lower limit of efficiency below which the community as a complete way of life cannot survive. Briefly, socialization

ROBERT A. STEBBINS

may be conceived of as the transformation of the biological person into the social person; mastery of nature is the effort put forth to meet the necessities of food and shelter; social control refers to institutions which make effective those decisions affecting the community as a whole.

This, in the barest outline, is the theory of community which forms the theoretical base of the present study. The essential elements needed to validate (or invalidate) the notions of the world of jazz as a community form have been summarized. We can now proceed to its application to jazz subculture.

THE JAZZ COMMUNITY

The jazz community is seen today at its most solidary and esoteric formation in those forms cast up by the modern jazz musician. The present study is concerned exclusively with the local jazz community and not with various national and international formations. At the local level the conflict between intrinsic values of jazz and instrumental values of commercial music is particularly intense. The local jazz community most clearly approximates a status community. In Max Weber's words:

> *Status groups* are normally communities. They are, however, often of an amorphous kind. In contrast to the purely economically determined "class situation," we wish to designate as "status situation" every typical component of the life fate of men that is determined by a specific, positive or negative, social estimation of honor.[2]

In the development of a status community two secondary principles of community formation are involved: social differentiation and closure. It can be said that all communities have systems of stratification based on the differential access to wealth, esteem and power, and that processes of differentiation occur in stratification competition. This principle of community formation (differentiation) provides some of the conditions necessary for the creation of specialized status communities.

Once status groups form, further processes of social differentiation continue to take place within them. Thus there is differentiation at two levels: within the larger community and within the status group. From whatever point it begins, fusion on all three dimensions can occur, thereby closing the circle. Closure is a conjoint operation of the principles of institutional stability and interinstitutional consistency which insures against disintegration from within and disruption from without.[3]

A further idea must be added to the general theory of community before our conception of the status community is complete. The concepts of "core" and "peripheral" institutions are useful in accounting for the fact that in any given community some institutions are more basic than others. The core institutions are relatively fixed; those which are peripheral surround the core and are characterized by a greater variation. There is a constant process of integration between these two types of institutions, and if there is no interference, they may arrive, in time, at a relatively stable balance.

Community structure is most fragmentary at its outer edges, and shows the greatest integration and consequently the greatest sensitivity in the central region. Institutional changes in the core affect the entire community. It is for this reason that social behavior is so highly structured here, while on the periphery there is a greater tolerance of variability.

CORE AND PERIPHERAL INSTITUTIONS IN THE JAZZ COMMUNITY

The following institutions are theorized to form the core and peripheral structures of the jazz community:

    I. *Core Institutions*
        A. Jazz jobs
        B. Jam sessions

ROBERT A. STEBBINS

C. After-hours social life
D. The musicians' union
E. The cliques (a secondary core institution)

II. *Peripheral Institutions*
A. The jazz musician's family
B. Commercial music jobs

It is now possible to review this theory in the light of current knowledge about jazz musicians.

THE JAZZ JOB

The form of employment which jazz musicians desire is the "job" which is hopefully one where jazz is played, but not always. Jobs may be one night affairs, such as dances, parties or a variety of special occasions calling for music, or they may constitute steady engagements involving one or more nights a week. To sustain life the jazz musician must work a full-time job usually consisting of 25 or more hours of paid playing a week. Whether the music played is jazz depends on a number of factors, such as the availability of such employment, the power of cliques, tolerance of insecurity and desire to play only jazz. Those in the top cliques usually find the most employment as jazz musicians, and also they can afford to be the least compromising when a situation prevails where there are no jazz jobs and they are forced to make the decision whether to play commercial music, join the ranks of the jobbing musicians or suffer unemployment until another attractive jazz job develops. If they opt the choice of jobbing, they are likely to play all types of jobs ranging along a continuum from genuine jazz to "sweet commercial." Commerical music may be defined as the two-beat dance music of the plush country clubs and society bands.

A jobbing musician is hired for one night to play a specific engagement which occurs only once. Usually it is a dance, although one may play for an occasional funeral, concert, style show or some other special event. Characteristically each job is unique for the jobbing musician. However, this work is ordinarily not enough to maintain minimum levels of living. Hence jobbing musicians are largely part-time workers and use professional music as a supplement to 40 hour a week daytime employment or as recreation.

The jazz job, then, is not something that supports all jazz musicians all of the time. Employment is spotty and may be punctuated by periods of work in the commercial and jobbing areas of music. Playing commercial music, however, is regarded as prostituting one's musical talent and is generally disapproved by others in the jazz community. There is often more pity than scorn for a well known jazz musician who goes commercial because he has a family to support and who, it is certain, will rejoin the ranks of his colleagues as soon as an opportunity presents itself. The least respect is accorded those who can play jazz, and possibly good jazz, but who prefer to play commercial music because of the money and social prestige.

The actual jazz job may involve playing jazz for listening or more frequently for dancing in some night club or tavern normally located in the transitional areas of the city. We include in our definition of the jazz job the jazz concert which is generally the most thrilling for musicians because the audience's attention is not distracted by liquor and conversation. The attractiveness of jazz jobs varies with the types of audience, "square" ones or those commercially minded being the worst. Working conditions, which involve a variety of physical aspects as well as the congeniality of the management, size of band stand, the condition of the piano, number of hours of employment per week and various other factors, are also components in the potential of a job.

In short, the job is significant because it supports the musician, and it may or may not be aesthetically meaningful, depending on whether jazz is played there. The jazz job

ROBERT A. STEBBINS

erases the line between work and leisure and transforms jazz, as professionally performed, into a continual pursuit of aesthetic values.

THE JAM SESSION

The jazz job as just described is relatively rare. There are few night clubs which permit musicians to play anything they like. This stems from the belief on the part of the management that there are few audiences that will tolerate what the musicians regard as good music. How "far out" a group of jazz musicians may play is a moot question and leads to considerable conflict between the employer and the employees. The operators of most of the night clubs featuring jazz and jazz-like dance music are too conservative for the majority of jazz musicians. Under these circumstances, the institution of the jam session becomes critical.

Ecologically, there is a tendency for jam sessions to occur in or near the transitional areas of a city.[4] Here, as on the genuine jazz job, it behooves the musician to produce as well as possible. Jam sessions most frequently occur within the cliques, as Nat Hentoff has indicated.[5] They provide a proving ground for upwardly mobile individuals within the jazz community. Here, as on the job, the newcomers must await an invitation to play, although the practice of "sitting in" makes entry into higher cliques somewhat easier through the job.

It may be seen that the jam session functions as the primary institution for aesthetic expression of the jazz musician; as a place where he can play the sort of music he likes, being responsible for his performance only to the jazz community.

AFTER HOURS SOCIAL LIFE

The jazz community is most alive and picturesque during the hours from 9 P.M. to about 5 or 6 A.M. Whether music is played for a living throughout this period depends on the city in which the jazz community is located. At whatever time the night clubs close, a sizeable after-hours social life flourishes until the early hours of the morning. It is a social life consisting of jam sessions, parties, gatherings at certain restaurants, coffee-houses and an occasional illegal after-hours drinking spot, sexual adventures or combinations of these. The core members of the jazz community are the mainstays of this institution which is in effect every night during the week except Sunday, when things start and end earlier. In some cities one can occasionally find a jam session late Sunday afternoon or in the evening before the taverns close.

It is not unreasonable to expect to find the jazz community physically located in some transitional area of the city, where much of the activity takes place both on and off the job.[6] Sometimes the boundaries of the physical community are not precise; many jazz musicians of Minneapolis lived in other parts of the city and had some after-hours "meccas" elsewhere and so forth, but there seems to be a tendency to concentrate the various affairs.

During the after-hours social life, the cliques and their functions are most in evidence. As will be seen later, the whole socialization process as well as the processes of social control are worked through these groupings which are most active at night and especially after the job is over.

THE MUSICIANS' UNION

Founded on November 6, 1896, the American Federation of Musicians (AFM) has over 275,000 members covering virtually all fields of professional music in North America. With hundreds of local unions spread throughout most urban centers, the jazz musician comes in contact with union government routinely.

Although the union is a core institution for musician circles generally, there are two good reasons why it might be considered as peripheral to the jazz community. One is the lack of interest among jazz musicians in local union govern-

ROBERT A. STEBBINS

ment. The other is the fact that the union does not guarantee the jazz musician the kinds of jobs most meaningful to him, namely, the jazz jobs.[7]

From another standpoint, however, the union plays a very central role among jazz musicians. It mediates conflict in at least three areas of professional and musical life: conflict between musicians over a certain job, conflict between the leader and his sidemen over wages, and conflict between the leader and the employer (in this case the night club owners) over wages.

Since jazz jobs are usually scarce, there is a temptation to undercover solicitation for a position within a band that is already working. Sometimes an attempt by similar means is made by a leader to move in on another band's job. There are two methods by which this may be done: playing under the minimum wage scale or secret bargaining with the night club's management. Both practices are forbidden in the union bylaws. If it can be proved by a dispossessed leader that he lost his job through such dealings, he may seek redress through the local union.

The union also frequently mediates wage claims of a sideman against his leader or a leader against his employer. If a leader does not pay the members of his band, he may be suspended from the union until he makes settlement. If an employer does not pay, he may be placed on the national "defaulters' list," a monthly statement prepared by the national union and circulated to all musicians who are members.

Most jazz musicians use the union under these circumstances if it is feasible, and for this reason it must be included among the core institutions of the jazz community.

CLIQUES

The cliques in the jazz community are its all-purpose institutions. They are institutions which have developed outside and around the institutions of the jazz job, the jam session and after-hours social life. Social interaction between jazz musicians in these areas has given rise to cliques, and in a fully developed jazz community the clique to which one belongs serves as the principal setting for almost all social and musical activities.

Jazz musicians' cliques are informal friendship groups based on common status aspirations within the jazz community and characterized by mutual obligations of job referral. The common status leading to the formation of the clique may be one or a combination of the following: a general level of musical skill, race or ethnicity, similar style and a common position in the hierarchy of jobs. In the larger jazz communities it is also possible that cliques may be structured along age lines.

Musicians like to play with others who are at least as competent as they themselves. An individual whose musical ability is not on the same level as others in the group is said to be a "drag" (does not play well), and is usually excluded from the clique. Thus forces are constantly at work to maintain a hierarchy of skills within the jazz community.

THE JOB HIERARCHY

Howard Becker has pointed out that a hierarchy of jobs exists in the world of professional dance music.[8] For the dance musician success consists in scaling an occupational ladder built on income, hours of work and wider community standards of achievement.

There are five levels of employment in this hierarchy: "jobbing" engagements, steady jobs in low level taverns and strip joints, neighborhood ballrooms and more respectable night clubs, well-known hotel ballrooms and staff employment by radio and television stations. Cliques form at each level in the job hierarchy. In this fashion it is possible to explain, in part, the skilled jazz musician's low prestige in society while attaining an almost charismatic quality in the jazz community.

ROBERT A. STEBBINS

CORE AND PERIPHERAL MEMBERSHIP

The jazz community takes form predominately among musicians at the second level of the hierarchy. These musicians are, for the most part, the core members. Some of the musicians at the other levels also hold membership in the jazz community, but such membership tends to be of a peripheral nature. The third level roughly corresponds with the notion of commercial music which has been developed in this study. These two levels of the job hierarchy have more members, both core and peripheral, than any of the others.

One point needs to be clarified in relation to core and peripheral membership in the jazz community. An individual who is playing a jazz job and making appearances at sessions and other forms of after-hours activity is par excellence a core member. However, jazz jobs are too rare to constitute a necessary component in this definition. For this reason a core member of the jazz community is defined as an individual who is considered by himself and by others in the jazz community as a musician who plays modern jazz and who plays jazz jobs and goes to sessions as often as possible. The word "possible" here refers to the relative frequency with which jazz jobs and jam sessions occur.

This definition takes account of the possibility that an individual can be employed at another level and still be a core member of the jazz community. A peripheral member is one who is also considered by himself and by others as a musician who is able to play jazz. The crucial distinction is that people in this group are in the process of leaving the jazz community, as seen in the increasingly lower rate of employment in jazz jobs and attendance of jazz community after-hours functions and in an increasingly higher rate of employment at the other levels.

AGE AND RACE HIERARCHIES

Nat Hentoff, a renowned jazz critic and oftentimes shrewd

observer, has noted that in New York cliques tend to form on the basis of shared styles.[9] There is nothing new about the observation that Dixieland, Swing and Modern Jazz musicians tend to associate only with their own kind. These, however, are more correctly depicted as types of jazz rather than styles. Hentoff is referring to a phenomenon which is possible only in the largest jazz communities: a proliferation of artistic forms within a type of jazz. Where this sort of arrangement appears, it is probably integrated with the skill and job hierarchies so that cliques are homogeneous with respect to relative skill and style at a given level of occupation. Hentoff observes that in New York clique formation is further carried out by age and race, a social grouping process which may be noticed in the larger jazz communities.

FAMILY LIFE

The number of jazz musicians who are legitimately married, with or without children, is not known, but they are probably in a minority. The status of "married" in the jazz world is a liability rather than an asset. Because of the low status of music as a profession, most families attempt to discourage their offspring from entering it as a career.[10]

The jazz musician finds he must put jazz first when he marries. "Marriage is likely to turn into a continuing struggle over this issue; the outcome of the struggle determines whether the man's musical career will be cut short or will continue. . . ."[11] The factor of insecurity in the world of music as a whole leads to family conflict, and in the case of the jazz musician it may force him into commercialism, out of the "music business" entirely or into the status of divorced. Certainly this situation must increase the jazz musician's interest in the less legitimate forms of marriage.

These sorts of demands which the jazz community makes on the individual help to explain the fact that where community formation is the strongest (or exists in any real sense), namely, among modern jazz artists, there is a

ROBERT A. STEBBINS

predominance of younger musicians (under forty).[12] It should also be noted that frequent style change forces the older musician out of the jazz community, for the reason that as time progresses his type of jazz becomes partially transformed into commercial music by the listening public.[13]

COMMERCIAL MUSIC

Commercialism dominates at all levels of the occupational hierarchy except the second, where the members of the jazz community are found. A musician who leaves jazz for the security of a commercial job or any of the music played at the other levels will, if he stays there long enough, eventually recede to a peripheral membership.

Commercial music is actually an institution in the jazz community, although it is definitely marginal. It enables a devoted jazz musician partially to withdraw when the going is tough in his art while still keeping up some of the old contacts by means of jam sessions and after-hours activities. The factors of family and age may operate to force him to stay on, in which case he may in time completely withdraw from the jazz world. However, he usually returns if he is young and single.

Perhaps an explanation is due as to why commercial music jobs are included as a peripheral institution while other forms of instrumental music jobs are omitted. Apparently it is preferable to remain with some kind of dance music if possible rather than journeying into the popular music field of rock-'n'-roll, country-western music and folk music. Also, some jazz musicians, if they are skilled in legitimate music, will revert to show and studio work as indicated earlier.

STABILITY, CONSISTENCY AND COMPLETENESS

In the preceding sections we discussed in some detail the characteristics of the core and peripheral institutions of the jazz community. These institutions are the standardized solutions to the problems of jazz subculture. It should be repeated that these solutions tend to reach stability under circumstances where disruptive social change is not taking place. The stable effect is achieved in the form of habits; the standardized solutions have become habitual.

There is also a considerable degree of interinstitutional consistency within the world of jazz. The most notable exceptions are found in the peripheral institutions of commercial music and the jazz musician's family. The family tends to take a form similar to that of the larger community, and here the values of being a good provider and being devoted to one's family clash with the values of the status community, such as those of playing jazz for its own sake. This difficulty is solved, in part, in the more casual and illegitimate forms of marriage which have fewer restrictive qualities about them.

There is in the jazz community a trend toward institutional completeness. The time has come to point out the basic institutions which must achieve a minimum level of completeness so that the community can remain intact.

THE SOCIALIZATION OF THE JAZZ MUSICIAN

The process of socialization is implemented through the secondary core institution of the cliques in the jazz community. It has already been pointed out how the higher cliques embody, at their fullest development, the basic values of musicianship, artistic creativity, and playing jazz for its intrinsic qualities. Everywhere a neophyte jazz musician goes within the jazz community, he comes in contact with these values which are also inherent, in a variety of forms, in the trade literature. Magazines such as *Down Beat* and *Metronome* have a national circualtion and are primarily interested in informing the serious jazz "buff" and the jazz musician where the national stars are working along with other news of interest to their readers. Jazz columns in local newspapers could also be viewed as supporting these values.

This type of socialization primarily concerns career formation. This is one way in which the jazz community may be

ROBERT A. STEBBINS

seen as an incomplete community. The young jazz musician typically comes to the jazz community as a late teenager, already socialized by the wider community. As a jazz musician he is resocialized; this involves a partial defection from his earliest set of values and an acquisition of a partially new set from a new set of significant others. It is in this context of an individual's value community composed of some old and some new values that we may interpret the remark made to this author by pianist Oscar Peterson to the effect that jazz musicians, not unlike many other Americans, want the better things of life, such as a home in the suburbs and a nice automobile.

These old and new values clash to a certain degree. The clash may be one factor in the attempt to escape through the use of narcotics, as found among some jazz musicians. To the extent that these values are of a material nature, they must be realized through the job. However, as will be seen shortly, the institutions for the mastery of nature are underdeveloped in the jazz community, and this leads to the basic theme in the sociology of jazz—the conflict between musical and commercial values. Anyone observing a jazz musician on a commercial music job will become well aware of this dilemma that confronts a vast majority of local jazz community members and all but the top national stars.

THE ECONOMICS OF JAZZ LIFE

The basic institution of the mastery of nature for the jazz musician is the job. Like its counterpart in most ethnic communities, this institution must depend on the patronage of the outside world. Both the ethnic community and the world of jazz have special products to offer which, in the case of those in jazz, must be purchased in some degree or the community will disintegrate. The idea of an incomplete community may easily apply here, for in the jazz world the institutions for the mastery of nature are now well developed; this is obvious in the scarcity of jazz jobs.

The following scheme outlines the means of social control in the jazz community:

I. *Agencies of Influence*[1][4]

    A. Communication

        1. Formal

            (a) trade publications

            (b) the union bulletin

        2. Informal

            (a) the job

            (b) jam sessions

            (c) after-hours social life

    B. Social Strata

    1. Cliques

II. *Institutions of Power*

    A. The musicians' union

The primary institutions and the cliques of the jazz community are the institutions of social control. Those musicians in the higher reaches of the jazz community have a pervasive influence in that, as already mentioned, they typify fundamental values. Those individuals set the standards and pass judgement on up-and-coming jazz musicians. At the local jazz community level, the opinions and attitudes of those most renowned are made known through social interaction on the job, at jam sessions, during after-hours gatherings and occasionally through the local union bulletins. The thoughts of those in other jazz communities, especially in New York, Chicago and Los Angeles, are revealed at the national level in the trade publications. Few, if any, jazz musicians climb to the top cliques in their jazz community without the approval of the individuals already in them.

The musicians' union is the only institution dealing in legitimate power, and as such its functions are limited. Dealing primarily in the regulation of wages, hours and

ROBERT A. STEBBINS

employment, it is able to apply three sanctions of increasing degrees of severity: fines, suspension and expulsion.

There are no institutions of legitimate power which insure conformity to the values and norms of the jazz community. Since the musicians' union is formed from a diverse body of performers in the popular, jazz, commercial and symphonic fields, there is probably no common set of values which every area of music honors, the principle of unionism notwith-standing.[15] Social control in this sphere is established through the agencies of influence, as just discussed. In the areas of behavior falling under the jurisdiction of outside power institutions, jazz musicians may or may not welcome intervention.

A recurrent theme in this discussion about the complete-ness of institutions has been the notion of the jazz community as a semicommunity. In each of the three areas of basic institutional development there is a degree of incompleteness which can be related to the larger society. An interesting observation is that this partial dependence on outside institutional forces creates conflict for the jazz musician. The desire for suburban living is one example of a clash between middle-class and jazz community values in which there is a fundamental economic incompatibility due to low and intermittent wages.

Also, the fact that the jazz musician is in many respects a member of a service trade makes him uncomfortably depend-ent on his audience for support.[16] This, in addition to the desire to promulgate his art to all those willing to listen, indicates that those who play jazz experience some conflict with respect to their listening public.[17] The jazz musician is anxious to play what the audience wants to hear. Yet their desires may lead him into commercialism or into the limbo of the latest dance crazes. Silbermann's idea of the reciprocal influence between the producers and consumers of music is also germane.[18] The solutions to those encounters with society are many and of only moderate success.

It will suffice to indicate that there is social differentiation within the jazz community. Jazz musicians were found to be higher on the special status community dimensions of wealth, prestige and power than were the commercial musicians.[19]

Closure is the general term for those institutional arrangements which prevent the community from being destroyed from within by some of its own members and which protect it from outside destruction. We have reviewed the system of values, norms and taboos in the world of jazz and need only to label them as a form of "generalized other" which guides the behavior of individual jazz musicians. An intriguing aspect of the jazz community is its esoteric qualities which have most meaning when presented as mechanisms for identifying outsiders, to protect it from external destruction. In this respect one is not worried about the expropriation of property, but rather, about the expropriation and dilution of values and institutions which make up the jazz community.

The "jive talk," or the parlance of the jazz musician, the various rituals of greeting, the private jokes and stories of the jazz world, the first name reference to national heroes, all may be best understood as ways of identifying the outsider as well as promoting an in-group feeling. There are, of course, other means by which this may be accomplished, such as by the requests made by a member of the audience or by how an individual plays when asked to "sit in" either on the job or at a session. The fear of the expropriation of values is most evident in Becker's observation that jazz musicians are highly suspicious of their audience, because of the former's belief that they have a special talent, and that they might have to sacrifice their standards of creativity to their listeners.[20] Closure as an operation is apparently quite successful in the jazz community in that it is especially tightly knit against internal and external disruption.

This chapter has endeavored to develop a special theory of the jazz community as a unique form of status community.

ROBERT A. STEBBINS

To this end, we have briefly outlined the general theory of community, defined what is meant by "status group," and applied these formulations to the world of jazz. It is evident, however, that the jazz community lacks institutional completeness: its solutions to the collective problems of socialization, mastery of nature and social control are inadequate in that the existence of the jazz community and its members is constantly threatened. For this reason, it is better to refer to the jazz community as a "semicommunity"; a tendency toward community formation which, because of the conditions of its origin, cannot become total.

It was posited at the beginning of this chapter that the theory developed here (without the jazz inserts) has validity in other areas of the sociology of deviance. The behavior of certain groups of narcotics addicts, homosexuals, criminals, bohemians, artists and perhaps devout radicals and reactionaries is amenable to study under this framework.

Reprinted from "A Theory of the Jazz Community," *The Sociological Quarterly*, Summer 1968. Copyright © The Sociological Quarterly.

The author is particularly indebted to Don Martindale for his advice and encouragement in this research.

NOTES

1. The conception of community employed here is drawn primarily from the work of Don Martindale, *Social Life and Cultural Change* (New York: Van Nostrand, 1962), p. 31-48.

2. Max Weber, *From Max Weber*, trans. by Hans Gerth and C. Wright Mills (New York: Oxford Univ. Press, 1958), p. 186-87.

3. Don Martindale, *American Social Structure, op. cit.*, p. 454-55.

4. William Bruce Cameron, "Sociological Notes on the Jam Session," *Social Forces*, 33:174 (1954).

5. Nat Hentoff, *The Jazz Life* (New York: Dail Press, 1961), p. 47.

6. Robert Stebbins, "The Conflict between Musical and Commercial Values in the Minneapolis Jazz Community," *Proceedings of the Minnesota Academy of Science*, 30:75 (1962).

7. For a discussion of the musicians' union the reader is urged to see, C. Lawrence Christensen, "Chicago Service Trades" in *How Collective Bargaining Works* (New York: Twentieth Century Fund, 1942); Robert D. Leiter, *The Musicians and Petrillo* (New York: Bookman Associates, 1953); Phillip Taft, *The Structure and Government of Labor Unions* (Cambridge, Mass.: Harvard University Press, 1954), p. 265.

8. Howard Becker, *Outsiders* (New York: The Free Press, 1963), pp. 103-14

9. Hentoff, *op. cit.,* p. 47.

10. Becker *op. cit.,* p. 115.

11. *Ibid.,* p. 117.

12. Robert A. Stebbins, "The Jazz Community; The Sociology of a Musical Sub-Culture" (Unpub. Ph.D. dissertation, University of Minnesota, 1964), p. 141.

13. This is not to say that those playing an older type of jazz, such as Dixieland, do not experience the conflict between the intrinsic and instrumental values. Probably the conflict is not as intense, since this music is the type that its contemporary patrons grew up with. The power of nostalgia works to some musicians' advantage. Still, this type of jazz is not very conducive to dinner conversation.

14. This outline, without the jazz community inserts, is made from lecture notes taken in a class by Professor Don Martindale, University of Minnesota, 1962.

15. Paul Carpenter's remark, ". . . jazz has not become an art form," stands as one example of this lack of consensus, *Music: An Art and A Business* (Norman, Okla.: University of Oklahoma Press, 1950), p. 78.

16. Howard Becker, "The Professional Dance Musician and His Audience," *American Journal of Sociology,* 72:176 (1951).

17. Stebbins, "The Conflict between Musicial and Commercial Values in the Minneapolis Jazz Community," *op. cit.,* p. 77.

18. Alphonse Silbermann, *The Sociology of Music,* trans. by Corbet Stewart (London: Routledge and Kegan Paul, 1963), p. 88.

19. Robert A. Stebbins, "Class, Status and Power among Jazz and Commercial Musicians," *The Sociological Quarterly,* 7:197-213 (1966).

20. Becker, "The Professional Dance Musician and His Audience," pp. 141, 143.

A Process Model of the Folk, Pop and Fine Art Phases of Jazz

RICHARD A. PETERSON

Ashes to ashes and dust to dust, if the liquor don't get you, the scholars must.

As with any creative process, jazz is produced by like-minded individuals who create, elaborate and break the conventions shared by the group.[1] Most academic research on jazz (including the studies by Howard Becker and Robert Stebbins reprinted in this volume) has looked at these group processes. Because of their microscopic focus on one or another particular community of jazz musicians, such studies often have a parochial ring[2] even though the processes they describe may be universal. Other scholars have set their studies into a matrix of larger ongoing societal trends. (See for example the studies by Neil Leonard and Irving Louis Horowitz in this volume.) Within this tradition, historical events and processes such as war, depression, technological change, audience taste, music industry reorganization and race discrimination, are seen as shaping and molding music from the outside.

This essay will use insights from both the micro- and the

macro-perspectives to search out the processes which have shaped and changed jazz over the past half century. In some ways our approach is not unique, for the best histories of jazz (Stearns, Modeir, Feather, Newton, Jones, Spellman, Wilson, Schuller) have melded both perspectives in order to give a complete picture. But our purpose is different from theirs in that we are less concerned with the descriptive detail necessary to trace the history of jazz than with discovering the underlying processes involved. Thus, this is less a *rewrite* of the "jazz story" than an attempt to *explain* the story. While much detail is lost thereby, there are gains as well. The model developed here should be helpful not only for better understanding the evolution of jazz but for tracing the emergence and diffusion of other cultural phenomena, such as rock music.

For at least a century there have been three distinct major streams of music in America. These are folk, pop and fine art music. Each of these could be further subdivided, for there are numerous distinct traditions in folk, varieties of format in pop and schools of fine art. Yet, the contexts in which music is created and consumed are quite similar from one variety to another *within* each major stream. Both fine and folk musics are sustained from generation to generation by social and cultural institutions. Fine art music has its conservatory, orchestra, patron, professional critic, virtuoso performer, audience and the mystique of "culture."[3] Each of the numerous folk traditions has its own mystique of ethnic "communion" and institutions comparable to those of fine music. The degree of role differentiation between the performer, creator, audience, critic and the rest is, however, not nearly so distinct.[4]

While folk and fine arts are nurtured by communities which are much alike in their social dynamics, popular music is the product of a mass-market industry which sells its product not to self-reproducing communities but to status

RICHARD A. PETERSON

groups which are defined primarily in terms of age and race with sex, social class and region playing secondary roles in differentiating markets.

Folk and fine music develop slowly by exploring and expanding the range of aesthetic possibilities in their respective forms. Pop music develops rather differently. While a consistently high proportion of all songs each year deals with one stage or another of the puppy love to divorce cycle,[5] there is a rapid succession of formats in which the formula tunes are packaged and there is a continual search for novel formats.[6] Thus, pop music is characterized by a succession of fads.[7] While most of these involve quite small differences, popular music has been open to major influences from beyond its bounds at certain historical periods. The "jazz age" of the 1920s and the "rock age" from 1955 through 1967 are the most prominent recent examples.

THE EVOLUTION OF MAJOR MUSICAL INNOVATIONS

Looked at in temporal perspective, folk, fine and popular music represent three parallel and independent streams. Jazz developed in the years just before World War I from a fusion of several different black folk forms and popular-based cabaret music.[8] It transformed and in turn was transformed by its fusion with popular music in the 1920s and has moved in several directions including that of classical music in recent years. A schematic representation of my view of the evolution of jazz is presented in Figure 1. The three continuing parallel streams are shown, as well as four less stable forms. These latter forms are designated "vital fad," "revival," "vital cult" and "new thing cult." The various arrows represent the *major* lines of influence set in time perspective. The scheme does not pretend to represent all crosscurrents within and between the various streams. It is derived from an examination of the evolution of jazz but hopefully would apply to the evolution of rock, or the waltz for that matter.

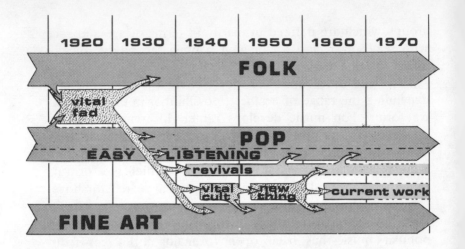

| 1920 | 1930 | 1940 | 1950 | 1960 | 1970 |

FOLK

vital fad

POP

EASY LISTENING

revivals

vital cult

new thing

current work

FINE ART

BIRTH OF THE VITAL FAD

The "vital fad" era of jazz in the 1920s witnessed a fusion of folk and pop elements. In its earliest stages it was taken from several black folk traditions with elements simplified and accentuated for a rapidly broadening primarily white mass audience. It had a simple driving rhythm and like the rhythm, lyrics tended to be specific and simple, focusing on real-life human problems. Performance tended to be amateurish and a humorous play element was quite pronounced. It was both repetitive and omnivorous of any style or technique which might contribute an exciting effect. Innovations developed rapidly and were copied and elaborated in a highly personalized contact between the various "hot" groups and performers. "Cutting contests," later stylized as a "battle of bands," were frequent.

Performers were drawn from blacks nurtured in several distinct black folk traditions and young white men who came from pop music but had had fortuitous exposure to a black folk tradition. The white musicians and a mass audience were drawn to this sort of music in large part because it symbolized to them rebellion and deviance from the prevailing Victorian mores.[9]

RICHARD A. PETERSON

Three quite different explanations can be proposed for the emergence of jazz as a vital fad in the years following World War I. My guess is that all played a role and, to make matters worse for those of us who like neat unifactor theories, they probably interacted one with another within a rather short timespan.

The first factor has to do with the dynamics of popular music fads. The cycle of Tin Pan Alley formula tunes which mixed sentimental ballads with "coon songs" and other ethnic stereotypes[10] had become repetitious and boring even to the relatively unsophisticated pop audience. And, a generation of star performers was growing old while its replacements were little more than pale imitations.[11] Finally, the audience's acceptance of jazz may have been preconditioned to the radically different beat and sound of jazz by the earlier incursions into pop music of ragtime and W. C. Handy-type blues.

A second line of explanation for the emergence of the vital fad era of jazz has to do with the social ferment of the times brought on by World War I, rapid urbanization and industrialization as well as the anguish over prohibition. A high degree of geographic mobility exposed black folk culture to white pop culture. What is more, jazz and the Roaring Twenties culture in which it became imbedded provided appropriate symbols of rebellion against the predominant middle-class Victorian mores dealing with sexual behavior, social class distinctions, racial attitudes, liquor, female liberation and intergenerational conflict.[12]

The third line of explanation focuses on dislocations in the industry which manufactured and disseminated popular music. The oligopolistic control which characterized the industry temporarily gave way to intense competition and thus the logic of producing carbon copies of proven hit formulas gave way to rapid experimentation.[13] Such competition was triggered by the rapid dissemination of new technologies, which in the post-World War I era meant the 78 rpm phonograph and the radio. These technologies profoundly changed the nature of performance and instrumentation and thus ushered in a whole new wave of performers. The rich operatic baritone which could fill a theater was replaced by the thin tenor voice which could carry over the surface noise of the shellac record. The changes also made possible the exploitation of new markets and marketing techniques for the products of the popular music industry. Where the prime product had been the sale of sheet music for dining hall and home-family piano performance in a predominately small town setting, the crucial new market was recorded music for college youth and urban performance in places featuring dancing and drinking.[14]

DEMISE OF THE FAD

The early vital period of jazz came to an end in the latter half of the 1920s. By this time it had diffused into and profoundly transformed popular music. The same three sorts of factors which brought the vital period into being may be invoked to suggest its demise. Seen as the evolution of a cultural form, clearly the novelty had worn off, the potentialities of the musical form and instrumentation of jazz as then defined had been thoroughly explored, and the music had become self conscious and "arty" and thus lost the essential element of excitement for the mass audience.[15] The tension between the audience (which wanted to dance and drink) and the musicians (who wanted to create good music) so characteristic of a later period[16] had already become quite pronounced.[17]

Second, the social ferment which fueled the interest in jazz had been dissipated. On the one hand, hard-core Victorianism had been defeated, while on the other, jazz had been sanitized of its symbolically rebellious elements by the successful efforts of the moralistic critics of the time.[18] What is more, the great depression brought to the fore questions of political and economic rather than cultural revolution.

RICHARD A. PETERSON

The third line of explanation for the demise of the vital fad would focus on the popular music industry. This can be characterized as a time of renewed oligopoly. The welter of independent radio stations was bought up and organized into networks. These developed a format not unlike that of network television today in which each radio network tried to capture the highest proportion of the general audience that was listening to the radio at any given time of day. There was no impetus to program anything that might be offensive to the predominantly adult, white, middle-class elements of the audience.

Increasingly, it became necessary to get radio airplay for phonograph records to become commercially successful. The innumerable small record companies were bought up by the emerging four giants of the industry who were financially linked to radio corporations or movie studios. Thus, record companies were reoriented to producing only those records which could be safely played on the air.[19] What is more, the newly formed Federal Communications Commission gained the power to give radio stations licenses to operate. Given these strictures network radio became supersensitive to moralistic criticism and developed a system of self-censorship which was not as centralized, but quite as tyrannical, as the Hayes office which enforced a code of ethics for the Hollywood movie industry.[20] The great depression also affected the market for jazz. It greatly reduced the purchasing power of those segments of the population, blacks and youths, who had financially sustained jazz.

It is hard to assess the full impact of economic and social events on the development of jazz. Perhaps bebop and its later developments would have emerged without the intercession of the great depression and World War II. During this long period jazz remained in the popular music tradition in the form of swing but could be heard with something like its original vitality only in the major urban ghettos and in "low-life" night spots. Jazz has never again had any comparable impact on popular music, and its subsequent musical developments have moved it in the direction of fine art music.[21]

SWING'S THE THING

Most of the swing that dominated the 1930s was pop music and never pretended to be anything but. This is not true, of course, of some of the work of Fletcher Henderson, Duke Ellington, Benny Goodman, Woody Herman, Count Basie of the Dorsey Brothers and others. These groups developed innovations in orchestration to allow free solos on top of large and rich ensemble playing. The result could be a fantastic driving and rich sound in live performance. Large band swing *jazz* did not reach the large popularity that its analogues have in the rock era, I believe, because of economic problems and technological limitations.

The large groups survived only because they traveled much of the time to perform dances for which a slow regular beat and sentimental mood were required.[22] A cynical format— "three for the bobby soxers and one for us"—was widely adopted. Second, these groups could not realize their *jazz* potential through records because the low fidelity, 78 rpm, ten-inch records of the era obscured most of the color and drive, and limited a performance to no more than three minutes. Third, live radio broadcast performances heard from prestigious dance halls over low fidelity AM radio suffered many of the same constraints.

It is interesting to ask what might have happened to this form if its inherent color, drive and excitement could have been captured on high fidelity LP stereo records and broadcast over FM stations By the time these technological advances were available, swing had degenerated into an urbane form of easy-listening music on the one hand or had become, on the other a component of fine art music. Meanwhile rock had taken the central stage for the mass audience.

REVIVALS

During the second World War two significant new move-

RICHARD A. PETERSON

ments emerged to reshape jazz. The first of these we call the revival tradition. An early manifestation of this movement was the 1938 Carnegie Hall concert by Benny Goodman which was devoted, in some part, to a "history of jazz." This signaled a revival of interest in classical New Orleans jazz. The revival was fostered by a number of New York club owners, festival promoters and record company executives,[23] but its appeal was to a coterie of collectors and preservers who were drawn to the music because of a romanticized identification with the antipuritanical associations of the early music, or because of their liberal identification with the black community which created the music. Like New York and California-based "folk" music, this jazz revival is more the province of zealous fans, curators, ideologues, collectors and historians than of professional musicians or the mass audience.[24] Over the years several other quite distinct revival cults have emerged which are as much like each other in their curatorial urges as they are unlike the communities of fans of other forms of music.

While it is tempting at first glance to write off revival musics as epiphenomenal throwbacks in the broader course of musical evolution, young recruits to these musics do not simply preserve the old styles. They also nurture and evolve new forms which may have a powerful influence on popular music. For example, musical styles and instrumental techniques which have been nurtured in various schools of urbane country and blues rivivals have greatly influenced pop and rock music since 1958.[25] Thus, revival traditions seem to be taking on much of the innovative functions of traditional folk musics which are withering under the corrosive impact of the mass media, urbanization and deghettoization.

VITAL CULTS

The innovations which gave jazz a whole new direction beginning in the early 1940s came not from swing or the New Orleans revival but from a reaction *against* modes. Bop, the second movement to emerge during World War II, came almost exclusively from young black musicians who congregated in New York City. Particularly in its early creative phases bebop was iconoclastic, humorous and irreverent. It was innovative in instrumentation, rhythm, technique, sound, color and the use of the human voice as an instrument. The music was not intended for dancing and the lyrics, though full of illusions, were unintelligible to the mass audience. Much of symbolism, associated with the vital cult was deviant from the dominant norms of the time and might have helped to attract a broader, youthful audience, but the musicians' rejection of the urban middle-class society was focused primarily in heroin,[26] a theme which then had no mass appeal.

The creative cult of bop was generated out of the racial, personal and artistic frustrations of a small group of musicians who became closely associated with one another.[27] Their goal was self expression with a conscious disdain of the mass audience. For this reason the term "cult" is used to describe the following of this period, in contrast to the earlier creative phase where "fad," connoting quick mass interest, seems a more appropriate term.[28]

Great advances in artistic expression were made at the expense of popular acceptance. The audience for this music was a small number of young New York educated blacks who developed the music and a somewhat larger group of white upper-middle-class liberal youth for whom the involvement with bop and its culture served as a form of racial self-hatred.[29] It is hard to set a date, but by 1950, the vital phase of the cult had come to an end. It diffused into cocktail club, easy-listening music via West Coast "cool jazz," became a species of revival music, became a staple of media background music,[30] evolved into an element of fine art music and spawned several new cults which developed for many of the original reasons that had brought the vital cult into being.

We will not deal with the "new thing cult" in any detail because it seems to follow the same dynamics as the vital cult

RICHARD A. PETERSON

of bop. Suffice it to say that each new cycle has been less rooted in the ghetto music of its day and more completely based on experimental music developments in the avant-garde jazz cult itself. Each new circle of black musicians has said, in effect, "We want to create a type of music whites won't understand, can't play and therefore can't steal from us." Each has created a sound that is appreciated by an ever smaller audience whether white or black. Each has been less commercially successful and more outspokenly hostile to white, bourgeois, capitalist society.[31]

JAZZ AS BLACK POWER

In this context the musicians tend to believe they are discriminated against because of their antiestablishment protestations and their race.[32] This is undoubtedly part of the story, but the evidence of radicalism in rock music suggests that club owner and record company executives are much less sensitive to radical sentiments *if* music of radicals sells well. If, for example, Mingus and Roach sold as well as Hendrix and Sly they would not have been blackballed by the industry.

Frank Kofsky deals with the community and culture which has generated various avant-garde cults.[33] He vividly describes the crucible of frustration that has placed the New York avant-garde jazz cult musicians in the vanguard of black nationalism over the past quarter of a century. It does not follow, contrary to Kofsky's line of reasoning, that postbop jazz has had *any* influence in fostering black nationalism in the ghettos. Since such jazz is not played, purchased or widely known in the ghetto (where it was replaced by rhythm and blues music after 1945) it could not have had significant influence.[34] If the music has had any influence on black nationalism beyond the circle of jazz performers it is through its impact on the east coast intellectuals of black nationalism. Even here it is, I believe, not the music itself but the exploitation of black talent by the music industry that is important.[35] For Malcolm X and others this microcosm is taken as a model of the economic, social and political travails of blacks generally.

JAZZ AS FINE ART

Jazz has long since moved out of folk and pop music except as it influences easy-listening music. Besides its revival and cult forms, it is much alive as an element in fine art music. By this I do not mean that the Cleveland Symphony Orchestra now plays the Thelonious Monk songbook; rather, Monk, Miles Davis, Archie Shepp, Duke Ellington, Don Ellis, the Modern Jazz Quartet and many other creative spirits of jazz and their protégés today work in a context much like that of other fine artists.[36]

There is a focus on technical mastery of instruments and the art form. There is self-conscious experimentation with conventions. Recruitment of jazz comes increasingly from school bands and academic conservatories. There is a formal split between practice and performance and performance tends to assume the norms of "classical" music. It takes place in concert halls, academic workshops and recording studios. The audience is expected to make an intellectual response rather than to be physically involved in the music; as a signal to this expectation, musicians perform without any except the mildest forms of showmanship. Rather than depending on a mass market for financial support, there is increasing dependence on patronage from universities, the government and foundations. As another attribute of fine art music, a group of professional critics develop. They focus attention on the perfection of musicianship, technical innovation and remaking the past and interpreting the future of the music in ways which link the music to positive cultural symbols.

This ideological redefinition of the meaning of jazz as an "art form" is most interesting. While an earlier generation of critics defined jazz as demoralizing low-life "nigger" music,[37] jazz is now interpreted in positive terms. It is often called

146   RICHARD A. PETERSON

"the only original American-bred art form" and "the great contribution of blacks to American culture." The sometimes shocking and self-destructive behavior of jazz musicians is now interpreted as the eccentric work of creative artists rather than, as it was earlier, the raving of demented fools. Jazz is exported around the world as a symbol of American freedom and cultural egalitarianism in contrast to the puritanical inhibitions of socialist realism. It is taught to American high school students as an antidote to the younger generation's infatuation with jazz's "stinking hippie" younger cousin, rock. As I have noted elsewhere,[38] the ideological interpretation of jazz in the cultural media has closely paralleled official attitudes towards blacks in this country.

JAZZ CIRCLES WITHOUT END

Rather than trying to find *the* jazz community we have traced the evolution of jazz in the belief that at different points in time and in different social contexts because of its place in widely differing sociocultural contexts. This has not been intended as a definitive statement, but rather as a sketch of a thesis deserving of much further attention by those fascinated with jazz, and with questions about the evolution of cultural forms generally.

The useful suggestions of Howard S. Becker, David G. Berger and Robert A. Stebbins on an earlier draft are gratefully acknowledged. The basic idea is derived from the author's "Cycles of Jazz: Ashes to Ashes and Dust to Dust, If the Liquor Don't Get You, the Scholars Must," a freshman English theme, Oberlin College, 1952.

NOTES

1. Thomas S. Kuhn, *The Structure of Scientific Revolutions*, (Chicago: University of Chicago Press, 1970), pp. 176-210.

2. William B. Cameron, "Sociological Notes on the Jam Session," *Social Forces*, vol. 33 (1954), pp. 177-182; Alan P. Merriam and Raymond W. Mack, "The Jazz Community," *Social Forces*, vol. 38 (1960), pp. 211-222.

3. Paul Carpenter, *Music: An Art and a Business*, (Norman, Oklahoma: University of Oklahoma Press, 1950; John H. Mueller, *The American Symphony Orchestra*, (Bloomington, Indiana: University of Indiana Press, 1951); Max Weber, *The Rational and Social Foundations of Music*, (Carbondale, Illinois: University of Southern Illinois Press, 1958); Leonard B. Meyer, *Music, the Arts, and Ideas*, (Chicago: University of Chicago Press, 1967); H. Wiley Hitchcock, *Music in the United States*, (Englewood Cliffs, N.J.: Prentice-Hall, 1969); Leonard Kasdan and Jon H. Appleton, "Tradition and Change: The Case of Music," *Comparative Studies in History and Society*, vol. 12 (January 1970), pp. 50-58.

4. LeRoi Jones, *Blues People*, (New York: William Morrow & Co., 1963); Charles Keil, *Urban Blues*, (Chicago: University of Chicago Press, 1966); Alan Lomax, *Folk Song Style and Culture*, (Washington, D.C.: AAAS, 1968).

5. Donald Horton, "The Dialogue of Courtship in Popular Songs," *American Journal of Sociology*, vol. 62 (1957), pp. 569-578; H. F. Mooney, "Popular Music Since the 1920's; The Significance of Shifting Taste," *American Quarterly*, vol. 20 (1968), pp. 67-85; James T. Carey, "Changing Courtship Patterns in the Popular Song," *American Journal of Sociology*, vol. 74 no. 6 (1969). pp. 720-731.

6. Richard A. Peterson and David G. Berger, "Entrepreneurship in Organizations: Evidence from the Popular Music Industry," *Administrative Science Quarterly*, (1971).

7. John Johnstone and Elihu Katz, "Youth and Popular Music: A Study in the Sociology of Taste," *American Journal of Sociology*, vol. 62 (1957), pp. 563-568; William N. McPhee, "'When Culture Becomes a Business," in *Sociological Theories in Progress*, edited by Joseph Berger *et al*, (New York: Houghton Mifflin, 1966).

8. Gunther Schuller, *Early Jazz: Its Roots and Musical Development*, (Oxford: University Press, 1968), pp. 63-88.

9. Norman M. Margolis, "A Theory on the Psychology of Jazz," *American Imago*, vol. 11 (Fall 1945), pp. 9-28; Neil Leonard, *Jazz and the White Americans: The Acceptance of a New Art Form*, (Chicago: University of Chicago Press, 1962).

10. Arthur Dorb, *How to Write Songs that Sell*, (New York: Greenberg, 1949).

11. David Ewens, *The History of Popular Music*, (New York: Barnes and Noble, 1961); Hitchcock, *Music in the United States*, pp. 91-126.

12. J. S. Slotkin, "Jazz and Its Forerunners as an Example of

Acculturation," *American Sociological Review*, vol. 8 (1943), pp. 570-575; Morroe Berger, "Jazz: Resistance to the Diffusion of a Culture Pattern," *Journal of Negro History*, vol. 32 (October 1947), pp. 461-494; Aaron H. Esman, "Jazz—A Study in Cultural Conflict," *American Imago*, vol. 8 (1951), pp. 221-225; Leonard, *Jazz and the White Americans.*

13. Richard A. Peterson and David B. Berger, "The Dollar and Pop Culture," in Peter K. Manning, ed., *Deviance and Social Change*, (New York: Prentice-Hall, 1971 (forthcoming)).

14. Ewens, *The History of Popular Music*, pp. 175-181.

15. Richard A. Peterson, "Taking Popular Music Too Seriously," *Journal of Popular Culture*, vol. 4 (1971), pp. 590-594.

16. Howard S. Becker, "The Professional Dance Musician and His Audience," *American Journal of Sociology*, (1951); Cameron, "Sociological Notes on the Jam Session; Anonymous, "Understanding the Jazz Musician: The Artist and His Problems" *Jazz Today*, vol. 2 (March 1956), pp. 41-56; Richard A. Peterson, "Audiences—and all that Jazz," *trans*action, vol. 1 (September-October 1964), pp. 31-32; Robert A. Stebbins, "Role Distance, Role Distance Behavior, and Jazz Musicians," *The British Journal of Sociology*, vol. 20 (1968), pp. 406-415.

17. Marshal Stearns, *The Story of Jazz*, (New York: Oxford University Press, 1956).

18. Leonard, *Jazz and the White Americans.*

19. Leonard, *Jazz and the White Americans.*

20. Richard S. Randall, *Censorship of the Movies*, (Madison: The University of Wisconsin Press, 1968).

21. By focusing on what is new, changing and at the forefront of attention in each era, this essay slights the persistent continuity of jazz-related styles as they are performed in thousands of school bands, road shows and drinking clubs around the country. While these are cultural backwaters, they are a vital spawning-ground of new talent and ideas.

22. Stearns, *The Story of Jazz*, pp. 140-148.

23. John S. Wilson, *Jazz: The Transition Years 1940-1960*, (New York: Appleton-Century-Crofts, 1966), pp. 139-57.

24. R. Serge Denisoff, *Folk Consciousness, The People's Music, and American Communism*, (Urbana: University of Illinois Press, 1971); Peterson, "Taking Popular Music Too Seriously."

25. Carl I. Belz, "Popular Music and the Folk Tradition," *Journal of*

American Folklore, vol. 80 (1967), pp. 130-42; Nik Cohn, *Rock From the Beginning,* (New York: Stein and Day, 1969); Ralph J. Gleason, *The Jefferson Airplane and the San Francisco Sound,* (New York: Ballantine, 1969); Paul Hemphill, *The Nashville Sound,* (New York: Simon and Schuster, 1970); Charlie Gillett, *The Sound of the City,* (New York: Outerbridge and Dienstfrey, 1970);R. Serge Denisoff and Richard A. Peterson, eds. *The Sounds of Social Change,* (Chicago: Rand McNally, 1972).

26. Charles Winick, "The Use of Drugs by Jazz Musicians," *Social Problems,* vol. 7 no. 3 (Winter 1960), pp. 223-230; Nat Hentoff, *The Jazz Life,* (New York: Dial, 1961), pp. 75-97.

27. Stearns, *The Story of Jazz;* Wilson, *Jazz: The Transition Years 1940-1960;* A. B. Spellman, *Four Lives in the Bebop Business,* (New York: Pantheon Books, 1966); C. Glenn Cambor, Gerald M. Lisowitz and Miles D. Miller, "Creative Jazz Musicians: A Clinical Study," *Psychiatry,* vol. 38 (1954), pp. 1-15.

28. Rolf Meyerson and Elihu Katz, "Notes on the Natural History of Fads," *American Journal of Sociology,* 1957.

29. Hentoff, *The Jazz Life,* pp. 15-22.

30. Robert A. Faulkner, *Hollywood Studio Musicians: Their Work and Career Contingencies in the Film Industry,* (Chicago: Aldine Press, 1971).

31. Lloyd Miller and James K. Skipper, Jr., "Sounds of Protest: Jazz and the Militant Avant-Garde," *Approaches to Deviance: Theories, Concepts, and Research Findings,* edited by Lefton, Skipper, Jr., and McCaghy, (Meredith Corp., 1968), pp. 129-140.

32. Jones, *Blues People;* LeRoi Jones, *"Jazz and the White Critic,"* *Downbeat,* (August 15, 1963), p. 16; Spellman, *Four Lives in the Bebop Business;* Roland Young, "Black Revolutionary Music," *Ramparts,* vol. 9 (March 1971), pp. 54-57.

33. Frank Kofsky, *Black Nationalism and the Revolution in Music,* (New York: Pathfinder Press, 1970).

34. Phyl Garland, *The Sound of Soul,* (Chicago: Henry Regenery Co., 1969).

35. Richard A. Peterson, "Jazz in Black and Red: Notes on a Theme by Kofsky," *trans*action, in press, 1971.

36. David L. Westby, "The Career Experience of the Symphony Musician," *Social Forces,* vol. 38 (March 1960), pp. 223-230; Alfred Schutz, "Making Music Together: A Study in Social Relationship," in

RICHARD A. PETERSON

Schutz, *Collected Papers: Studies in Social Theory,* vol. 2, Arvid Brodessen, ed., (The Hague: Martinus Nijhoff, 1964), pp. 159-178; Geraldine Pelles, *Art, Artists and Society: Origins of a Modern Dilemma,* (Englewood Cliffs, N.J.: Prentice-Hall, 1963); Leonard B. Meyer, *Emotion and Meaning in Music,* (Chicago: University of Chicago Press, 1956).

37. Leonard, *Jazz and the White Americans.*

38. Richard A. Peterson, "Market and Moralist Censors of a Rising Art Form: *Jazz,"* *Arts in Society,* vol. 4 (Summer 1967), pp. 253-264.

Jazz and
the Other Arts
NEIL LEONARD

Relationships between jazz and the other arts cover a very large area. I have limited myself here to a survey of considerations which have interested me for some time and which, as far as I can gather, have been relatively unexplored. This chapter should therefore be read not as an attempt to arrive at definitive conclusions but as an indicator of a neglected field of study, which will hopefully stimulate further discussion.

Connections between jazz and the other arts have been neglected for at least two reasons. First, comparisons between different art forms tend to be fuzzy and tricky. Lately the field of comparative arts has been primarily the stepchild of literary history, and most of its research reflects this orientation. In a single essay it is impossible to review the literature of the field and discuss its problems, although a few scholars have begun the attempt. [1]

A second reason is that many regard jazz as *sui generis,* not really art at all but merely popular music or, worse, a wild weed flourishing without cultivation at the expense of the flowers in the garden of the arts. Despite growing recognition, jazz is still the victim of these judgments. One measure of this is that the music is still largely neglected in the academic community. Few colleges or universities give courses in jazz, and often the scholars interested in it are not in the music department.

But if academics have not paid much attention to jazz as an art, a number of artists have, and it is possible to draw some useful connections between jazz and the other arts.

When we think of jazz and literature, novels such as Dorothy Baker's *Young Man with a Horn* (1938) and John Clellon Holmes's *The Horn* (1963) come to mind right away. Richard E. Hawes has made a surprisingly long list of these novels. Although most of them are of little interest in themselves, their wide popular appeal has done much to enhance the image of the jazzman as a naive genius manqué or maudit who fits into a continuing Romantic tradition. This image warrants further study, for it has influenced the picture and role of the jazzman as seen by his audience and himself.

Literary historians have pointed to the connections between Romanticism and philosophical naturalism,[2] and it is worth mentioning that many of the novels about the jazzman are in a neonaturalistic vein. Their values are close to those of the classic blues of, say, Bessie Smith. Like the blues they are often hard-boiled statements of elemental facts, with frank treatment of sex, violence and infidelity and with a cynical view of human nature motivated by self-interest and animal appetites in a deterministic and materialistic world. In both the blues and naturalism the style tends to be simple, spare and direct, if sometimes awkward, and a sense of resignation and understatement evokes feelings of pathos, bordering on tragedy. Not surprisingly, near the turn of the century traditionalists responded to the naturalistic novel much as they would to the blues later on.

The connection between jazz and poetry has also been significant. The words of the blues, of course, are a form of poetry and they, along with the music of jazz, have attracted a number of poets and affected their work in several ways. Langston Hughes's *Weary Blues* (1926) provides a good case in point, but it is not difficult to think of other poems directly influenced by jazz or what passed for it. But there have been more subtle influences; for instance, the pervasiveness of jazz-like rhythms in the work of major poets. These have been perhaps most often observed in the poems of e. e. cummings, yet they are also evident in more conservative poetry.

As an indication of their pervasiveness, let us look at the poems of T. S. Eliot, a conservative in social, religious and political matters, who had no special fondness for jazz. We tend not to associate him with jazz beyond the lines in *The Waste Land*: "O O O O O that Shakespeherian Rag—/ It's so elegant/ So intelligent." But if he had little regard for ragtime, he recognized the significance of its rhythms and their roots. In 1923 in an article called "The Beating of a Drum," he observed that poetry began "with a savage beating a drum in the jungle, and it retains that essential of percussion and rhythm,"[3] and in general he recognized the importance of such rhythms in all modern art and gave them a significant place in his poetry and plays. His use of "The Shakespherian Rag" (there really was such a song[4]) and other suggestions of jazz evoke what he took to be the superficiality and mechanical nature of modern life, and at the same time emphasized the primitive urges of some of his characters. This was particularly true in the dramatic fragments of "Sweeney Agonistes" (1927), originally called "Wanna Go Home, Baby?," which dealt with two prostitutes and their friends in a London flat, and utilized an under-pattern from the Greek drama. "I had intended the whole play to be accompanied by light drum taps to accentuate the beats (esp. the chorus, which ought to have noise like a street drill),"[5] wrote Eliot, who hoped to engage the audience's unconscious participation by involving its sense of rhythm. The kind of rhythm he had in mind resembled that of

NEIL LEONARD

commercial jazz of the twenties, the sort sung by music-hall singers like Marie Lloyd. One of his essays of this time dealt with her, and he believed that the catchy songs of vaudeville contained a device for giving poetic drama a broad appeal. Eliot wanted to hold the playgoer's attention not only with jazzy rhythms but other music-hall clichés too, and in the process expose him to the profounder material beneath the surface. This use of the musical vernacular reflected his idea that in "the music of poetry" the poet must take into account everyday speech in his "melody and harmony."[6] "Sweeney Agonistes" used a good deal of the vernacular, both musical and verbal. In one of its songs one character plays tambo, another bones, while the rest join in the syncopated nonsense—somewhat akin to scat singing—based on a familiar song. The first verse goes:

Under the bamboo
Bamboo bamboo
Under the bamboo tree
Two live as one
One lives as two
Two live as three
Under the bam
Under the boo
Under the bamboo tree.

Another song and for that matter much of the dialogue of the drama has similar rhythmic patterns together with antiphonal techniques which we associate with jazz and African music. These techniques continued to occupy Eliot into the 1930s. There are antiphonal lines in *Murder in the Cathedral* (1934) alternately intoned by the drunken knights who enter the cathedral to kill Becket. The third stanza of their chorus reads:

Where is Becket the Cheapside brat
Where is Becket the faithless priest
Come down Daniel to the lion's Den
Come down Daniel and join the feast.

Grover Smith, the leading authority on the sources of Eliot's numerous borrowings, argues that these lines were derived from Vachel Lindsay's "Daniel," part of which Lindsay designated to be read "with a touch of 'Alexander's Ragtime Band.' "[7]

I am suggesting here that jazz was an important element in the sensibility of the Atlantic community in the first part of this century and that the new music, however diluted, found its way into the works of artists who did not necessarily like it or its derivatives.

So much, for the moment, for jazz and literature. Now let us look at the sorts of connections we can make between jazz and painting.

Several jazz musicians have concerned themselves with the fine arts, Duke Ellington being a good case in point. As a young man growing up in Washington, Ellington liked to draw and paint, and in high school concentrated on courses in design. He almost turned to the graphic arts as a career when he won a poster contest sponsored by the NAACP which awarded him a scholarship to Pratt Institute. He decided to turn instead to music but after making this decision continued to draw and for a time was a partner in a successful poster business. Later he designed covers for some of the sheet music of his compositions. More important, his fascination for the pictorial affected his music. As Ellington explained:

> In my writing there is always a mental picture. That's the way I was raised up in music. In the old days, when a guy made a lick, he'd say what it reminded him of. He'd make a lick and say, "It sounds like my old man falling down stairs" or "It sounds like a crazy guy doing this or that." I remember ole Bubber Miley taking a lick and saying "that reminds me of Miss Jones singin' in church." That's the way I was raised up in music. I always have a mental picture.[8]

Thus, of "East St. Louis Toodle-oo" Ellington declared, "The

NEIL LEONARD

title meant for me the broken walk of a man who had worked all day in the sun and was leaving the field at sunset."[9] And the other members of the Ellington band, which sometimes composed things collectively, relied on mental pictures too. "The guys," Ellington said, "would be walking up Broadway after work and they see this old man coming down the street, and there was the beginning of 'Old Man Blues.' "[10]

Critics have compared Ellington to Debussy and Delius. How much these composers affected him is not fully clear, but we do know that he learned about Debussy early in his career from the Broadway arranger and orchestra leader, Will Vodrey, and certainly recordings such as "Misty Morning," "Rainy Nights," "Swampy River," "Azure" and "Dusk" suggest a link with impressionism, both musical and painterly. Along with impressionistic painters Ellington emphasized the importance of color. "I like to think of music in terms of color," he said, "and I like to see the flames licking yellow in the dark and then pulsing down to a red glow."[11] He believed that such imaginings stimulated his creative capacities.

These brief remarks about Ellington have indicated some of the ways in which painting and visual matters have influenced jazz. Now I want to look at the problem from the opposite direction, using Stuart Davis, a friend of Ellington, to show how jazz affected painting.

Throughout his career Davis was much interested in jazz, and while still in his teens he had sought it out in the New York area, sometimes accompanied by fellow painter Glenn Coleman (a member of the Ash Can School). As he later recalled, "Coleman and I were particularly hep to the jive for that period and spent much time listening to Negro piano players in Newark dives. . . . it was necessary to go to the source to dig it."[12] Not only did Davis like the music and affect some of the jazzmen's talk but he took special pride in his friendships with them. Besides Ellington he knew Louis

Armstrong, James P. Johnson, Pete Johnson, George Wettling and Earl Hines, for whom he named his son. Partial to pianists, he once declared, "I had jazz all my life—I almost breathed it like the air. . . . I think all my paintings, at least in part, came from this influence, though of course I have never tried to paint a jazz scene. . . . It was the *tradition* that affected me."[13] Thus it is not surprising that several of his pictures have jazzy-sounding titles, most obviously "Swing Landscape," and others, some reminiscent of Ellington, e.g., "The Mellow Pad," "Owh in San Pao!" and "Something on the 8 Ball."

Davis liked to think of his art in terms of music. Jazzmen, including Ellington and Pete Johnson, played at the openings of two of his one-man shows, and Davis hoped the audience would see the analogies he found between the paintings and music. Among other things he thought that his irregular geometric shapes and piebald colors echoed the rhythm and tempo of the music. Assuming that music and art had a good deal in common, he felt that neither should try to tell a story; pictures and music had lives of their own and existed in and for themselves. He further believed that we appreciate painting and music in pretty much the same way. "The eye," he asserted, "travels through a picture in a period of time just as [the ear] follows the tonal intervals in music as they are progressively played in a sequence of time."[14] According to him, both music and painting were comprised of tonal intervals, the various sounds in music being analogous to color, contrast, size and direction in painting. In his "Hot Still-scape for Six Colors" he claimed to use colors just as a musician uses instruments "when the tone color variety results from the simultaneous juxtaposition of different instrumental groups."[15] Moreover Davis found in jazz parallels for the subject matter of his paintings. He hoped to convey what he discovered in the work of Louis Armstrong, "The American Spirit," which he defined as a new sense of reality forced upon us by the pace of modern life with its

NEIL LEONARD

"hundreds of diverse scenes, sounds and ideas in a juxtaposition that has never before been possible."[16] Equally important, jazz pointed the way to something which he had seen in Gaugin, Van Gogh and the Fauves, an absolute order without reference to any particular subject matter. He heard this first in Newark in the "numerical precision" of the black piano players, which had a "formal" or "classical" quality. "This is the reason I like jazz, which has influenced my work deeply," he explained. "Jazz sets up a simple form within which it establishes a freedom."[17] Davis' analogies sometimes seem vague or farfetched, and I do not mean to suggest that they are necessarily valid. But true or not, they affected his painting and throw an interesting light on it.

In general, drawing analogies between different art forms raises big problems. Too often the results are overly subjective, fanciful or nebulous. This seems true of Madame de Stael's dictum that music is frozen architecture, and Oswald Spengler's assertions about "the visible chamber music" of bent furniture of the eighteenth century, "the Titian style of the madrigal," *allegro feroce* of Frans Hals and the *andante con moto* of Van Dyke."[18] Moreover, it seems mistaken to make very much of analogies between concepts such as realism or impressionism in painting, music or literature. Not only are the terms used differently in the various art forms but the arts may be quite separate in nature and tradition. Despite their interrelationships, art forms do not necessarily develop at the same pace or manner, but according to their own rules and patterns, and those of the culture which nourishes them.

In spite of such pitfalls I believe a few comparisons and analogies can be made between jazz, literature and painting. Again it seems helpful to use, insofar as possible, influential artists to illustrate my points, and I want to call once more on Eliot to represent literature and to use John Marin for painting. Both men were working in the first 40 years of the twentieth century, which saw important developments in jazz. Jazzmen during these years were by and large verbally inarticulate, so it is difficult to rely on any one of them in this context, but I think that after examining some of the things Eliot and Marin had in common we shall be able to fit jazz into some general tendencies.

Eliot's poems and Marin's pictures departed broadly from convention, and both men tried to explain their intentions. Eliot maintained that the radical innovations in modern poetry sprang from deep changes in society which necessarily drove the artist to new forms and techniques. "Our civilization," he claimed, "comprehends great variety and complexity which playing on a refined sensibility must produce complex results."[19] Marin too spoke of his art as a response to the complexities of modern life. Some of his best-known, early paintings are of New York City, which he called "the land of Jazz—lights and movies." Discussing these pictures, he wrote: "The life of today so keyed up, so seeming unreal yet so real and the eye with so much to see and the ear to hear. Things happening most weirdly upside down, that its all—what is it? But the seeing eye and the hearing ear become attuned. Then comes Expression:

taut, taut loose and taut electric staccato.[20]

Jazz seems to have been a response to the sorts of things Eliot and Marin had in mind. From the time of the First World War on, critics have called the music a sensitive reaction to the chaos and complexities of modern experience, and the early records of the Original Dixieland Jazz Band (ODJB), the first out-and-out jazz recordings, made in 1917, suggest the electric and staccato qualities and the simultaneous tautness and looseness which Marin had mentioned four years earlier. The first recorded blues were also a reaction to modern anxieties, and when jazzmen did talk about their work, they sometimes spoke of it in these terms. Ellington's comments about "Eerie Moan" (1933) and "Harlem Air Shaft" (1940), for example, express his reac-

NEIL LEONARD

tions to the life of New York City. His compositions found inspiration not only in elderly men walking home at sunset or down city streets but also in other images, sounds and smells of the contemporary environment.

Again, both Eliot and Marin felt that the artist had to experiment with new forms and techniques. Eliot declared that "the poet must become more and more allusive, more indirect, in order to force, to dislocate if necessary, language into its meaning."[21] *The Waste Land* with its fragmentation, altered contexts, ambiguities and obliqueness offers a good illustration of what he had in mind. Marin too found it necessary to distort and disjoin conventional symbols. Many of his pictures have things in common with analytic cubism, for instance, his early etching "Grain Elevator in Wee-hawken" (1915) and later his city pictures such as "Street Crossing, New York" (1928). In these one finds twisted images, jagged angles, chevrons and other spiky forms which contributed to a pictorial shorthand uniquely his own. Jazzmen too experimented, however unconsciously, with new forms and techniques. Bessie Smith forced and dislocated musical language into its meaning through a variety of techniques including unorthodox rhythmic and tonal devices and unconventional timbres, while the ODJB conveyed a strong sense of fragmentation with some of the same techniques. Its recordings, which abound with interrupted melodic lines and rhythms, abrupt, frenetic, and without clear transitions, often seem to verge on chaos but seldom disintegrate into it.

At the core of these innovations was another which also reflected an awareness of the variousness and complexity of modern life: the expression of multiple facets of material from different points of view simultaneously, or as nearly so as the medium allowed. Eliot's poetry strongly implied his "feeling that the whole of the literature of Europe since Homer and within it the whole of literature of one's country has a simultaneous existence and simultaneous order.[23] He liked the way James Joyce conveyed "the sense of everything happening at once"[23] in *Ulysses,* and his own poetry and drama evoke a strong sense of simultaneity through such devices as double entendre; borrowings from earlier artists; shifting identities; interplaying voices; ambiguous references to space and time; and mythological prototypes and under-patterns—all of which suggest more than one level of meaning. He noted how Joyce had used the mythological method of "manipulating a continuous parallel between contemporaneity and antiquity," and believed that other modern artists were bound to employ this technique developed by Yeats. "It is," concluded Eliot, "simply a way of controlling, of ordering, of giving shape and significance to the immense futility and anarchy of contemporary history .... It is, I seriously believe, a step toward making the modern world possible in art."[24] With the help of such integrating devices Eliot was able to fuse a wide variety of different kinds of experience using what he called a "logic of imagination" quite different from the ordinary "logic of concepts."[25]

In his own way Marin did similar things. He too recognized the necessity of indirection and made his audience "look around a little"[26] in his pictures, and he emphasized multiplicity and simultaneity. In connection with his early New York City water colors he wrote:

> I see great forces at work; great movements; the large buildings and the small buildings; the warring of the great and the small; influences of one mass on another greater or smaller mass. Feelings are aroused which give me the desire to express the reaction of these "pull forces," those influences which play with one another; great masses pulling smaller masses, each subject in some degree to the others' power. ... While these powers are at work pushing, pulling, sideways, downwards, upwards, I can hear the sound of their strife and there is a great music being played.[27]

Marin felt that imaginative art involved "a composite of influences of things seen,"[28] and he sometimes made up to 20 quick pictures of a boat or other subject as it moved before his easel. But more often he put more than one image on a single paper or canvas. One of his greatest difficulties was to get a picture "to travel in its planes," as he put it. His biographer, MacKinley Helm, points out that this meant getting the several views to coexist more or less independently without interfering with one another, so that any of them might be lifted off the paper without disturbing the others.[29] The overall effect is of seeing different aspects of the subject from different points of view at the same time. Marin contained and controlled his multiple images by painting frames around his pictures and balancing the opposing and dissimilar elements in an intuitive synthesis reminiscent of Eliot's "logic of imagination."

Certain aspects of jazz also reflect the trend toward multiplicity and simultaneity. The records of the ODJB and the recordings of the Eureka Jazz Band of New Orleans, which indicate how jazz sounded before 1917, reveal the shift away from traditional homophony in which one instrument carries the melody and the others accompany it in unison or supporting harmony. The Eureka Band played homophonous versions of traditional marches and hymns but it also used these and other forms of popular music as bases for jazz renditions. A hymn tune such as "Just a Closer Walk with Thee" was jazzed up with several devices involving simultaneity. One was close to polyphony, the use of more than one melody at a time, the lead instruments, trumpet or cornet, clarinet and trombone (the Eureka Band often had more than one of each) playing different, though related, melodies. For academically trained ears especially, early jazz was polytonal, not only because its practitioners used "blues scales" or "blue" microtones along with the orthodox diatonic sounds but because the self-taught musicians sometimes played out of tune unintentionally. Simultaneity also manifested itself in jazz rhythms, in syncopation insofar as it implied more than one rhythm, and more explicitly in polyrhythm, i.e., two or more independent rhythms played at the same time. Furthermore, simultaneity appeared in the dynamic interplay of the different instruments in jazz, an interplay reminiscent of the various voices in *The Waste Land* and not entirely unrelated to the interaction of forces Marin imagined in the city.

Finally I want to speculate, although the evidence here is slim, that the jazzman synthesized the multiple aspects of his material in much the same way as Marin and Eliot did. The harmonic pattern underlying a "Just a Closer Walk with Thee" or "Tiger Rag" performs a unifying function, a point of reference relating the different voices, not entirely unlike the mythological underpatterns of *The Waste Land* or *The Family Reunion*. Such devices bespeak a highly associational kind of logic, which we connect primarily with music. Eliot and Marin discussed the organization and structure of their work in terms of music, and the jazzman used something akin to Eliot's or Marin's logic of imagination. Speaking of the integrative method of modern poetry, Eliot said, "The sequence of images coincides and concentrates into one intense impression. . . . The reader has to allow the images to fall into his memory successively without questioning the reasonableness of each at the moment, so that, at the end, a total effect is produced."[30] Perhaps this is what happens to us when we view a Marin picture. After "looking around a little," we find the images coinciding into one intense impression. And possibly the same is true of jazz. Its elements fall into our unquestioning memories and the total effect in the end is an intense impression, although of course this does not rule out moments of recognition and gratification along the way. "Harlem Air Shaft" provides an indication of this. As Ellington wrote:

> So much goes on in a Harlem air shaft. You get the full
> essence of Harlem in an air shaft. You hear fights, you

smell dinner, you hear people making love. You hear intimate gossip floating down. You hear the radio. An air shaft is one great big loud-speaker. You see your neighbours' laundry. You hear the janitor's dogs. The man upstairs' aerial falls down and breaks your window. You smell coffee. A wonderful thing, is that smell. An air shaft has got every contrast. One guy is cooking dried fish and rice and another guy's got a great big turkey. Guy-with-fish's wife is a terrific cooker but the guy's wife with the turkey is doing a sad job. . . . You hear people praying, fighting, snoring. Jitterbugs are jumping up and down always over you, never below you. That's a funny thing about jitterbugs. They're always above you. I tried to put all that in "Harlem Air Shaft."[3] [1]

Eliot and Marin also sought "to get it all in," to evoke as much of the variousness and complexity as they could, and certainly one of the striking things about "Harlem Air Shaft" is that it conveys something, however fragmentary, of several different kinds of experience, juxtaposing and superimposing them without formal transitional devices and fusing them through an associational logic of imagination which evokes a single intense impression.

NOTES

1. René Wellek and Austin Warren, "Literature and the Other Arts," Chapter 11 of their *Theory of Literature* (1942), and Mary Gaither, "Literature and the Arts" in Newton P. Stallknecht and Horst Frenz, eds., *Comparative Literature* (1961). Also helpful is the section on music and literature in the bibliography titled *Literature and the Other Arts* brought out in 1959 by the New York Public Library under the auspices of the Modern Language Association.

2. See, for example, Charles C. Walcutt, *American Literary Naturalism. A Divided Stream* (Minneapolis, 1956), *passim*.

3. T. S. Eliot, "The Beating of a Drum," *Nation and Athenaeum*, XXXIV (Oct. 6, 1923), 11-12; see also Morris Freedman, "Jazz

Rhythms and T. S. Eliot," *South Atlantic Quarterly,* LI (Summer, 1957), 419-35.

4. R. B. Elderry, "Eliot's Shakespeherian Rag," *American Quarterly, (Summer, 1957), pp. 185-86.*

5. Quoted by Hallie Flanagan, *Dynamo* (New York, 1943), p. 82.

6. T. S. Eliot, "The Music of Poetry," *Partisan Review* IX (Nov.-Dec., *1942), p. 485.*

7. Grover Smith, *T. S. Eliot's Poetry and Plays* (Chicago, 1956), p. 182; Vachel Lindsay, *Collected Poems* (New York, 1955), p. 159.

8. Quoted in Richard O. Boyer, "Hot Bach," Pt. II, *The New Yorker, XX (July 1, 1947), p. 27.*

9. Quoted by Stanley Dance in liner notes for "Duke Ellington and his Orchestra, 1927-1940," C3L27.

10. *Ibid.*

11. Boyer, Pt. I, June 24, p. 29.

12. Stuart Davis, *Stuart Davis* (New York, 1945), pp. 2-3.

13. Quoted in Katharine Kuh, ed., *The Artist's Voice* (New York, 1962), p. 53.

14. See Edwin Alden Jewell, "Abstraction and Music," *New York Times*, August 6, 1939, Sec. 9, p. 7.

15. "Stuart Davis," *Parnassus,* XII (Dec., 1940), p. 6.

16. Stuart Davis, "Self Interview," *Creative Arts,* IX (Sept., 1931), p. 211.

17. Stuart Davis, "Is Today's Artist With or Against the Art of the Past?" *Art News,* LVII (Summer, 1958), p. 43.

18. Quoted in René Wellek and Austin Warren, *Theory of Literature* (New York, 1942), p. 131.

19. T. S. Eliot, *Selected Essays* (New York, 1932), p. 248.

20. Dorothy Norman, ed., *Selected Writings of John Marin* (New York, 1945), pp. 100, 125.

21. Eliot, *Selected Essays,* p. 248.

22. *Ibid.,* p. 4.

23. T. S. Eliot, "Ulysses, Order, and Myth," *Dial,* LXXV (Nov. 23, 1923), pp. 480-83.

24. *Ibid.*

25. Preface to St. J. Perse, *Anabasis,* trans. by T. S. Eliot (New York, 1938, p. 8.

26. MacKinley Helm, *John Marin* (Boston, 1948), p. 20.

27.Norman, p. 4.

28. *Ibid.*, p. 87.

29. Helm, pp. 97-98.

30. Perse, p. 8.

31. Boyer, Pt. II, p. 30.

Jazz and
All That Sociology

CHARLES NANRY

One of my favorite fables is the one about groping blind men and elephants. It illustrates my belief that when one realizes he has only a small part of the whole in hand, he is bound to undertake re-evaluation and aim for fresh perspectives. What follows is but one small part of the whole elephant called jazz; but it is my hope that this small beginning will open new areas of inquiry and understanding.

In 1967 I undertook a pilot study which attempted to establish whether critical states in the careers of jazz musicians could be isolated. I had hoped to discover types of musicians who were at clearly different points in their jazz career. The study was successful: I found that two career stages, clearly separable, marked some musicians as aspiring candidates and others as established professionals. The candidates fell into two subcategories: those who had achieved some degree of success (candidate successes) and those who had not (candidate failures). I called this major independent variable Occupational Status.[1]

This study was expanded in 1969 to compare candidate successes and failures with professionals on a variety of

CHARLES NANRY

attitudes. When groups were controlled for race, age and occupational status, there were significant differences among them. In fact, I found that most professional musicians are hard working, adaptable and bureaucratically oriented—a clear contradiction of much of the available jazz literature, which embodies what I call the Jazz Myth.

The jazz myth is a constellation of presumed deviant attitudes and behaviors on the part of jazzmen. It has resulted in part from overly romantic and celebrationist notions about jazz and jazzmen. The jazz myth to some degree stems from a lack of critical and academic concern with jazz. Some jazz writers, sympathetic to black culture and/or deviance, have understandably failed to be analytical and critical about jazz. Many writers with critical and analytic ability have opted for more prestigious art forms. It has taken jazz a long time to be recognized as a legitimate art form. Part of the reaction to jazz can be attributed to racism; part to its origins as black American folk music. But whatever the reasons, many jazz writers have had limited knowledge about jazz as music. Many have been rank amateurs in music, writing and/or critical ability.

Jazz musicians themselves have also contributed to the myth. An example of the myth in action among jazzmen is the "beautiful syndrome." The beautiful syndrome represents a penchant on the part of many jazz musicians to be uncritical of one another. If you ask one jazz musician about another's playing, the most likely response is: "Man, he's beautiful." In the beginning of my research I assumed that this response was reserved for outsiders. It is not. Jazzmen also "jive" each other because they do not want to risk alienating anyone, including fellow musicians, who might control employment. Sociologists writing about jazz have not altogether escaped the myth.

As jazz writers, sociologists may be conveniently divided into two schools or "styles." The first is the "subculture school" exemplified by the jazz writings of Lastrucci,[2]

Becker,[3] Cameron,[4] Merriam and Mack[5] and Stebbins.[6] This school views jazz musicians as constituting deviant subcultures. Their major emphasis is on those characteristics that set jazzmen apart from others.

The second style of jazz and sociology writing, what I call the "assimilationist school," is more historically oriented. In general, authors who belong to this school tend to see jazz as part of macrosociology. Their emphasis is typically on the place of jazz in the larger context of American society. These authors are usually concerned with the impact of social change on jazz and, in general, they paint on a larger canvas than the subculturists. Sociologists like Berger,[7] Leonard,[8] Harvey[9] and Peterson[10] exemplify this tradition.

It is unfair, however, to compare directly members of the two schools since they typically consider different issues. Little is to be gained from simply disputing what they have said. The central problem for all sociologists who write about jazz is the same: representative sampling. The sampling frame is often unspecified or simply assumed.

Part of the problem is that no one has yet come up with a satisfactory definition of jazz. Without that definition it is difficult to type jazz musicians. Perhaps we ought to follow Waller's—or was it Armstrong's—apocryphal injunction "not to mess with it." I think not; but we ought to recognize that jazz is not one music but many. One man's jazz may be another's commercial pap. Self-definition is one way out of the dilemma; namely, those who call themselves jazz musicians are jazz musicians. The assumption here is that a self-definition will be difficult to maintain if others do not agree. But this "solution" does not fully solve the critical sampling problem either. We need a typology of jazzmen and reliable techniques for selecting representative samples. The goal of this chapter will be to develop that typology.

My own data indicate that relatively few musicians call themselves jazz musicians. Most prefer to be labeled as musicians who play jazz. Some black musicians find they cannot shake the jazz label; some whites cannot earn it. Miles

Davis and Duke Ellington have rejected the jazz label but their audiences refuse to follow suit. "Other" as well as self-definition is obviously involved. Below is my proposal: a modest strategy for sampling that may help. It is based on the assumption that jazz researchers have identified types of jazz musicians but that the existing literature must be reorganized. The two schools of jazz and sociology, the subculture school and the assimilationist school, typically discuss different types of musicians. By way of example and in order to clarify the thrust of these schools, I will briefly discuss the work of Howard Becker, representing the subculturists, and Morroe Berger, representing the assimilationists.

Becker's major theoretical concern, as expressed in *Outsiders,* is with deviance:

> social groups create deviance by making the rules whose infraction constitutes deviance, . . . (deviance is) . . . a consequence of the application by others of rules and sanctions to an "offender."[1]

Jazz values are opposed to commercial values by Becker in order to illustrate the labeling process. Becker talks about dance musicians who have either artistic values (which he equates with jazz) or commercial values. His study is not, nor does it pretend to be, a comprehensive study of jazzmen. Jazz for Becker is free self-expression, artistry; commercial music is music susceptible to outside pressure and compromise. The true jazzman is presumed to be an artist; the commercial musician a craftsman.

Although Becker does not give us data on the race and age of the musicians he discusses, I think it is reasonable to assume that he is talking about frustrated dance bandsmen who hold the artistic value of freedom of expression in a restrictive musical context. These deviants are dance musicians, not jazz musicians, who use a hypothetical reference group of idealized jazzmen. They are musicians caught up in the jazz myth.

The subculturists in general talk about scattered coteries of musicians caught up in the lonely value of artistic self-expression. The assimilationists, on the other hand, are more concerned with the historical contexts of black jazz. In "Jazz: Resistance to The Diffusion of a Culture-Pattern" Morroe Berger states the theme most clearly:

The purpose of this paper is to examine the implications, for the diffusion of jazz, of the fact that the Negroes, with whom jazz is correctly associated, are a low-status group in the United States. The evidence to be presented will confirm the hypothesis that in the diffusion process the prestige of the donors has considerable bearing on the way in which a borrowing group reacts to cultural traits of other groups.[1][2]

It serves no useful purpose to fault the assimilationists because of "historical bias," i.e., their nonsystematic selection of data. It is sufficient to say that, like the subculturists, they have not solved the sampling problem.

A new synthesis is needed to properly "place" the existing literature as well as extend it. Critics of the jazz and sociology literature are often uneasy because what they read fails to describe jazz as they know it. In order for that criticism to be constructive, however, they must re-analyze what others have done rather than cast it aside. The sampling problem may never adequately be solved in any case, for the jazz label is "unprotected" by licensing procedures. But we must be able to categorize those about whom we speak.

Certain values long associated in the minds of jazz insiders with the art form—the jazz myth—are, in reality, values that belong only to a segment of those who have traditionally been labeled as jazzmen. Frustrated dance band musicians do not, and have not, fairly represented jazz. Except as role models, men like Louis Armstrong, Duke Ellington, Miles Davis and John Coltrane do not fairly represent jazz either. The many kinds of music we think of as jazz must be analytically distinguished before they can be linked together. The same is true for types of jazzmen. If we fail in either

CHARLES NANRY

effort, arbitrary and sterile generalization may result. A typology of jazzmen must reflect the complexity of jazz, otherwise we will be describing a jazz world as falsely monolithic as, say, the "communist world."

Jazz does not exist in a social and cultural vacuum. The assimilationist school has given us ample evidence of the impact of social and technological change on jazz.[13] The subculture school has documented the dynamic tension between the role of performer and the role of creator. But confusion has resulted from accepting either as typical of all jazz. The Gordian knot may be cut by making a series of analytical and heuristic distinctions which can ultimately be tested.

The first distinction I would propose is that jazz as a musical category be separated from notions about particular jazzmen constituting social groups. Jazz as a musical category is an art form, distinguishable from other musics, normative and learned, i.e., it represents values that must be transmitted. As a category it has the characteristics of Durkheim's social facts, that is, it is outside of any single individual and constrains behavior. The consideration of jazz as a musical category leads ultimately to a musicological problem: consideration of it, on the other hand, as a group phenomenon leads to a sociological one.

Jazzmen in social groups interact. One thing which presumably brings them together is their relation to the category of music called jazz. But other nonmusical characteristics such as race and age have an impact on group behavior and attitudes. Jazz is but one of many social facts that concern the jazzman. Any group of jazzmen will, therefore, be affected by one or more overlapping sets of interactive social facts. It is possible to study jazzmen and the effect of their jazz identification only if some of the major influences are untangled. In considering jazzmen we ought to keep in mind that we are dealing with men who are musicians who play jazz. Every school child who learns music is a potential jazz musician. Most kids who play music, however, do not become jazz musicians. Black kids, for example, are more likely than white kids to be exposed to jazz. Given the recent American opportunity structure for blacks what other art forms were open to them? Jazz selects blacks, whites select jazz.

But these facts must be linked to a theoretical perspective that may "explain" their interrelationships. In my own research, reference group theory has served that purpose.

I see nothing mysterious about the notion of reference groups. From one point of view the notion is simply an extension of the idea of group culture. In industrial societies there are competing ways of doing things, hence alternative models of behavior are at least potentially available. Reference group theory is an attempt to discover the process whereby one group's values are adopted rather than another's. Manford Kuhn in *The Dictionary of The Social Sciences* defines reference group this way:

> The term denotes a social group with which an individual feels identified and to which he aspires to relate his identity. A person derives from his reference groups his norms, attitudes and values and the social objects these create. He also derives significant social categories, both the ones to which he is assigned and the ones with which he is, in one way or another, contrasted.[14]

Whether subcultures may develop based on membership in reference groups is questionable, since one may also refer to nonexistent reference others—to a "paper eternity." Jazzmen may think of Buddy Bolden as an "other" in the same way that a poet may refer his work to Homer.

Jazzmen may refer themselves to other jazzmen. But when they do, they will not, in all likelihood, refer themselves to all of jazz (past and present) or emulate all of those who call themselves jazzmen. The question is how any jazz musician relates to jazz as a category or art form *and* how he relates to existing groups of jazz players. Of course there is a synergistic effect on the individual adjusting both to the form and to others. Jazz worlds, therefore, have their own internal dynamic which we may call the "within jazz" structure.

But jazzmen have always had to articulate their expression within the larger world of entertainment. This articulation has created modes of accomodation to, for example, the music industry.[15] This adds a "between jazz and nonjazz structures" dimension to our analysis.

Jazz worlds with their own internal dynamics may be distinguished from and related to other "worlds" which the musician's life cycle carries him through. But the relationships are far from simple. The history of jazz confronts us with many puzzling facts. Most jazzmen have been part of the larger world of entertainment in America. With the growth of the mass media the demand for skill, for example, the ability to read music well, has increased. Under the impact of industrialization in America, the professionalization of the entertainment sector, and of jazz, has grown apace. Yet at the same time, jazzmen continue to innovate within jazz and to change and revitalize the art form. Jazz, in other words, has never been simply swallowed up by mass entertainment in America.

A partial explanation of this phenomenon comes from an understanding of the impact of racism in the United States. Black musicians were usually not allowed to become too prominent within the overall structure of mass entertainment. Of course they had to be creative in order to survive, since mere competence was not enough; but the very small number of black musicians who did achieve a noticeable success—Louis Armstrong is the best example—won their triumphs by a strategy of accommodation, striking their bargains with the devil of *kitsch*.[16]

In addition to reference group theory another theoretical perspective that intruded upon my thinking at this point was Max Weber's theory of bureaucracy. Weber's general thesis[17] is that there is a "strain for rationality" in the West which constantly pressures institutional areas toward bureaucratic organization. Yet pure bureaucracy, by definition, is unable to cope adequately with major social changes. Changing technology, industrialization and urbanization demand innovation in social structure. One way out of the dilemma of rationality is through the development of charisma.[18] In the aesthetic area, as in others, pure bureaucracy by itself would eventually bring everything to a halt.

In a masterful analysis of music in the West, *Rational and Social Foundations of Music,*[19] Weber put his notion of alternating rationality and irrationality in music to the test. Weber analyzes the development of Western music and attempts to demonstrate that, in spite of increasing rationalization (for example, the development to the well-tempered scale), certain elements kept escaping the process (for example, the "irrational" properties of the dominant seventh chord). Some "irrationalities" have social origins. The difficulties incurred in attempting to coordinate male and female voices or the need to tune instruments for ensemble playing are but two examples cited by Weber.

The application of Weber's theory of bureaucracy to jazz is delightfully straightforward. The dominant internal career structure of those labeled as jazz musicians at any given moment represents the authoritative bureaucracy.[20] *Any* variation from that "received structure" may represent a charismatic challenge. The charismatic challenge, however, will not be felt unless that charisma is *routinized.*[21]

The routinization of charisma in this case involves the founding of schools of jazzmen through mechanisms like playing together. It also affects jazz as a musical category through the establishment of styles.

It may also be that certain individual musicians or groups of musicians can build a power base outside of jazz itself by parlaying "audience rewards" to the point where jazz itself is forced into accomodation. Jazz which has freely used folk, popular or "classical" music elements as source material may be particularly vulnerable to this criticism.

It is not my intention to claim isomorphism between Weber's analysis of the ideal typical bureaucracy and the threats to it from charisma and jazz. But the jazz mainstream or establishment continues to have its *avant garde* threat. The Weberian perspective offers an opening gambit. Its application suggests the eventual need for serious *audience* research. We must know what segments of the jazz and/or other audiences tend to support what types of bureaucratic or charismatic jazz players. For example, in my research I found evidence to indicate that radical polarization is occurring within jazz with young black players perceiving their music as black music. Young whites are more likely to value "artistic" or "jazz myth" orientations.[23] Both perceptions of what is true jazz represent clearly differentiated charismatic challenges to the jazz establishment.

With the development of rock as an outlet for white creativity, jazz may become whatever black musicians play. The growth of black militancy has had and will continue to have an impact on jazz. It would be surprising if this were not so. The black side of the jazz myth is that only blacks can play it because only blacks have "soul." Jazz proficiency is assumed to be ascribed by some blacks; it is assumed to be achievable by most whites. Writers like LeRoi Jones[24] are quite explicit about this. Obviously the twin principles of the definition of the situation and the self-fulfilling prophecy are at work here.

This "split" is not a new phenomenon in music. Something along the same lines happened with the development of Bop in the 1940s. That music was partially a reaction against the "bureaucratization" of swing. Bop represented both musical and social protest. Bop musicians reacted against all too predictable and heavily ritualized swing arrangements as well as "Uncle Tom" expectations on the part of audiences for black musicians. Boppers, musicians and nonmusicians alike, saw themselves as the antithesis of a complacent and desiccated society and its popular art. The dialectic continues, alternating between establishment jazz and charismatic challenge based on nonmusical as well as musical developments.

The critical issue here revolves around where and how charismatics recruit their audiences. The next step that must be taken is serious audience research. That step has not been taken.

Since I have no direct evidence on the audience response let us turn our attention, for the moment, to the place of jazz vis-à-vis the American music industry. At this point one aspect of the reference group perspective becomes useful.

An important development within reference group theory has been the elaboration of the "local-cosmopolitan" continuum.[2 5] The dimension along which this continuum is organized represents one's general orientation. A local is one who is oriented toward those around him; a cosmopolitan to a larger grouping usually based on specialized interests. The popular metaphor of the big frog in the little pond (presumably a successful local) and the little frog in the big pond (presumably a less than successful cosmopolitan) captures the spirit of this useful typology.

Alvin Gouldner has explicitly included a reference group aspect in his empirically operationalized definition of this continuum. Gouldner's interest is in specifying aspects of manifest and latent roles. The issue for him pivots upon what social identities are called upon in the reference group process. He defines the poles of the continuum as follows:

> 1) Cosmopolitan: those low on loyalty to the employing organization, high on commitment to specialized role skills and likely to use an outer reference group.

> 2) Locals: those high on loyality to the employing organization, low on commitment to specialized role skills and likely to use an inner reference group orientation.[2 6]

CHARLES NANRY

By "inner reference group" Gouldner means face-to-face or membership groups while "outer reference groups" are those that are more "universalistic".

Figure 1 illustrates in a graphic way the cross-classification of these two dimensions, that is, the bureaucratic-charismatic and the local-cosmopolitan. This cross-classification creates a property space which permits us to name types of musicians who might be found where these dimensions intersect. The bureaucratic-charismatic dimension refers to the internal structure of jazz. The local-cosmopolitan dimension refers to the relationship of jazz to other structures. The former dimension is internal; the latter external. Both have self-other and social organization implications.

Figure 1
A Typology of Jazz Musicians

Within Jazz	Between Jazz and Other Musicians	
	Local	Cosmopolitan
Bureaucratic	Dance Band Musicians and other "Club Date" Musicians	The "Studio" Jazzmen/Craftsmen
Charismatic	"Free Jazz" Players In Non-Jazz Bands	The Jazz "Innovator"

The cross-classification of the two variables outlined above is grounded in my own empirical investigations. It developed out of thinking about the contradictory material in the sociological and psychological literature on jazz. Rather than presumptuously characterizing that literature as "wrong," the better strategy became one of placing or specifying the generalizations within a theoretical framework that reduced the apparant contradictions.

Becker, Stebbins, Merriam and Mack and the other members of what I have labeled the "subculture school" are writing mostly about the frustrations of local-bureaucratic musicians. In terms of the above typology, the musicians who

operating in the music business as there are in others. You are an old ball player at 35 but a young philosopher. Only empirical investigation can resolve this issue.

The generation of typologies out of existing literature, however, leads to other problems. The typology generated in this way has been "imposed" even if it is empirically derived. The four "boxes" in either of my cross-classifications have a kind of artificiality about them. I propose that they represent "theoretical subcultures" and demand further investigation of a special kind. They do, however, also represent the beginning of grounded theory. I say this because these categorizations have grown out of my own research. Dividing my sample on the basis of these analytic dimensions made sense out of what otherwise tended to be anomalous findings.

In my study successful candidates moved from local-bureaucratic position to the cosmopolitan-bureaucratic stage pausing at the local-charismatic stage only long enough to acquire improvisational technique. Young black musicians seemed to do this more easily than young whites. Many young white musicians got caught in the jazz myth, represented here as a local-charismatic orientation. For candidate failures in general, jazz becomes an end rather than a means. This is in part because hiring practices in jazz tend to be informal and clique-ridden. It is easy to get "bum steers" in jazz because communication is often nonverbal and, presuming competence, who you know is more than what you know.

Most pros are bureaucratic-cosmopolitans with a few influential inside "stars" becoming charismatic-cosmopolitans, that is, having purely artistic values and reference others. Their innovations tend to be absorbed slowly, however, like those of other creative artists.

The theoretical subcultures described here permit the researcher to use stratified sampling techniques based on the dimensions of the typology itself. The methodology required for this kind of study demands that characteristics of each "subculture" be investigated and not presumed. This can be accomplished by collecting data related to the presumed dimensions of the cross-classification.[27]

In my own work I have developed a research strategy to "liberate" derived typologies, i.e., reduce the likelihood that a typology, clever as it may be, will end up distorting reality. The secret is a simple one: let the subjects in on the research process. Many of the people we are interested in knowing about are themselves interested in sociology; many have had undergraduate courses in the subject. One well-known jazzman, a key informant in my own research, held a master's degree in the sociology of education. But I propose something more than the use of a key informant; more than, for example, William F. Whyte's Doc in *Street Corner Society.*

Presuming that many of the people we are interested in are intelligent and educated, it is not difficult to give them a "minicourse" in sociology. It is not too different than teaching Introductory Sociology, or, better, than training a research assistant.

This technique, of course, presupposes participant observation. It is necessary to gain the trust, interest and enthusiasm of some key informants. It also implies trusting the informants to gather data and conduct interviews. Employing the layman as sociologist enables a researcher to indirectly interview respondents who might otherwise be inaccessible.

In my own research, for example, I found it impossible to get to certain key black jazzmen who were hostile to a white non-jazz-playing sociologist. Data from these men were collected for me by a respected black jazzman with whom I had become friendly and for whom I had secured employment.[28]

At an early stage in my research I also asked some jazz musicians with whom I had established rapport to read over some of the literature on jazz and then tape recorded their critical comments. It was from a noted saxophonist, in fact, that I first got the idea of dividing the literature into "schools."

We ought to bring the musicians back in. Jazz results from

patterned social interaction. It is the product of dedicated craftsmen as well as creative geniuses. It involves technique as well as mystique. What musicians do and think is the most neglected area of jazz research. Speculation abounds; data do not.

NOTES

1. These categories are not unlike those of other empirical typologies widely used in occupational sociology. Many occupational studies in sociology have developed some model of career stages. See: Basil J. Sherlock and Richard T. Morris, "The Evolution of the Professional: A Paradigm" in *Sociological Inquiry*, Vol. 37, No. 1, Winter 1967; Oswald Hall, "The Stages of a Medical Career," *American Journal of Sociology*, Vol. 53, No. 5, March 1948, pp. 327-336; Dan Lortie, "Layman to Lawman: Law Schools, Careers and Professional Socialization," *Harvard Educational Review*, Vol. 29, Fall 1969. For industrial workers the classic statement is by Delbert C. Miller and William H. Form, *Industrial Sociology*, New York, Harper and Row, 1964, p. 541.

2. Carlo Lastrucci, "The Professional Dance Musician," *Journal of Musicology*, III, Winter, 1941, pp. 169-172.

3. Howard S. Becker, "The Professional Dance Musician and His Audience," *American Journal of Sociology*, Vol. 57, 1951, pp. 136-144; Howard S. Becker, "Some Contingencies of the Professional Dance Musician's Career," *Social Problems*, Vol. 3, July, 1955, pp. 18-24; Howard S. Becker, *Outsiders: Studies in the Sociology of Deviance* (New York: The Free Press, 1963), pp. 79-119.

4. William Bruce Cameron, "Sociological Notes on the Jam Session," *Informal Sociology: A Casual Introduction to Sociological Thinking*, (New York: Random House, 1963). This is a reprint, with minor additions, of the *Social Forces* article.

5. Alan Merriam and Raymond Mack, "The Jazz Community," *Social Forces*, Vol. 38, No. 3, March 1960, p. 211.

6. Robert Stebbins, *The Jazz Community: The Sociology of a Musical Subculture*, unpublished Ph.D. dissertation, The University of Minnesota 1964; and Stebbins, "The Theory of the Jazz Community," *Sociological Quarterly*, Vol. 9, 1968, pp. 461-494.

7. Morroe Berger, *New Leader*, December 28, 1942; and Berger,

CHARLES NANRY

"Jazz: Resistance to the Diffusion of a Culture Pattern," *Journal of Negro History*, XXXII, October, 1947, pp. 461-494.

8. Neil Leonard, *Jazz and The White Americans: The Acceptance of a New Art Form* (Chicago: The University of Chicago Press, 1962).

9. Edward Harvey, "Social Change and The Jazz Musician," *Social Forces*, Vol. 46, No. 1, September, 1967, pp. 34-42.

10. Richard A. Peterson, "Artistic Creativity and Alienation," *Arts in Society*, 1965, pp. 244-248; and Richard A. Peterson, "Critics and Promoters, the Moralizers of Art: Their Impact on Jazz," Mimeo, Vanderbilt University, n.d.

11. Howard S. Becker, *Outsiders, op. cit.*, p. 9.

12. Morroe Berger, "Jazz: Resistance to the Diffusion of a Culture Pattern," *loc. cit.*

13. Neil Leonard, *op. cit.*, pp. 90-107.

14. Manford Kuhn, "Reference Groups" in *Dictionary of the Social Sciences* (Gould and Kolb, eds.), (Glencoe: The Free Press, 1964), p. 581.

15. Richard Peterson, "Critics and Promoters. . .," *loc. cit.*

16. Neil Leonard, *op. cit.*, pp. 108-132.

17. Max Weber, *The Protestant Ethic and The Spirit of Capitalism* (New York: Scribners, T. Parsons [trans.]), 1958, passim.

18. Max Weber, *The Theory of Social and Economic Organization* (Glencoe: The Free Press, Henderson and Parsons [trans.]), 1947, pp. 358-363.

19. Max Weber, *The Rational and Social Foundations of Music* (Carbondale: Southern Illinois University Press, Martindale, Riedel and Neuwirth [trans.]), 1958.

20. Max Weber, *The Theory of Social and Economic Organization, loc. cit.;* and Gerth and Mills, eds. *From Max Weber, Essays in Sociology,* Oxford University Press, 1946, pp. 196-198.

21. Max Weber, *The Theory of Social and Economic Organization, op. cit.*, pp. 363-386.

22. Theodore Kemper, "Reference Groups, Socialization and Achieve-

ment," *American Journal of Sociology*, Vol. 33, No. 1, February 1968, pp. 31-45.

23. My own research indicates that the general racial polarization occurring in American society has deeply affected young people and their music. Young white musicians turn toward as an outlet for creativity. Young blacks may find more "payoffs" in assuming a race-conscious posture. See: Charles Nanry, *The Occupational Subculture of the Jazz Musician: Myth and Reality,* Unpublished Ph.D. dissertation, Rutgers University, 1970, Chapter 7.

24. LeRoi Jones, Blues People (New York: Morrow, 1963); and Jones, Black Music (New York: Morrow [Appolo], 1967); for a contrasting view see Marshall Stearns, *The Story of Jazz* (New York: Oxford University Press, 1970) and Barry Ulanov, *A History of Jazz in America* (New York: Viking, 1952).

25. Robert Merton, "Patterns of Influence: Local and Cosmopolitan Influentials," in Herbert H. Hyman and Eleanor Singer, *Readings in Reference Group Theory and Research* (New York: The Free Press, 1968), pp. 281-290.

26. Alvin Gouldner, "Cosmopolitans and Locals: Toward an Analysis of Latent Social Roles," I, II, *Administrative Science Quarterly*, Vol. 2, 1957-1958, pp. 281-306; pp. 444-480.

27. The empirical definition of a typology is perhaps the most difficult problem in deductive social science. See: Theodore Ferdinand, *Typologies of Delinquency* (New York: Random House, 1966).

28. Since work in the jazz world is dependent on informal cliques and networks one proves his sincerity by securing employment and "calling someone on a gig." See: Nanry, *op. cit.*

CHARLES NANRY

Part II:
The Beat Goes On:
Rock Comes of Age

The second part of this volume considers the historical shift to rock as the "new" American popular music. Rock represents the rediscovery of roots, for it draws heavily on black folk music for inspiration and propulsion. Like jazz, rock is an amalgam of other forms and like jazz it tends to be fueled by other forms. The recent vogue among many rock groups for country and western music is an example of this. Although historical analogies are dangerous, many parallels between the development of rock and jazz are evident. Both musics initially depended on the development of a popular base rather than an elite one. Both suffered through a period of rejection because the canons used by jazz and rock musicians were unorthodox. Both musics relied on technical innovation and both were considered the music of outsiders. That is, jazz was black music; rock was and generally still is the music of the young.

Chris White has prepared an epistle for this volume addressed to musicians. His perception of where the jazzman stands today is an important and passionate restatement of the artist's dilemma in general and the black artist's dilemma in particular. This chapter provides an important bridge for taking the musician's point of view into account and understanding where jazz "is at" in the age of rock. Professor White assures jazz players that now is the time to take things into their own hands in shaping the future of their music.

If we are to understand where today's musician "pays his dues" it is essential to understand the workings of the recording studio. An important statement on this work context is included here. Robert Faulkner provides a sociological analysis of the modern recording studio which describes this most important context of professional American music. Other contexts—night clubs, college concerts and other "live" performances—have come to depend more and more on the selling of records to a mass audience. The studio is the place from whence music is packaged for mass distribution. Increasingly musicians must make it in the studio if they are to make it at all.

Howard Junker (the fifties) and Jon Landau (music in 1970) provide the historical perspective so necessary to understanding the present state of rock. Without the kind of background provided so brilliantly by Junker and Landau the present music scene makes little sense.

The final chapter in this book is written by Irving Louis Horowitz, the veritable guru of what's happening now. Horowitz brings us full circle by tracing parallels in the development of jazz and rock and some interesting insights into parallel developments in the two forms; for example, the erosion of a popular base for both musics as they ceased to be music for dancing. Horowitz' closing words provide a useful summary for this Introduction:

> Hard rock may be done in by popularity, commercialism and festivals. More likely it will collapse from internal ailments: becoming too artsy-craftsy or removed from the dance form that gave rise to jazz and rock alike, and thus distancing itself from the folk sources of its original inspiration. But in the meantime, this is the most significant music having a mass social base yet to appear in American society.

Check Yourself!

CHRISTOPHER WHITE

I have seen too many angry, confused and bitter jazz musicians. They were usually good musicians who had spent a fair amount of time at mastering their instruments. They went about doing all the things that they were told they ought to do in order to "make it." They practiced, stayed clean and created music that was truly representative of themselves. If they were lucky, they were just barely able to make ends meet; if not, they suffered the economic fate of the unskilled, "unprofessional" laborer in this society.

Perhaps they were not the innovators of their time. (By innovator I mean the person who changes the direction of jazz by the influence of his style alone—for example, Louis Armstrong, Charlie Parker, John Coltrane.) But they were competent, skilled musicians nonetheless. It was easy for them to measure their failure; all they had to do was compare what they were making with what a comparable musician involved in other forms of entertainment music was making. The difference was so great that jazz players were without a doubt aware that something was wrong.

This essay is addressed to these musicians. I have been

fortunate enough to escape the problem that I have outlined above because, in part, I was able to recognize that there was a gap between what I *thought* was happening in the field and what actually was happening. Once I saw and understood the nature of the disparity, I was able to adjust my point of view and values in some instances, and attempt to work as much as I could for changes outside myself and in other areas. I know that what I have to say is by no means definitive; however, I would like to share my observations in the hope that they may help other musicians to evaluate more accurately their situations. Perhaps some of the alternatives I have personally recognized might lead others to courses of action that will work for them.

When it dawned on me that I didn't want to spend the rest of my life playing two-week stands, trying to support my family at home and myself on the road on two hundred dollars a week (before taxes), I decided to take a look at the nature of the business I was in. Although the music I was involved in was enjoyable enough to make, the life style it engendered left a lot to be desired. However, music was my life and even if I had wanted to start a totally new career, it would have taken longer than I could afford to learn how to do something else.

On the other hand, at this time (the 1960s) even the big names in the field were finding it hard to keep working. Jazz clubs all around the country were going out of business and record companies were starting to chop up their jazz catalogs. On all sides, businessmen and musicians alike were saying that jazz was dying. Yet I still heard a certain vitality in the music. Whenever people, young and old alike, were exposed to jazz, they enjoyed it. Moreover, given a positive environment, I still derived a great deal of pleasure in creating the music. Further, I felt the same "vibrations" from my fellow musicians.

A closer look at the various contexts which for a time provided income for the creators of jazz reveals that the

CHRISTOPHER WHITE

music was never what the owners of these establishments were selling. They were running dance halls, brothels or night clubs. All of these enterprises depended on certain aspects of jazz but not the personal dimension of improvisation. As long as the bulk of their patrons were able to dance to, feel safe with or in some way identify with the "unusual" through music, then everything was fine. However, times change and there is a new music, rock, for the rebellious, nonconforming majority to identify with.[1]

However, the conditions and point of view that enabled Jelly Roll Morton to produce a "King Porter Stomp" or John Coltrane a "Love Supreme" still exist for those on the outside looking in. The real spirit of jazz was never accepted or even considered (there was no need to) by the music business. It was a music that became popular like so many other fads—like the more recent bossa nova, the meringue or the cha-cha-cha: in order to be milked for as much as it was worth. And it was. Most of its techniques have been and even are still being "borrowed" by those who play popular music.

The rub is that jazz has grown and now expresses meaningful nuances that require even those who try to ignore or discredit it to consider it an art form. However, the truth of this fact put those musicians who played jazz in a "trick bag." The opportunity to develop further and to expose the music was thwarted by the profit motive. The relationship between jazz and club owners was, after all, leech-like. As soon as the club owners, like the dance hall operators before them, thought that jazz was not pulling its own weight (that is, bringing in as many spending patrons as other forms of entertainment could), they severed the relationship. This left many musicians jobless and bewildered, trying to make a living playing other kinds of music or leaving the field altogether. Some still have not recognized the fact that their music has become independent of the club or the dance hall and are desperately trying to recreate that kind of setting albeit with little success.

CHECK YOURSELF!

That jazz *is* art does not mean that it is *not* entertainment. There are many fine jazz players whose music still draws enough of a particular kind of spending audience that clubs who cater to that audience can still make money. But these clubs are few, and only the well established names in the music field seem to be of interest to their owners. These established groups are usually either the ones led by the innovators of jazz in the forties through the early sixties, or commercial quasi-jazz groups. However, today's amalgamator (the musician who combines many styles to make his own) has little opportunity to play and perhaps develop into the innovator of tomorrow. Chances are that even his fellow musicians are putting him down if his music is looked upon as experimental.

The word "entertainment" in its current usage, particularly when applied to performances, is synonymous with amusement. Moreover, it seems that modern man equates the stimulation of thought with the waning of amusement. For better or worse, the jazz player, the entertainer of yesterday, *is* a stimulating, thought-provoking artist today and subject to all of the difficulties and to none of the advantages of the artist in this country.

The Rockefeller Brothers Fund published in 1965 a comprehensive report that was the result of discourse among many people involved with the performing arts as performers and administrators. The findings of the various panels on the performing arts paint a gloomy picture of what it means to be a performing artist in America. Briefly, all of the major institutions dedicated to the preservation of the arts find themselves with fewer and fewer wealthy patrons, while materials and services cost more and audiences dwindle. The corporations who now control the resources (instead of those wealthy philanthropists who used to support the arts) want to play the numbers game with the performing arts. They ask: How many people attend, on the average, a performance of the Metropolitan Opera? The more enlightened corporate

CHRISTOPHER WHITE

donors (like Standard Oil of New Jersey) are as involved with perpetuating and basking in the glory of the western art tradition (which by and large isn't ours) as much as supporting art for its own sake, so that the corporate image emerges as the primary consideration in whether or not support is granted. The state and federal governments are dragging their feet with respect to the arts and consider them unnecessary "fringe" items at best.

The reasons for the general condition of the arts in the United States are as varied as there are people; however, it is certain that the relationship of the arts to the popular general culture of this society is closely dependent upon the concept of profit as the ultimate value. The arts take the subordinate role of providing images that do not mirror what in fact is the operant value system. Consequently, the arts that are supported reflect only those aspects of the human condition that are required, for whatever purposes, by those who are able to support the arts. Moreover, only the most visible and viable of these artistic disciplines is supported, and at a level that places them constantly on the brink of nonexistence.

But the most telling point is simply that the Rockefeller Panel Report, for all its comprehensiveness, makes no mention whatsoever of jazz. The panel claimed to have chosen to deal only with the "live performing arts"[2] and further they concentrated on "the professional organizations that sponsor and present opera, drama, instrumental and choral music and dance. We do so because this is where the need is greatest. . . . These are, in effect the public arts."[3] I don't know whether jazz was excluded because there were no professional organizations that represented it, but I am certain that jazz is a "public art" that, for whatever reason, was not included in the report.

The problem then is clear: jazz, a music developed primarily by Afro-Americans, is in the same position that Afro-Americans find themselves in in this country. Jazz has been kept separate from but dependent upon external systems that control it. Further, the musicians who make it have of necessity been preoccupied with competing in a commercial environment with musicians whose traditions and value systems allow them to view economic success as a measure for musical accomplishment, an environment which does not afford the jazz player the opportunity to acquire comparable financial rewards. In addition, constant creativity and ingenuity are demanded of the jazz musician simply in order to allow him to compete. When the jazz player turns to the arts or the world of "serious" music, if he is allowed to function in it at all, he is judged by standards and systems that again do not apply to his music. Unfortunately, most jazz musicians have been so busy trying to survive that they have not enjoyed the advantage of examining their own music's history and traditions, and have thereby failed to achieve a perspective on the relationship of their music to the overall historical development of jazz. This perspective is necessary in order to isolate, organize and articulate effectively the misconceptions that are held by others who attempt to evaluate the worth of their jazz. This dilemma has been stated succinctly by Julius Lester:

> They heard jazz in New Orleans and tried to imitate it. They couldn't, but they recorded it, got the money, and had their thing called "legitimate." This process has never abated. . . . The music of black people is recognized today. . . but now the ploy is to say, well, it may be true that this is Negro music, but now it belongs to the world. Says who? We didn't give it to anybody. You came and got it, took the money and the credit, and then come back and tell me what a great thing I've done by giving the world this music.[4]

The solution like the problem is so closely linked to the position of the Afro-American in the United States that to offer any course of action without considering race and bigotry would be foolish. However, the key in Lester's statement is that "they" always come back—not only to tell

CHRISTOPHER WHITE

jazz musicians how nice they are to offer such a lovely gift but also to observe and perhaps select another present to "give" to the world (if they can't get away with taking it without telling where they got it).

Since we are the source from whence flow such bountiful gifts, should we not consider ways of patting ourselves on the back instead of seeking external acknowledgement that is always too little and too late? For external acknowledgments are too often given by singling out one person or a select group and giving them a taste of what is commonplace for most musicians of their caliber in either the commercial or artistic world: media exposure, notoriety and some financial success; such recognition thereby creates the illusion that, in order for us to be successful, we must continue to relate to systems that do not operate on the same premises we do. We therefore strive and strain to produce that "make-the-money" tune and wonder why our record company never really promotes it the way they do some of the other groups' tunes which contain so many of our musical ideas.

Our bewilderment stems from the fact that the record company is not interested in selling us or our music. We are a tax write-off and are recorded in order to "document" a musical achievement. Among the ways documents are used is research, and that is what has been going on. Those musicians who the record companies believe will produce more market-able products are thus regarded because they have, more often than not, researched our music, but their attitudes toward money and music can be expressed in exactly that order of priority: money, then music. And all the time we thought it was the other way around; we created *our* music and, if it was true to our high musical standards and if we worked hard and toed the mark, we would be financially rewarded. Right? Wrong!

It is tempting then to approach the music from the monied point of view. But to do that would be to play the majority's game on their own home ground, and those two circumstances, plus having to fight one's own inner motivation toward creativity, would make three strikes—you're out. We must create our own rules and train and recognize our own musical authorities because we have already created the music; it's called jazz.

We are not going to change the way things are until we, the musicians, begin to document an aesthetic system for our music. Although critics and musicians involved with "serious" music may disagree on whose music is really creative and whose music is fraudulent, both groups have critics and theorists to whom they can turn for support. All we, the jazz musicians, have are the statements of famous players that historians or journalists quote, usually out of context, to prove damn near anything they want to. Thus, historians and journalists have controlled the information available to laymen. The musicians have felt that jazz had enough musicial substance; that it was unnecessary for us also to be verbal. We overlooked the fact that, although all music is subjective, the tradition of understanding in the West heavily relies on objective commentary, which is conspicuously lacking for jazz. Therefore, we, the makers of the music, have never really had a chance to make known what it is we and our music are about. Although many words are written and spoken publicly about jazz each week in this country, I would venture to say that very little of that commentary comes from jazz musicians. Moreover, most communication about our music is only incidentally focused on the continuity of its development from various root sources to the present.

The need for a center of aesthetic study is acute. The musicians who constitute the music (jazz is a music, that develops in direct proportion to the musical skill of those who perform it)[5] are involved in the very real and almost totally time-consuming activity that is called personal musical development. Yet these are the same people who should be involved with establishing such a center and working within it. A proposal should be developed and funds sought so that stipends could be offered to a number of musicians, enabling them to devote full time to their interest in this area. The need for a national organization toward this center is indicated; perhaps the newly formed Institute of Black American Music can place this endeavor among the other activities it has already identified as its concerns.

Currently, there are many organizations which are being initiated by jazz musicians to deal with areas of concern to them. Rhythm Associates, Inc., my own firm, concerns itself with education, not only instrumental instruction, but also the introduction of jazz as an art form to the classroom and regular curriculum of schools from kindergarten through college and into communities throughout New York state. The Collective Black Artists are beginning to deal with some of the fiscal problems with which we are confronted; they are doing this by developing a distribution network through which they can market records and music they have produced. They are also publishing a newspaper and giving classes on the business aspects of being a musician, addressing the problems of contract law, copyrights and publishing. And Jazzmobile is still bringing jazz performances to the communities from which jazz comes by means of outdoor concerts given during the summer on mobile stages and indoor concerts during the winter in school assemblies. Jazzmobile also gives free instrumental instruction by means of their workshop program. There are many organizations that are more or less geared to the propagation of jazz as an art form through the creation of work for musicians. This is usually accomplished by a concert series. Jazz Interactions is the first of these organizations; they have been conducting this type of presentation longer than any other organization that I know, and since their administrative body includes many musicians, they are able to offer varied kinds of programming over and above the concert series. The Left Bank Jazz Society of Baltimore and the Hartford Jazz

CHECK YOURSELF! 197

Society have been very similarly active over the years. There are many performing organizations which are developing repertory and presentations that enhance the chances for earning a living. The Jazz Composers Orchestra and the New York Bass Violin Choir are two examples.

All of the musicians who are connected with the groups described above sooner or later realize that they have to make some financial adjustments until they become established in the new thrust of their profession. The gigs in the colleges, community centers or workshops do not come in as soon as one begins, but the concept is important enough to make some sacrifices for it. Once jazz musicians understand that their earning capacity can expand in direct relationship to how much they do to relate what the music is about to as many people as possible, then the fight is easier and their income will increase.

The hardest thing for me when I started Rhythm Associates was keeping a teaching staff. At the time I was sharing with the teachers any fees that the school received. We had too few students to keep a musician who had been offered a week's work on the road. Yet the musician who made his living playing jazz was the backbone of the school. The solution was to secure a grant that would enable the school to offer a base income that would enable the musician to stay in town and work a weekend in addition to his teaching and make a living wage. We were able to do that when we established the Jazz Workshop for MUSE, the Brooklyn Children's Neighborhod Museum.

The point is that we musicians must take a firm hand in the structuring of organizations that address themselves to our problems. We must take a good hard look at ourselves and try to see how we relate to all the activities that are going on that have something to do with the music we are making. The days of the jazz musician who only wants to do his gig, without any concern for what his gig *really* is now and will be next year, are over.

The prediction is easy: either we get ourselves together or

CHRISTOPHER WHITE

not only will we be devoured but so will be our music. The world of technology is enabling those people who regard musicians as controllable objects, whose most endearing qualities are their abilities to assimilate and then regurgitate whatever they hear, to make creativity obsolete and to sell that heartless product as creativity because they control all channels to the audience. The art world has not been given a common language with which to establish a basis of communication with the jazz world. Worst of all, no one is exposing the music to the public and creating a new young audience. *We* must supply that language and start developing an audience. Where do you fit? What can you do to help put yourself into that picture? Once you make the choice, straight ahead—and don't get weary, children!

NOTES

1. The electronic technology of the majority's world impinges upon the environment of the have-nots as well. Their buying power is not changed, but their appetites are whetted. A sociologist of some note pointed out recently at a Rutgers Institute of Jazz Studies symposium that most jazz players have resisted the use of electric instruments and that a 13-year-old kid probably knows more about electronics than do most jazz musicians. The assumption of the charge (and it was made indignantly, why I'm not sure) is so gross that it requires no comment; however, I wonder if he ever stopped to think that the 13-year-old's father bought that electronic equipment with considerable ease-compared to the fact that most jazz players and the bulk of people residing in the neighborhoods from which jazz stems and which it represents would have to spend more for that equipment than the instrument's added ability to help tell his story through music would be worth.

2. Rockefeller Brothers Fund, Inc., *The Performing Arts-Problems and Prospects* (New York, 1965), p. 9.

3. *Ibid.*, p. 9.

4. Julius Lester, *Look Out, Whitey! Black Power's Gon' Get Your Mama* (New York, 1968), p. 86.

5. Written music grows in direct proportion to what the composer calls upon the performer to produce. What he writes may or may not be in reaction to his exposure to a virtuoso performer. Improvised instrumental music, however, grows with the skill of the people who make it.

Hollywood Studio Musicians:

Making It in the Los Angeles Film and Recording Industry

ROBERT R. FAULKNER

It would be difficult to go through a day in this country without being exposed to the work of studio musicians. From motion picture and television film background music to an endless variety of phonograph recordings and seemingly unrelenting radio and television jingles, the work of studio musicians is packaged into countless forms. Studio performers represent the elite of a highly competitive and cutthroat business. Yet while they are professionals in their line of work, few people out of the mass media industries even know that they exist. They are always audible, but rarely heard. They are even less often seen. Even on the late night talk shows, their job is to perform between the chatter; only occasionally are they before the camera for a sustained amount of time. Media performance time—conversation before the microphones—is typically permitted only to the orchestra leader. While his day's work may consist of high voltage performances on records, television, film and jingles, the performer's name is rarely mentioned on record jackets, and never in film and TV series credits.

Studio performers who work in the Los Angeles industries

possess a unique combination of artistic talent, long training and perfected skills utilized in a highly complex production process, a rather turbulent economic environment and a free-lance hiring system. In the commercial music business, as noted above, studio work is an all-inclusive term: it designates motion picture and television film jobs, live and taped TV, record dates, and radio and television jingles. Free-lancing refers both to hiring on a wage or job-by-job basis, and to an area of work performance. Contracts between an employer and a musician cover only the studio work immediately at hand; they terminate when the job is completed and the musician is paid. Unlike symphony musicians or those who hold staff positions in radio and television and legitimate theaters, the free-lancer in Hollywood has no long term contract with any one organization or commercial studio. Like free-lance writers, photographers and detectives, he competes for jobs in a market where his ability, reputation, tact and social contacts determine the nature and volume of his work. He is a musical entrepreneur, a musician for hire.

To the outsider, free-lance hiring seems hopelessly fragmented and unorganized. But while studio employment is predominantly casual in nature, within the recording settings one finds informal orbits of power, privilege and prestige which shape the work and careers of commercial musicians in Los Angeles.

A key figure on the free-lance scene is the music contractor, who is in charge of hiring musicians for record dates, film and jingles. His job requires that he be familiar with the available talent, know the individual skills of the performers and understand the needs and desires of the composer, conductor and artist and repertoire man. On the basis of his experience and bargaining power he hires the best musicians he can.

The market value of some players on the free-lance stock exchange is considerable; so much so that performers who are in high demand for studio work can be said to constitute an "inner circle." While there is considerable intrigue and competition for studio jobs, there is no actual conspiracy of the few against others. The inner circle is really a loosely organized group of colleagues in high demand who handle a large volume of work. Their occupational success separates them from others on the musical scene, and organizes the free lance labor market.

Musicians who are on call at the studios occupy a privileged position; they are on a contractor's list as those musicians he prefers to hire. The higher on the list, the more work one does, the more lists one is on, the more chances one has of being called. Below the inner circle free-lancers are the musicians who fill out the work call. Still very much in demand for studio work, they are hired after the "cream of the crop." These overlapping groups of players do all the film and recording dates in Los Angeles. Supplementing them are musicians at various stages of their careers: some have lost their market value or popularity; others are doing casual work in local orchestras, big bands, rehearsal groups, nightclub gigs and dances. But no matter what stage a free-lancer has reached, his career is interdependent on his colleagues' careers, as well as on what is happening to contractors, composers and arrangers.

One can predict crucial points in a musician's career—his speed of advancement, and his ultimate achievement—by knowing how often and by what studios he is called. Free-lance workers hold conventional understandings about why some work more than others, why some get work and lose it, which contractors are loyal, which ones are disagreeable SOBs, and the musicians who are cutthroats or, conversely, not aggressive enough. Members' problems vary with position. Considerable strain, intrigue and style arise from studio players' efforts to maintain some sustained control over their chances in the hiring-power game.

At the top of free-lance work are the players who work in the motion picture, television film and recording studios.

ROBERT R. FAULKNER

These musicians are chosen by contractors, leaders and composers. Those most in demand have access to the best paying and often most musically interesting work. They are frequently requested by the studios, and when a contractor puts together an orchestra they are the first to be considered. In Los Angeles there are 15 to 20 major contractors who allocate the work in the studios, and they are in frequent competition for the services of the same group of popular musicians.

Some film studios have a "first-call" policy in which musicians informally assure the contractor that they will accept all of his (and the studio's) calls as long as they are notified 96 hours before the work date begins. After that time, they are free to accept other calls. In exchange, the free-lancer is assured that he will work whenever the production scores call for his instrument. This formal system within the informal free-lance structure is left over from the days of the contract studio orchestra, when the major studios had a stable orchestra of musicians. With the end of the contracts in the late fifties, some studios retained their instrumentalists by means of the first-call policy. Those film enterprises with more productions and more work for musicians were, of course, in a better position to establish and sustain the 96-hour agreement. Generally, however, the changeover to the new noncontractual system has radically changed the overall employment situation for the musician.

Composers and conductors hired to do a film score frequently prefer some musicians over others. During their work in the industry, they come to feel more confident conducting particular players; they often write instrumental parts with particular musicians in mind, or simply like the sound, efficiency and personality of center instrumentalists. Unlike the contract studio orchestras, free-lance orchestras are subject to the preferences of composers and conductors. Thus a musician on call at one studio can be hired to play at another if requested by the composer-conductor, whereas under the contract orchestra system, union regulations and quota restrictions constrained musicians to work in their home studio.

Related to the choices of composers, conductors and contractors is the status structure within the orchestra. Tension and problems can result from where one sits in an orchestra: ecological position closely matches social position. The terms "first chair," "second chair," "section man," "first chair soloist" or the more familiar "concertmaster" reflect the prestige given to which part one plays. Presumably the more important (more exposed) the part, the more competent the player. The contractor is interested in hiring the best players; at the top of the list are those who can play principal parts, typically the preferred studio pros. In hiring he begins with the concertmaster, then second chair and down the list; he might even ask the concertmaster what musicians he would prefer. Naturally, in this status game of musical chairs, some acquire reputations as top players or section men. They are those pros who are cool and poised under pressure, who can play any part under any conditions and who are of proven worth. They make few mistakes. The contractor's job is made easier and more efficient by the weight of precedent, and thus he turns automatically to the stable, studio men, the inner circle, even though others on the list might well be of equal or greater ability.

If musicians are subject to the preferences of contractors, the contractor is subject to the evaluation of those who depend on his talents. His position of prestige and authority rests on the quality of the solo men, a well-run hiring setup, and his ability to please the composer who has written the music and the conductor who must direct the studio performance of it. His job is full of tension and intrigue, for studio success depends on his ability to coordinate the schedules of a group of highly talented, sensitive and busy musical entrepreneurs. He uses a wide spectrum of techniques to get the musicians he wants in the orchestra he puts together. The basic medium is exchange. By offering assur-

ROBERT R. FAULKNER

ances of future calls, by cashing in on past alliances and by tactful negotiation with other contractors, he exchanges high-paying studio work for loyalty. The more loyalty he receives, the more the free-lancer is likely to be near the top of the list. The contractor is jealous of his prerogatives and protective of the musicians in "his stable"; and the promises and threats which are part of this exchange relationship can reassure or irritate musicians.

Wage scales and working conditions for the motion picture and television film studios are set by collective bargaining agreements between the studios and the American Federation of Musicians. The agreements do not, however, contain any stipulations about the minimum number of musicians to be used on production calls, nor can the union demand that a studio or contractor hire a particular number of musicians or sanction employers for any unjust hiring or firing episodes. Unlike other craft unions, the musicians' union has little control over the labor market, offers no apprenticeship program, and since the days of the contract orchestras, provides only wage scales, rest periods and minimum scoring hours and amount of music per TV series. Success, then, is dependent on sponsorship, loyalty and reputation; colleagues, contractors, composers and conductors shape the career movement of individuals and, thereby, the larger studio scene.

CAREER FOOTHOLDS AND GETTING IN

When he seeks to enter studio work, the unestablished recruit sees his career as contingent upon his ability to develop the proper web of contacts with those who control access to jobs. Sponsorship is the major social mechanism which brings him to their attention, allows him to establish a reputation as a solid and dependable performer, and prepares him to cope with the various pressures of the work itself. From the viewpoint of the sponsors, several important conditions must be attended to: 1) the young musician must be sponsored in such a way that established colleagues are not threatened with loss of power and privilege; 2) contractors and leaders must be convinced that the recruit is competent and can be depended upon; 3) the appropriate timing and pacing of the candidate's introduction into the division of studio labor must be determined and implemented and 4) the candidate must learn the subtle etiquette of the referral system and, most importantly, that sponsorship is a process of reciprocal exchange.

Breaking into the informal web of relations in the studios requires a combination of entrepreneurial zeal, aggressive self-advertisement, ability to handle interpersonal competition with grace and coolness, and performing talent. The reputation a player is likely to acquire depends upon several factors. Other persons assess his ability to read music quickly and accurately and to play under pressure before audiences of colleagues, and whether he can be moved into the existing allocation of statuses or roles. Free-lancers assess their position vis-à-vis others in terms of the number of calls they get, the quality of the work call, and informal assurances by a contractor or contractors that they will be called by him. "Breaking in" means waiting for an opening, being sponsored and successfully moving into the circle. The candidate must spend time working his way through the network of casual gigs, rehearsal bands, club dates, jobbing dance bands, orchestras and so forth. In doing so, he indicates his willingness to undergo the ceremonial period of putting in his time. Implicitly he demonstrates to those behind him or others just starting that he occupies a given position in free-lance work.

If breaking into the inner circle were simply a matter of putting in time, there would be less competition and hostility between musicians. Instead, some recruits move up faster than others, and some candidates get "frozen" at particular stages of their career. Sponsorship is the major mechanism for the regulation of human traffic into the inner circle of the

ROBERT R. FAULKNER

studios. The musician must come to the attention of significant inner circle members who will recommend him to other players and hiring contractors. This process is similar to the system of "tapping" found in the military and industrial management.[1] The sponsor sets the appropriate timing and pacing of the protégé's entry and subsequent advancement.[2] Because considerable risk is introduced when someone is moved along faster than he "deserves," timing and a common sense notion of distributive justice, of correspondence between efforts and reward are primary concerns.[3] The timing of career movements is dependent upon the number of people whose fates are affected by the introduction of a new member. Those solidly "in" have less to worry about than those on the edges of the inner circle. The sponsor must be careful not to move the candidate too quickly into these areas if he expects the reciprocal approval of his colleagues. He and his protégé have nothing to gain and much to lose if they fracture the link between the time and effort invested in "getting in" and "making it."

An example of the link between the etiquette of timing, handling the perceived suspiciousness of colleagues and putting in considerable investments is an outgoing and gregarious brass player who discussed with me some of the problems involved in getting a foot on the inner-circle ladder. He talked about the "moral division of labor" and the casual "dirty work"[4] he did before beginning to ease into the better jobs of studio labor.

> You're called to work when work occurs. You can't sell yourself as a musician as you would something else, like I had a degree from such and such. Your fellow musicians recommend you here and there, they see if you can do the work, and if you can, pretty soon you get more calls. You know, you do bar-mitzvahs, dances, dumb things, but eventually you start doing better work in films, rock and roll recordings. So, slowly I would get called, somebody couldn't make it, somebody was

unavailable. My first job was at X studio. The contractor liked what I did and from then on things built up.

This musician pointed out that the movement into the existing arrangement of colleagues is slow and dependent on the actions of others. A reed player who had just made it in the studios also talked about the problem of breaking into the division of labor and the importance of pacing and timing in advance.

You put in a certain amount of time before other players will recommend you to the good jobs. I mean, I had to work my way into it. When you come into a town as a strange musician, you get strange reactions, people don't want to just welcome you with open arms. You have to prove yourself and you have to run the gamut of suspicion from other players because someone thinks you're going to take away jobs from him. That has to be worked out. You can't be a threat to the established players; if it's your turn and you're called and nobody's being aced out, then there's encouragement and no resentment.

Informal organization is most telling under conditions of uncertainty: first, the problem of taking away someone's work, but more importantly, incurring dislike for doing so; and second, as a "rookie," the problem of what will actually be the consequences to others of one's own advancement. Considerable apprehension also centers around the support a musician can expect from sponsors if he is seen as "moving too fast" or "acing someone out."

Colleagues can help the sponsor move the protégé across the plans and paths of others into the existing network. But they are also potential exploiters. The etiquette of sponsorship forms part of what has been called the "almost instinctive attempts of a group to cushion themselves against the hazards of their careers."[5] Colleagues are concerned about their own careers. They can resist or even "dump on" players by specific acts of neglect. The most obvious instance

ROBERT R. FAULKNER

is when a player attempts to break in without the explicit recommendation of another musician who performs on a similar instrument, who may reason that his own position is being threatened.

One of the most powerful members of the inner circle candidly described appropriate ways of "making it." He then discussed some of the more unpleasant types of political maneuvering which can take place in free-lance work and the resources the inner fraternity can bring to bear on these blatant attempts at career advancement.

Getting into this jungle is very, very difficult. You have to be very smart. Two things count. You have to have knowledge of your employers, who you are working for, the leader on the date, what they want, how best you can contribute to their music. The next thing is knowledge of the methods, the subtle methods, of contact in this work. One way is to play and be seen in bands, orchestras, wherever work is. You create your own product.

Some players come into town and try to undercut the guys already established out here; they don't survive one week, they're through before they start. You see, we know what's happening and how a guy is operating. If you're smart you'll get encouragement from other players; if you're not, forget it, you'll just cut your own throat in a hurry. For instance, some guys come into town, call up every goddamn contractor and say "A told me to call you, B said this and that, you know . . . use me. . . ." And then on a date a contractor comes up to you and asks you if the guy was recommended by you. If we don't know him or didn't recommend him, well that guy's in trouble, and he'll have problems getting any work with us and the top contractors.

It might seem logical that if one is going to risk breaking into the inner circle, he might as well move in at its center rather than the edges. However, this respondent indicates that there is more policing among the elite at the center than on the edges, and more power and influence to be exercised vis-à-vis hiring contractors. "Playing it smart" means knowing what the rules are and how they operate to reduce risk. The free-lancer is obliged to follow informal rules in regard to others; in turn, he expects that others will cooperate as he advances.

If sponsorship is widespread, all members become concerned because their informal positions are vulnerable. While many free-lancers in the inner circle are reluctant to get involved in sponsorship, they all share an interest in controlling the flow of recruits into their circle. Many do not actively sponsor because they must not only put a new recruit before their colleagues, but also invest part of their reputation in doing so. Those who have the most influence and status with contractors and important others find it easiest to take an active role in recommending new players. They have, in a sense, more social credit. But because social credit can be used up quickly in the process of asking for preferential treatment for a protégé, the number of potential candidates remains low. Meanwhile, the fear of "blowing" a call, of folding up under pressure, of being unable to "cut" a difficult part intensifies. If a recruit fails to live up to the expectation of his sponsor or sponsors, and reflects negatively on their judgment, others may be reluctant to accept any future recommendations.[6]

A young musician who is outside of the inner circle explained a dramatic instance of failure to use a break set up for him by a powerful, elite performer.

> About three years ago, I met M at C Studios, he's a very popular player in the studios, very much in demand. He heard about my playing and later set up a date with me on it. It was handled very nice. He set it up with the contractor, arranged it with him and everything, he told the contractor I could do the job. I got the music a couple of days before the date. It was difficult and I

　　　　　　　　　　　　ROBERT R. FAULKNER

practiced it four or five hours a day. It was full of up-tempos for a film they were shooting. He said it was easy and I would have no trouble. Well, it would have been easy for *him,* but not for me . . . at least not at that time. I didn't have any confidence in my playing. I backed out of the date. I just had to call him and say I couldn't do it. So he called the contractor and the contractor got pissed off at him and everyone got bugged with me. What a mess. If I could have done it, I would now be on call at that studio and into the scene, but I backed out at the wrong time and that was that. I've never got a call from them since. . . . I can play that piece of music in my sleep now.

The significance of this episode is not the rather frank admission of being unable to play the music, but the fact that he was not able to play it according to his own standards of professional excellence. This musician emphasized that failure to handle the opening breaks can significantly slow down or ruin a career in the free-lance scene. The connection between musicians and contractors is so all-important that the consequences of both good and bad studio performance quickly reverberate throughout the whole system.

A young player who has been more successful than the musician above pointed out how he negotiated similar terrain just a few years earlier:

The first job is the hardest, you're on trial. Nobody wants to hire someone for the first time unless they think you have a reputation. It's very hard for a new player to get in, but you got to be ready when the time comes, if you goof it, well. . . . This is something that players don't talk about, but they feel it, you know it's there and nobody says anything. It takes a pretty strong ego to put up with this pressure and the silence that goes along with it. The greatest fear in this business is the fear of the unknown. You never know what they're going to throw at you to play. So over a period of time you get a feeling of satisfaction that you're able to make it, and it shows you've gone through the waiting, the pressure and all of it. You never know whether you've made it or not, no one says it. It's just the fact that you stood there on one leg for so long and nobody told you you could put the other one down.

This musician and the majority of respondents agree that building a reputation is difficult, pressure-ridden and often uncertain. The gradual approval of colleagues, increase in calls and calls with inner-circle members symbolize achievement in a musician's career. But, as the above respondent noted, there are no formal entrance criteria, certificates of "making it" or tenure other than how often one is called by contractors. The player compares himself to others: some he has moved ahead of, others he is in competition with and still others are more solidly in demand than himself. Such a system of referral and the fluid criteria of success tend to magnify the sense of injustice felt by those who have not yet made it into the existing allocation of jobs or who have been left behind. Predictably, the most common reason given for their comparative failure has been power possessed by contractors and the differential influence in sponsorship possessed by some free-lancers. Predictably, the more open resentment is directed toward those in the inner-circle: "The all-stars who get all the work while the rest of us are struggling."

The "all-stars" and "cream of the crop" are not the only actors who actively sponsor musicians. Composers and studio conductors frequently take an interest in moving a recruit along by putting pressure on contractors to hire him, and the more powerful the sponsor, the greater the likelihood his efforts will be successful. This can create resentment among both contractors and performers. One string player, who shares with the other respondents an appreciation of the subtleties of hiring etiquette, reported how an influential composer-conductor with many famous films to his credit actively shaped the beginning of his career in Hollywood.

> I had been playing in various places and some of my good friends were composers and arrangers. One was instrumental in helping me, he told a couple of contractors to use me, you know the whole routine, "He's good, use him, help him." Well, being recommended doesn't automatically mean you're going to do all the contractor's work right away. It's hard to break into his steady group of people. But eventually I was used if some of the first players were busy, if they had other calls that day. I wasn't interested in cutting into their work and stirring up a lot of hostility. But eventually things started to fall into shape, I did the work, people liked my sound, and that was it.

This respondent noted the contractors' interest in perpetuating the existing informal organization of work and their implicit reluctance to bring new players in. They have built up arrangements with a steady "stable" of players, and in handling their own work contingencies turn automatically to these studio pros. With either a performer or composer-conductor for a sponsor, breaking into such an arrangement without creating enmity is an important part of free-lance etiquette, and a crucial career turning point.

Entrance into the inner circle depends not only upon ability and one's sponsor's power, but also on the degree of commitment of the contractor to his stable of players, and the amount of studio work available to musicians. In other occupations, such as medicine, pool hustling and the academic world, colleagues exercise major control over recruitment and the pacing and timing of career advancement. Free-lance studio work presents multiple sanctions and influences, illustrated in the various bargainings and agreements which go on between performers, contractors, composers and conductors. The number of participants in these agreements increases the uncertainty of a recruit's career fate by adding to the contingencies which he must handle.

Free-lancers not only must cushion themselves against the hazards of competition, but also the potential erosion of career success as a result of the demands of studio work.

Like policemen, reporters, doctors and air-traffic controllers, free-lancers must be prepared to handle a wide variety of uncertainties in performing their jobs. The established free-lancer as well as the new recruit must be in shape, both physically and mentally, for endurance, stamina and concentration are demanded. One established player talked about some of the work and career strains; in doing so he developed the theme of supply and demand found throughout the interviews: "The contractor can always turn to other musicians."

> You get called for a date, the music is in front of you and you have to knock it off like that . . . right on the spot, read it immediately, and if you get into trouble, you've had it, and that's why we're there. You have to be ready and equipped, and have practiced, and be warmed up and you can't say, "Well, today I don't feel so good, I had a fight with my wife or I'm nervous or I had another call and I'm tired." The contractor doesn't want to hear it, the leader doesn't want to hear it. So there's a lot of pressure for the guy just breaking in, the clock is going and you're sitting with a 50-piece orchestra, and you're getting paid over 30 bucks an hour, it's expensive and there are these moments . . . if you can't do it there are 50 other guys waiting to have a shot at it.

The economics of recording, the continuous pressure to be ready to play anything, and the muted fear of competitors were picked up enthusiastically, if somewhat sarcastically, in the responses of some musicians. Because the supply of musicians and eager recruits far outstrips the number of available work calls or positions on a contractor's list, mistakes at work can lead to the contractor's calling other,

ROBERT R. FAULKNER

and from his viewpoint more competent, players. Contractors are viewed as important arbiters of what is a good performance, but most are not active performers themselves. In the musicians' discussions of contractors, they are usually viewed as ignorant and generally unaware of musical or artistic values and problems, much as jazz musicians discuss problems concerning "squares," or rock performers complain about "teeny-boppers."

A brass player explained the pressures of uncertainty on studio calls and how one can be only as good as his last performance under the microphones.

> You can't hide too long in this business. Composers write for all the stands and if you don't play much music one day, the next day . . . you never know, you might be on the first stand, and with a solo to play, and there you are. You either do it or you don't. You're continuously exposed, so you have to have good chops, stamina, everything right for each call. It's accepted that everyone have that, if not, they won't make it. Look . . . it's simple, if tomorrow I don't play well, the contractor might say, "What the hell's wrong with him?" He'll never think of the last three years where you've never made a mistake. So you can lose it all in a day, I honestly believe it. You can come in a bar too soon, like you play a perfect recording and miss a note or page-turn and the guy looks up and says, "I won't use him anymore."

Even when a career is fairly well sustained and the musician enjoys considerable security, particular problems can be traumatic. A most dramatic turning point was reported by an older player. The incident involved a composer-conductor at one of the major studios and demonstrates how the musician sitting next to the player is a potential competitor. We were talking about the steps that led to his work in the commercial field.

> It was strange the way it happened. We were doing a

picture and the first chair player was having trouble that day. The director looked over and said, ". . .you're flat, godammit, you're flat and you know it, ever since we started this picture." Well, this guy gets up from his chair and goes over to the water cooler, gets a drink and the director says, "Are you ready to make this take now?" And he said, "I can't make it now, I'm so nervous." And I'll never forget that . . . he pointed to me and said, "You play first chair." And this take was a fast sequence, very tricky. I played it, that was it. I didn't realize it at the time, I didn't see the importance of it all . . . if I had missed that thing, well. . . . I played it, not perfect, but well enough to satisfy the conductor I guess. We only made one take and he said "print it."

Studio calls are precarious because, as one player put it, "We never know what they're going to throw at us." Each call is important; in most instances the players cannot practice their parts at home, as they can in the symphony orchestra. And for the established studio "pros" as well as for those breaking in, work problems put the contractors, composers, conductors and colleagues continually on the spot. No one wants to be responsible for "clams" (audible errors). They are costly to the producer and they increase the tension on subsequent takes for the work group.

Much of the music free-lancers perform does not require them to use their skills, talent and endurance to the upper limits. This is in itself a major work contingency: one cannot let his skills slip or minimize the danger that difficult calls can present. A former orchestra musician indicated how the contractor plays such an important role and compared free-lance work to the orchestra.

You can go for weeks, months, without anything to play, just whole notes, dumb music. Then one day you walk into a call and have to play a solo. So you never stop being discovered and by God, you play it better than the guy who played it yesterday, and the con-tractor—who you've known for years—will say, "Boy,

ROBERT R. FAULKNER

that sounds beautiful," you know, like "I didn't know you could play that good." So you get called on and you better do it. That's one way of making a name and one way, I might add, of destroying yourself. You see, you're playing with some of the best musicians around. The challenge is to stay on top, to keep ahead of your instrument. There are many good players out here and the competition is tremendous. This is a completely different experience from what you go through in a symphony. It's very acute. Once you play your audition and pass your second or third year, you're there, you're in no matter how many people are waiting behind you. In this business you're only as good as your last call, only your last one. In many cases not even a second chance is allowed. I know of a couple of guys from an excellent orchestra who had some trouble with the dates at one of the studios, and that's it. That's all it took, just once or twice.

Despite the rather self-serving argument that while others have failed, he has made it, the implication is clear: a musician cannot rest on his laurels, at least not for long. Neither can he feign expertise, that is, come on strong as a backstage soloist but fail to deliver when the red light for recording comes on.

A theme heard many times was that "you're only as good as your last call." One musician qualified this statement, but endorsed it as a principle under which contractors operate.

It's a few mistakes and you're likely to be in trouble. You might find yourself not being called by that contractor, or requested by that composer if you goof up his date. Word gets around, for both good and bad jobs. It all depends. Some guys say, "All right, he goofed but I know it was a bad day." Others aren't so tolerant and say, "Why should I tolerate that when there are 15 other guys I can call who maybe won't make any mistakes?"

Free-lancers must also face work contingencies introduced

by the economic position of individual studios, the economic health of the film and recording industry and more immediate concerns, such as the budget expenditures for composers and performers and fads and fashions in musical styles. Control over these external aspects is largely out of the hands of the free-lancer. Their personal impact depends on the individual's status in the informal hierarchy of studio work. For example, one interviewee, a brass player, was very much in demand by contractors and composers. If he accepted all his calls, he could have worked almost around the clock. He is in his mid-forties and has been successful in the scene for over 15 years. Here he points to the importance of having many accounts, knowing many contractors and being aggressive in going after calls. He comes closest to being the most intense rate-buster among all the musicians we interviewed.

You work according to what instruments a composer writes for, and the studio gives the composer 17 men, and he might not use my instrument, so I don't work that call. The big secret is to work for as many different people as you can. You have to spread your accounts. You may be first call with five, maybe ten, contractors and composers, which means when they put out a call, you will be asked for first. I'd just as soon be second or third call with 20 or 30 composers and a lot of contractors, which I think I am. I wish all the calls would fall into place one year. I think that's the trouble with a lot of guys, they get stuck in one place, they depend on one contractor, and when he falls through, or the studio goes quiet, they don't work. So you learn to juggle your dates, get around and be in demand. To be a success you have to be a businessman.

The following respondent is a free-lancer who is informally tied to one or two contractors. He has informal links to a studio which last year started to use fewer strings, which he plays, and more brass, percussion and woodwind instrumentalists. Unlike his colleague above, he cannot muster much of an argument about the virtue of aggressiveness and working

218   ROBERT R. FAULKNER

for many contractors. When he does refer to colleagues, the highly demanded "star concertmasters" are mentioned with a bit of envy. He nostalgically looks back on the contract orchestras. This was clearly the best work and money he ever had in the studios. Many violin, viola and cello players not in the inner elite circle of string musicians sound much like this respondent.

My work dropped off last year. The studio cut out my instrument, so no violins were used. To have a violin section that sounds like anything, you've got to have at least six to eight players. The studio couldn't afford it for these series, they cut costs by reducing the section. They used a band instead.

Q: What did you do then?

What did I do? Nothing. You stay home and wait for the phone to ring, what can you do? I think cello is more popular now among composers, with four cellos you can get a sound. The big name concertmasters work you know (he gives names of ten musicians) . . . mostly on the big productions, maybe some TV, but most TV doesn't use many violins or violas. Hell, I'm lucky if I can get a call once a week at X Studio.

Both of these musicians face problems inherent in free-lance work. But the second respondent lacked a sustained series of contacts with those who hire. The sure-fire entrepreneurial tone is unmistakably missing from his language. In contrast, his colleague actively cultivated informal influence and leverage with several contractors. In this way he spread the risks inherent in his hiring network. By building up his "accounts" he cushioned himself against the fluctuations in studio productions, market demand for various series and potential competition for valued calls.

Members of the inner circle must work to keep the system intact and to maximize studio calls. Individually, a performer does this by spreading his accounts and risks across a number of hiring agents, a privilege built into being a "star" in the inner elite. Collectively, members attempt to control the number of recruits into their circle.

Like all occupations, studio work generates a set of routine contingencies which must be negotiated, handled, and rendered as predictable or manageable as possible. One persistent problem centers around the *control* musicians have over the conditions of work, the composers and conductors they play under, the studios they perform in, the colleagues they work with. Another problem is tied to their *skills* and musical talents: the misuse and underuse of their abilities in studio work, the imposing technological conditions under which they must work, their uncertainty about which skills will be demanded from day to day and the fluctuation between routine and crisis at work. Third, a level of personal *honor* is claimed and socially accorded by colleagues, which gives the musician his position in the studio pecking order and his perception of being inside or outside influential circles. Recurrent concerns also revolve around the *market situation* of the individual performer in the occupation and that of the occupation in the industry: the structure and intensity of competition for scarce jobs and monetary rewards, the fluctuations in music budgets in mass media production, and the consequences of greater consumer demand for these entertainments. The career problems faced by the protégé or recruit attempting to break into the inner circle must be seen against the individual and collective attempts of inner-circle colleagues to build and sustain a form of social insurance, and to cushion themselves against the hazards of present and potential competitors, mistakes at work and the precarious nature of free-lance employment.

A Note on Methodology

A systematic sampling of studio musicians was impossible because the actual size and composition of the universe was uncertain. No complete listing of free-lance musicians working in the studios, for example, was available, and only a very rough estimate could be made concerning the actual number of players who were called for available recording jobs.

Taking the size of the studio orchestras during the contract days as a rough indicator of the number of musicians in the motion picture and

ROBERT R. FAULKNER

television-film area (they naturally overlap with other free-lance work, such as phonograph recordings), we obtained a total of around 360 players. Within the 360 I located a group of about 190 "inner-circle" or preferred players. The final sample of musicians consists of a group of high-ranking musicians in the free-lance system. Fifty-nine (or 81 percent) of the final sample were players identified by their colleagues as being "among the busier players in commercial work."

Reputational questions were asked of half of our total sample of 75; by this point (N=36), there were few names being added to our list of "top players" and these questions were subsequently omitted from the interview.

Instrument	Reputational Approach: Named Within the "Top Group of Musicians"	Total Interviewed of "Top Group"	Final Sample
Violin	20	8	14
Viola	11	1	3
Cello	15	5	6
Bass	14	3	3
			26
Tuba	4	1	1
Trumpet	23	5	5
Trombone	16	4	4
Sax-doublers	25	8	9
Percussion-drums	19	5	6
			25
Clarinet	9	4	4
Flute	9	5	6
Bassoon	6	4	4
Oboe	5	2	2
French horn	12	4	6
			22
Total	188	59	73

Three out of the 73 in the final sample were women. The average age for all players was 46 years; the string musicians were slightly older (average age 47, range of 33 to 57) as were the brass, saxophone and percussionists (average age 45, range from 29 to 52).

Thirty-one performers had completed either a four-year college or conservatory type of instruction. Twenty-one players spent three or more years in major symphony orchestras such as the Boston Symphony, Philadelphia Orchestra, Pittsburgh Symphony, Rochester

Philharmonic, Seattle Symphony and others. Sixteen of these persons had held principal or assistant principal positions in their respective orchestral sections during their careers. Since entering studio work, several had been offered positions in major orchestras. Nineteen musicians had worked three or more years in the big bands (Glenn Miller, Woody Herman, Claude Thornbill, Benny Goodman, Paul Whiteman, and other famous bands). Twelve of these respondents had played either the lead (first) or solo, jazz "chair." The remaining players had worked less than three years in the orchestras, big bands or as concert soloists before moving into commercial work in New York, Chicago and Los Angeles.

The income for respondents in 1965, which included income from all types of free-lance employment, ranged from $7,000 to $62,000 with a mean income of $27,800 and a median of $26,000. Over 80 percent of these players earned 60 percent or more of their total earnings from work in the motion picture and television-film area of free-lance work. The rest was divided among phonograph recordings, jingles and other types of calls, including outside "leisure employment" in chamber symphonies, recitals, jazz dates and various "casual" calls. This figure suggests, quite independently of reputation, that I have selected a group of performers who are among the busiest musicians in this type of work.

This chapter is based upon material in Robert R. Faulkner, *Hollywood Studio Musicians,* Copyright © 1971 by Aldine-Atherton Publishing Company, Chicago.

NOTES

1. Morris Janowitz, *The Professional Soldier* (New York: Free Press, 1969), pp. 145, 151.

2. Howard S. Becker and Anselm L. Strauss, "Careers, Personality and Adult Socialization," *American Journal of Sociology,* LXII (November, 1956), 253-263; Norman H. Martin and Anselm L. Strauss, "Patterns of Mobility within Industrial Organization," in *Industrial Man* (New York: Harper and Brothers, 1959), pp. 81-89.

3. George C. Homans, *Social Behavior: Its Elementary Forms* (New York: Harcourt, 1961).

4. Everett Cherrington Hughes, *Men and Their Work* (Glencoe, Illinois: Free Press, 1958), p. 108.

5. *Ibid.,* p. 108.

6. Oswald Hall, "The Stages of a Medical Career," *American Journal of Sociology,* LIII (March, 1948), p. 336.

ROBERT R. FAULKNER

Ah, the Unsung Glories of Pre-Rock

HOWARD JUNKER

Hail, hail rock 'n' roll
Deliver me from the days of old.

—Chuck Berry

I didn't mind the days of old (the pre-rock fifties). Of course, I was too young (ten in 1950) to be really oppressed by the diminution and souring of postwar dreams.

But I remember that even as late as 1956, the year McCartney, Harrison and Lennon first met and Doris Day's soppy "Whatever Will Be, Will Be" sold ahead of "Heartbreak Hotel," federal troops were sent into Little Rock—*on the side of* the revolution. Take only three more examples. I admire Harry Truman for having vetoed the McCarran Act (which required Commies to register) and for recalling MacArthur (as a warmonger). I would take Adlai Stevenson over Gene McCarthy any day and even Ike, the one-time (interim) president of Columbia University, over Tricky Dick.

The music wasn't that bad, either. For one thing, it was used differently. Silence was not so unbearable (unattainable). Life was not so externalized and intense that an artificial pacemaker (the transistor) was necessary. You could get by on your own juices. So music was still a little special, something to live with, not in. Radios were just becoming standard "extras"—along with heaters! and white-walls. One of our family's two radios had a clock that would wake you up to music, start the coffee, etc. The other was an old "portable," a machine too huge to lug—we never used it with batteries—with a top that rolled down (over the dial) like a desk.

Still, I heard music all the time, incessantly. Even today I live with a built-in sound track, always zinging and humming through my cortex, a better clue than dreams to the state of my psyche. And I didn't go ape over music that much. And I hated dancing.

In those days you had to be carefully taught—at "dancing class." ("Help me solve the mystery of it./Teach me tonight.") The reason you couldn't figure it out for yourself —you had to dance the adult dances, just like Little League expected you to play Big League ball. Ballroom technique (the big New York City DJ show was called *Make-Believe Ballroom*) included the waltz (remember the great compromise of '55, Kay Starr's "Rock 'n' Roll Waltz"), the foxtrot and your basic box step. Fortunately, for those like me who couldn't count "one-two-side-together," there were really only two kinds of dances, fast and slow.

Fast dancing was mostly left over from that 1927-commemorative, the Lindy Hop, which celebrated Lindbergh's flight across the ocean. And from the jitterbug, another leftover from the jazz-me-baby days. I guess some people did the Bop, but nobody I knew. In slow dancing, you could almost get by with anything, including putting both arms around the girl. "When we're dancing and you're dangerously near me. . . ." Unfortunately, whenever I tried to get by without moving my feet at all (perhaps dropping my hands down there below the waist), the whistle was always blown. "But you're not dancing," she said.

Speaking of conversation: in those days you had to converse while dancing. There was no faking social inter-

HOWARD JUNKER

course in a stoned trance. I used to try to think up riffs beforehand, but the best way out was to hum—in your partner's ear. Singing in her ear was also good, if you could remember the words. Also it was preppy to bob your left arm in time with the music. And then there was the Dip. I was saved, though, by novelty dances, namely the Mexican Hat Dance and the Bunny Hop. The Mexican Hat Dance was the only Latin number I ever mastered. It required nothing more, nothing less, than hopping from one foot to the other for a long time and then swinging your partner for a long time.

Square dancing, in those days, was not square. It was a legit form of social expression and had nothing to do with the early influence of bluegrass. We just did it, without question, during sock hops in the gym, for example. And there was something courtly about it—bow to your partner . . . now second gent . . . honor your corner lady, grand right and . . . —and there was something tricky (and satisfying) in following a good caller, whose vast repertory supplied surprises—and challenges—that fast dancing never did.

The Bunny Hop was all that let me survive that (tuxedo) Cotillion I had to go to every Christmas. (That was from '54 on, if you're keeping score.) At these "formals," it was not unusual for young studs, like myself, to wear jock straps beneath their cummerbunds. The girls, miracle of miracles, wore straplesses, which always stayed up (how?). And at the Junior Prom at the H.S. there was a stagline, i.e., bird dogs, and the girls had "dance cards," numbered one through eight, as in save the waltz or Number Six or the last dance for me. The way you knew it was the last dance was that the band played "Good Night, Ladies."

In the Bunny Hop you got to jump around and get sweaty and the band always took a break afterward (so you could cool off, sneak a joint, i.e., a cigarette). I suppose the Bunny Hop was a somewhat embellished, organization man version of the farout kicking of early jitterbugging. You all got in line, boy-girl-boy-girl, hands on the shoulders or, if you were a guy, on the waist—or *hips*—of the person in front. Then you kicked twice to the left, twice to the right, hopped forward, backward, hop, hop, hop. Each round increasing in volume and tempo. If the band was the greatest, the sax (the key early fifties "ax"—homage to The Bird) would trot out in front of the line, oh when the Saints/come marching in. . . .

Remember that even late-fifties rock dancing was not all that athletic. It was pretty cool. (It was the twist that introduced onanistic frenzy.) Fast dancing in the fifties was so controlled, so repetitive, so much bopping and twirling, I thought it very boring. The only move of any worth—and it remains an absolute classic—was the crossover-down-the-arm slide. Listen closely: You began from that two handed back-and-forth pump. Without letting go, you lifted her left hand up and behind her head and your left up and behind your head (girls weren't supposed to lead); then, releasing both hands (dropping the left altogether) you slid the right arm-and-hand back down and along hers. Man, was that sexy.

But you're still not convinced there was anything back there that deserves nostalgia. And I admit, it is possible to view pre-rock as a bottomless abyss between the golden youth of Frank Sinatra, a distant era now beyond rancor, and the night Elvis appeared on Ed Sullivan, the camera quietly deleting his pelvis. (It should be recalled that Presley had first appeared—opposite Sullivan—on Steve Allen's show and gotten huge ratings. Hi ho, Steverino!)

Sure it's possible not to want to swoon again, all that smooth syrup of all those crooners, those greasy Italian baritones, that ethnic crowd (mob) of Vic Damone, Perry Como, Dean Martin, Julius La Rosa, Tony Martin, Al Martino, Tony Bennett, Mel Torme (he was Jewish, of course, but then again Billy Eckstine was a Whiteman's Negro and Harry Belafonte a colored white).

My hero, circa 1952, was Johnny Ray. Of whom I could do a pretty good imitation. So could everybody else. Eeeeeeef yooar swwweeett hhhhhaaaarrrrttt sennnnnnnzzz a lllleeeeettttttaaa uuuufffff gooooobbbbyyyeeee. Just take off

HOWARD JUNKER

your jacket, loosen your tie, take *it* off, unbutton your shirt, take *it*. . . . And tear your hair out and cryeeee. (A very strange gesture in those days, not manly, you know, Marlon "wallowing in insolence" Brando, the first motorcycle hipster in *The Wild Ones,* used to room in Greenwich Village with the guy who became Mr. Peepers.) Nobody, nobody has ever put more outrageous super-dramatics into a song than Johnny Ray. Hell, Sinatra used to hide behind the mike. As for your moderns, say, James Brown, next to a real Actors' Studio master like Ray, Brown comes on like Rocky Marciano in drag.

On the distaff side—yes, they said that—the lineup was chockablock with squeaky-clean "vocalists" whose first names sounded as if they ended with "ie"—Joni James, Kitty Kallen, Patti Page, Peggy Lee and Rosemary Clooney. And Her Nibs, Miss Georgia Gibbs. Plus all those so harmonious sisters, The Andrews, McGuire, Fontane, King, De John, De Castro . . . Sisters. Men placed less emphasis on family ties (beyond the Mills and Ames Brothers) mostly favoring schoolboyish names, like The Crewcuts and all those Fours— The Four Freshmen, Preps, Lads. . . . Needless to say, the black groups were a good deal more sinister, e.g., The Four Aces, the Inkspots. . . .

And just for a moment rehearse Sinatra's own revival in the early fifties, first as Best Supporting Actor in *From Here to Eternity* (1953). Then as the mellow, swinging, that is to say, experienced—in the Playboy sense—singer of "Learnin' the Blues." (Playboy arrived in an undated issue late in '54 with La Monroe on the cover. Tits and ass were big at the time; every record jacket of the era has girls looking back over their shoulder, their boobs in profile, their haunches full-face.)

The main point about pre-rock culture, though, is that the society conducted itself as if it were homogeneous. At least that was very much the overt goal: conformity, desegregation, togetherness, the United Nations.

" 'I'd give anything to belong . . .' she sighed as she looked enviously through the window at a happy group of boys and girls heading for the bowling alley. Listerine Antiseptic clinically proved four times better than tooth paste."

So great was the impulse towards social leveling that snob-appeal was flipped on its ass, with the likes of Mrs. Francis Irenee du Pont II of Wilmington and New York, one of Society's most charming young matrons, declaring, "We wouldn't be without Camels in our home."

Other women, probably influenced by Mary Martin in *South Pacific* (and *Peter Pan*) got crew-cuts, like everybody else, so that one columnist remarked, "You have to ask for a draft card to tell the boys from the girls."

It was, in brief, theoretically possible for everyone to dig the common culture. The eggheads were constantly debating masscult(ure), Malcolm X had his hair processed, and the entire family, from 6 to 60, tuned in to *Your Hit Parade*.

Your Hit Parade, which was simply TV's ratification of the charts (the Top Seven), worked very effectively until the kids demanded music the family couldn't take. (At which point exit *Your Hit Parade*, enter Lawrence Welk.) Namely, rock: "The Hit Parade Singers . . . began to look harassed. Finally the pimple burst. Snooky Lanson, the creepiest of the four, stood up in front of one of those cardboard sets they used, and sang out 'You ain't nothin' but a hound dog' with a shit-eating Lucky Strike grin on his face." For the young rock critic who wrote that, even the attempt of a mainstream (adult) creep to sing rock was disgusting. Consensus culture was over.

(Out in Hollywood there was *Juke Box Jury*, as in "put another nickel in/in the nickelodeon/all I want is having you and/music, music, music." The MC of this show claimed that R&B records were "dirty and as bad for kids as dope.")

Your Hit Parade was only one symptom of TV's effect on pop music. *American Bandstand* was even more crucial; it was the first show specifically dedicated to teenies. The same parochial school kids showed up every day down there in

228   HOWARD JUNKER

Philly, and you got to know who could dance, who was going with whom, and who did well on yesterday's social studies test. You could also, if you needed it, learn how to dress and how to dance. I'd rate that about 87. It had rhythm; I could dance to it. In short, the image of Youth was set loose in the land. . . . But there was something else. By taking over "programming" from radio (*Amos and Andy* reached its 10,000th performance on November 16, 1952), TV let radio become the music medium. Please play our song, Mr. Record Man. Ultimately, the Establishment abandoned the medium to the kids who, after a generation of radio-rock, learned how to turn it into Art.

Actually, the way DJs knew what to play was quickly systematized by the Charts—a merchandising device incorporated into the act of promotion. As one station manager put it, "If you're playing the 35th worst record in town, and somebody else is playing the 87th worst record in town, you're better off than they are." So you heard what was popular, which then became your favorite, which. . . . Which meant that the circle was very vicious indeed, manipulative and short circuiting. The early effect of the intense feedback of record promo was payola (bribing a DJ or distributor to plug—or push—your product), which finally broke as a scandal in the late fifties (but only *after* the quiz show scandal).

At another level, the intense feedback meant that songs became ever more deeply drilled into the subconscious. So they went out quicker, which increased the demand for new models. Ten songs hit Billboard's weekly No. 1 in 1951; 19 made it in 1960. Further, the kids began to get economic power, which along with cheap and portable radios, gave them the power to get a sound of their own (like their own room, their own car).

The introduction of the 45 gave them a record format of their own. It looked, felt, played and cost cheap. Shuffling through a thumbful of 45s was as easy as riffling a pack of bubblegum baseball cards, easier than mixing up a canasta deck. You had a stack you liked to hear and when you got tired of one side, you pulled it out and threw it away. (It was normal practice to release a dog—or a standard—on the flip side, thus forcing you to buy more.) And in this manner, the old, scratched and nicked 78 was launched as the world's first frisbee. The 33, introduced simultaneously, became the format for serious music and "easy listening" (so you didn't have to interrupt your make-out session, getting off the couch to attend the phonograph).

It took a long time for musicians to grasp the potential of tape and amplification, although here again there were isolated instances in pre-rock. Les Paul not only played an electric guitar, he pioneered in overdubbing, thus turning himself into a one-man band and his wife, the singer Mary Ford, into the Ford Sisters. Les Paul and Mary Ford sound very thin in the 16-track era, but reverb was fresh then and sound was not considered something to be manipulated (except by the avant-garde of Cage, Varese and Stockhausen, who it should be said, had already explored in the fifties such sixties rock inventions as the light show, amplified instruments and multiple-speaker systems).

The development of amplification obviously provided a way past the big band—four cats on amplifiers could fill a big room. So, too, the development of stereo-hi-fi tuned people in to pure sound—*Hi-Fi Drums* and *The Sounds of Sebring* (a race track in Florida). Thus, the record player became more than a piece of furniture, it became electronic equipment, although the popular teenie infatuation was not with such contemporary technology, but with the antique, the hot rod.

As for the aesthetic of pre-rock, when you get down to it, as we must at last, it was pretty goopy. But there are not a few surprises.

Consider the all-but-forgotten "Rag Mop" of 1949. It was bouncy jazz-scat. "R . . . r-a-g . . . r-a-g-g-m-o-pp, Rag Mop . . . doodleyopbopadooppa." From "Rag Mop," obviously,

HOWARD JUNKER

comes the spelling bee lyric of "Respect" and earlier, all
those other nonsense syllables that proto-rock used to break
up the lyric line, freeing it from the rhyming couplets that
had (admittedly) become so ossified in the Tin Pan Alley
ballad:

Pepsi Cola Hits the spot
12 full ounces, that's a lot
twice as much and better too
Pepsi Cola is the drink for you!

And do you think that folk sprang full-blown from the
Clancy Brothers, Odetta and the Kingston Trio? Please
remember that one of the biggest groups in the early fifties
was the Weavers, which included (the blacklisted) Pete
Seeger. And that in 1950 the Weavers made Leadbelly's
"Goodnight, Irene" the top single of the year. That the next
year, Patti Page's "Tennessee Waltz" was the first of the
all-time, nationwide Nashville hits. And that the Weavers also
scored with Woodie Guthrie's "So Long It's Been Good To
Know You" (a song whose Depression significance completely escaped me at the time), "On Top of Old Smokey"
and "Tzena, Tzena" (which had, for me, no Israeli overtones
until a Barnard girl taught me how to hora).

And do you think that mature Beatles-Zappa eclecticism
was the first pop music that ranged far and wide in its
inspiration? Pre-rock had opera singers on the charts (Mario
Lanza with "Be My Love") and opera-inspired tunes: Sammy
Kay's waltz "You" came from *La Boheme.*. "Stranger in
Paradise," (which I will always remember fondly from New
Year's Eve in Suzie's basement; that's the song by which I
first frenched Anne R.), was taken from Borodin's *Prince
Igor* (via *Kismet*). And in '54 there was "Napoleon," better
known (by some) as *The 1812 Overture*.

William Saroyan wrote "Come On-a My House" with his
cousin on a 1939 cross-country motor trip, but the song,
having been used in an off-B'way production of a Saroyan
play, was popularized in 1950 by Rosemary Clooney, whose

"Italian Mambo" so sorely offended Italianos that they forced many radio stations to keep it off the air. Even Uncle Miltie wrote a pop hit, "I." (Jackie Gleason, at the time, was not only a comic slob but a reasonably trim, "mood music" bandleader, a kind of ballsy Montovani/Andre Kostelanetz. "Send only $2.50 to 63 Central Ave., Ossining, N.Y. and receive your own authentic, autographed Liberace miniature piano, gorgeous as a candy, jewel, thread or cigarette box, in ivory or mahogany plastic. What a conversation piece!")

The taste of the day was definitely eclectic. Movie themes were frequent pop hits—"The Third Man," "Moulin Rouge," "High Noon." And there remained, perhaps as a dying tribute to Tin Pan Alley, a direct line to Broadway show tunes— "Lullaby of Broadway"—of which I'll mention only "A Bushel and a Peck," "Hernando's Hideaway" and "I Love Paris." (B'way didn't peak out until '56 with *My Fair Lady* and then *West Side Story*.)

From far away (and anywhere across the sea was far away because pre-rock was pre-jet—remember "26 miles across the sea Santa Catalina is waiting for me" and "See the pyramids along the Nile . . . see the tropics when they're wet with rain/just remember when you're home again/you belong to me") came such exotica as: "C'est Si Bon," Vaya con Dios," "Eh, Cumpari," "Glow Worm" (from the German, *Glüh-wurmchen*), "Uska Dara" (that's Turkish) and "Gomen-Nasai," which means "Forgive Me" in Japanese (it was written by a G.I. helping occupy Japan). ("Just Walking in the Rain" was written by a group of inmates of Tennessee State Pen who called themselves the Prisonaires—this was well before Chuck Berry got canned for transporting a 15-year-old girl across state lines, to say nothing of Johnny Cash.)

There was a larger dimension to this cosmopolitanism namely, all those Latin rhythms: tango, mambo, samba, conga, rumba, merengue and cha-cha. There was a fad a year and all those footwork diagrams in Arthur Murray ads. "See for Yourself How a Few Hours at Arthur Murray's Opens the

232   HOWARD JUNKER

Door to Good Times and Popularity!" Lady of Spain, I adore you. Pull down your pants, I'll explore you. Played on the accordion, of course.

Further, pre-rock included a sense of humor, i.e., novelty numbers: Red Buttons' curiously pre-Dylan "Strange Things Are Happening," the cutesy "How Much is That Doggie in the Window," the monstrously chilling "The Thing"—"Get out of here with that bum-bum-bum before I call the cops"—the O. Henryesque "The Naughty Lady of Shady Lane"—"and she's only five days old." And the broad parody of Stan Freberg, the poor man's Tom Lehrer, whose "St. George and the Dragonet," just the facts, ma'am, played four weeks at the top of the charts.

And there was a yearly procession of Christmas cuties: "Santa Claus is Coming to Town" through "All I Want for Christmas is My Two Front Teeth," "Rudolph, the Red Nosed Reindeer" (Gene Autry rides again). "I Saw Mommy Kissing Santa Claus," and, finally, Eartha Kitt's profane "Santa Baby" ("A '54 convertible would be so nice . . . so hurry down the chimney to me"). After awhile it became impossible to promote a Christmas number sufficiently— without starting in late July. Meanwhile the tunes that did make it were interpreted as hymns to the (much decried) commercialization of Xmas—or the vanguard of an attack on American institutions. (*White Christmas* was finally filmed in '54.)

And now back to Video Central: TV also spawned a few pop hits. The first, in '55 was "Blue Star," the theme of the first "doctor" series, *Medic*. Also that year a '53 nowhere tune, rewritten on Mitch Miller's suggestion for a Studio One play about a DJ, "Let Me Go, Lover," hit the top in a version by Joan Weber, although it was also "covered," in typical practice of the times, by Teresa Brewer, Sunny Gale, Peggy Lee and Patti Page.

"Covering" meant recording someone else's hit in your style, a deed that could be done with such ease and frequency because 1) artists didn't write their own material, they did what the A&R man told them to do; 2) artists didn't even play an instrument, they were "vocalists"—I think the first group to play *and* sing were the Four Freshmen; and 3) the various markets were extremely segregated, thus when R&B started selling (on small, out-of-town labels) the white artists would cover the breakout numbers. (Between '49 and '54, 49 country songs sold a million records.) R&B, you may recall, had been called "race music" in the forties, and it took an older teenager—the category that replaced the "bobby-soxer" of the Sinatra era—to find the black station, if there was one, on the radio dial.

There was not a lot of social consciousness surging through the early fifties, as is well known. TV peeked at organized crime with Senator Kefauver, who thereby vaulted into contention as a presidential candidate. But by and large, there was McCarthyism. Woodstock, you may not recall, was then the name of the typewriter owned by Alger Hiss, convicted of perjury (for denying he had been in cahoots with the Commies). Perjury was very popular in the early fifties; so were the crimes of contempt, for refusing to say whether you were or ever had been . . . and income tax evasion, if they couldn't prove you were a racketeer.

Pop music tended to look the other way, which was partly a legacy of the Depression's sense of forced optimism: "Bye-Bye Blues," "(All You Really Need Is) Heart." The world is waiting for the sunrise. Pretend you're happy when you're blue. Tennessee Ernie Ford's "Sixteen Tons" sounded more like bluegrass machismo than an indictment of mining conditions. And if you want a fine example of glorious racial obliviousness, try the Bingo's "Chattanoogie Shoe Shine Boy." Oh them colored folks, ain't they got rhythm and blues.

Religiosity simmered mighty close to the early fifties surface. Tricky Dick meet Billy Graham. In 1950, Kitty Kallen delivered "Our Lady of Fatima," a song which has happily slipped from mind. But who could forget such

HOWARD JUNKER

devotionals as Eddie Fisher's advising insomniacs to count their blessings instead of sheep. (Eddie was then admired for his marriages, as with Debbie Reynolds. In 1950, Liz was 18, the bride of Nicky Hilton.) Yes, brethren, there was Frankie Laine intoning "I believe for every drop of rain that falls, a flower grows," Kay Starr asking "Have you talked to the Man upstairs, he will always see you through"; and Don Cornell asking-telling "How do I know? The Bible tells me so." For good measure, I throw in, "Be sure it's true when you say, 'I love you.' It's a sin to tell a lie."

Needless to say, by 1956 such piety had been transmogrified by a lot of things and the Platters into "My Prayer"—"is to linger with you in the still of the night"—which was actually the son of "Teen-Age Prayer" from the year before. (For the record, there was also "Teen Age Crush" and "Teen-Age Love" in '55, "A Teenager's Romance" in '57 and "Teen Angel," "A Teenager in Love" and "Teen Beat" in '59. As for Frankie Lymon, whose group was called The Teenagers, he was a mere Harlem 13-year-old when he wrote "Why Do Fools Fall in Love?" in 1956. Falsetto was big in the mid-fifties, partly because, for a lot of guys, like Lymon, their voice hadn't changed. Also falsetto was a way past the dreary normalcy of crooning.

Pre-rock went through a lot of growing pains getting straight about age. Mostly, of course, there was the growing sense that what we wanted to do was not allowed by the adult world. Too young to go steady. And everything else. (The Philadelphia Phillies of Robin Roberts and Richie Ashburn were so young when they rose up to challenge the indomitable Yanks, they were called the Whiz Kids, a corruption, of course, of the Quiz Kids, of radio fame.) In general, the assumption was that the world would last, if it did, in much the same way as it always had been. Thus, you could afford to wait—grow up—and so things would last.

"They tried to tell us we're too young, too young to really be in love."

In the fifties myth, you could have sex, but only if love

endured. ("I don't want a ricochet romance.") "Love and marriage," as Sinatra said (I don't think with much cynicism), "go together like a horse and carriage . . . you can't have one without the other." (Oh yes, I gotta admit, innuendo was big. Arthur Buy-Em-By-the-Carton Godfrey, the ukelele kid, was scolded for making dirty cracks on the air. Faye Emerson and Dagmar let much of it hang out on TV. And Jo Stafford pleaded, "Make Love to Me.")

The key early fifties song about age, though, was not the Rosemary Clooney/Marlene Dietrich duet, "Too Old to Cut the Mustard." Nor was it "Old Soldiers Never Die," revived, unmelodically, by MacArthur while addressing a joint session of Congress and made a hit by Vaughan Monroe, the John Wayne of pop—"their faces gaunt, their eyes were blurred, their shirts all soaked with sweat. They gotta catch those riders but they ain't caught 'em yet. . . ." No, the key song was Sinatra's "Young at Heart" (1954). This was absolutely the last ditch suggestion that age is in the mind, that "you could survive till a hundred and five, if you're young at heart."

It marked the end of the unified sensibility, the homogeneous culture. From then on, the gaps, first identified as an intellectual gap between the eggheads and everybody else, just proliferated. (In those days we were still trying to build a better bomb; the Bikini took its name from the South Pacific atoll on which much H-bomb testing was done. Presumably it had the impact of same.)

And now, let us close this album from yesteryear with a word about nostalgia itself.

Nostalgia became the trivia industry in the mid-sixties but it did not exist in the early fifties. There was not that much to look back to—the War, the Depression. Two generations of Americans never had a childhood, didn't have much fun at all, which is a major reason They don't understand Us now. . . .

Tin Pan Alley had always acknowledged the existence of

timeless standards, but the first album called "oldies but goodies" wasn't released until 1959. It included "Earth Angel" from '54 and "Dance with Me, Henry" from '55. The term was then corrupted to old or solid gold (million dollar weekend), although Old Gold, in pre-rock days, meant a cigarette "for a treat instead of a treatment."

And by the late sixties, Murray the K was poormouthing "We ran goldies into the ground back in '63. . . ." Actually, by the mid-fifties, there was a glimmering awareness of Instant Nostalgia, a sense that life was passing by very fast and that contemporary events would soon enough become objects of intense historical longing: "The day we tore the goal posts down . . . we will have these moments to remember. . . ." (I solemnly swear that on the evening of Nov. 7, 1970, I heard a DJ say, "And now from 1970, remember Three Dog Night with. . . .")

And so today we have Memory Lane as an adjunct to Wall Street. Last August, a Cashbox editorial detected "old-time music publishers" again looking into their vaults for gold, "convinced that this material, much of it revolutionary in its day-and-age, should not lie fallow, but should be exploited anew for youthful audiences. . . . Management also feels that many of these songs are not dated, but timeless in their appeal. They simply require tender, loving care, or as Famous Music put it recently, the desire to 'put diamonds in new settings.' "

And so the dog returns to its vomit. . . .

Ah, the unsung glories of pre-rock. . . .

Rock 1970 –
It's Too Late to
Stop Now

JON LANDAU

There is a lack of excitement in the air, like the days before the Beatles. Bob Dylan has lost much of his impact, even though his records sell more than ever. The end of the Beatles as a group is now irreversible. Even the Stones have fallen into the ranks of the merely human, unable to sustain the fantasies of a new generation the way they did those of mine. There are no longer any superhumans to focus on. And the wellspring of rock has failed in the last three years to produce a new, dynamic R&B singer with anything approaching mass appeal.

Creative moments come at long intervals and last a short time in any popular culture. Rock 'n' roll was a distinct musical form for only a few years—according to Charlie Gillett, 1954-1958. The years 1959 through 1963 were years of transition in which the music manipulators became temporarily more important than the artists themselves and in which the artistry of the rock 'n' roll years was formalized and plasticized by unimaginative record companies and A&R men.

Only in the hands of a few independent minded artists like

Phil Spector and the Beach Boys, and companies like Atlantic and Motown, did the music continue to grow. In 1963 the Beatles shattered the dreariness of the music business. And with them came rock, the music of the sixties, and a music quite different from rock 'n' roll.

Of the two, rock is a music of far greater surface seriousness and lyric complexity. It is the product of a more self-aware and self-conscious group of musicians. It is far more a middle-class music than the lower-class one its predecessor certainly was. And, while it borrowed extensively from rock 'n' roll styles, it was a fundamentally different kind of music.

It was mainly played on guitars instead of pianos and horns, mainly by whites instead of blacks, mainly in groups of three, four or five musicians, instead of in nine and ten piece bands, mainly on FM radio (after 1964) instead of AM, and mainly in concert halls and specialized clubs, instead of in bars and state fairs. To replace record hops, liquor and transistor radios there were light shows, dope and head-phones.

And yet both were essentially folk musics. The best music in both idioms came from men who recorded their own material, or worked very closely with a collaborator on it. While producers have been important in both fields, the music was essentially controlled by the performing artist—unlike the music from 1959-63. And in both situations there existed a strong bond between performer and audience, a natural kinship, a sense that the stars weren't being imposed from above but had sprung up from out of our own ranks. We could identify with them unhesitatingly.

As we move into a new decade and the Beatles recede into our musical past, one gets the sense we are moving into a new, constructive period of transition—a prelude to some new approach to music in the seventies. It may well be that when someone writes a history of rock ten years from now he will identify its creative period as 1964-68. Certainly the year 1970 will be viewed as one of the decline of one set of artists (groups) and the emergence of a new set (individuals, solo artists, acoustic artists).

Looking back at the last ten years, it seems obvious that the atmosphere of low expectation, common during the early sixties, contributed to the growth of many artists who became popular in the later sixties. It gave them time to learn their craft in an unhurried and unpressurized period. When fame finally summoned many of them in the wake of the Beatles, a surprising number were more than ready with their *own* musical statements.

In America, colleges, coffee houses and independent record companies like Elektra, Prestige and Vanguard became the haven of aspiring musicians seeking refuge from the poverty of commercial recording scenes during those years. In England, the established music scene was dominated by people even stodgier than their American counterparts. With Cliff Richard's self-righteousness acting as a kind of norm of acceptability, few new groups were even given an opportunity to record. And yet, despite its inaccessibility through records, increasingly well-educated British young people turned away from pop and found a haven in small clubs where groups like the Stones, Animals and Mayall's various bands played blues and early American rock 'n' roll.

In England as in the States, the commercial potential of this new thing was ignored by established companies, which in turn gave musicians a chance to grow without being hustled into record contracts prematurely. The Beatles themselves were the classic example. It is therefore not surprising that when the Beatles proved the commercial viability of rock in 1964, there were so many groups prepared to follow through with their own distinctive music.

THE BRITISH INVASION

The Beatles established rock with the finality that Presley had established rock 'n' roll. In their wake came two types of

JON LANDAU

groups: the forerunners of mid-sixties FM rock, including the Yardbirds; then, the Pretty Things, Manfred Man, the Who, the Animals, the Stones and the rest—the pop establishment's attempt to update itself without accepting the cultural changes implied in the styles of the more adventurous and innovative groups. These children of Cliff Richard included Billy J. Kramer and the Dakotas, the Searchers, Freddie and the Dreamers, Herman's Hermits, and Gerry and the Pacemakers. Through the mid-sixties these two different styles achieved high levels of popularity.

So many of the most popular groups of the late sixties came from England because in that country they could remain sheltered from American audiences until they were well prepared. American groups had to make their debuts and mistakes in front of the audience that counted most. In addition, English groups have been more obviously theatrical, the usual explanation for it having to do with English vaudeville traditions.

American groups were often more natural but less interesting on stage. Mick Jagger's command of the stage may have been programmed but it was perfect. Jim Morrison's spontaneous, debauched style was merely vulgar. English groups were comfortable with their pop-star identities. American groups would be considered *dressed up* if they appeared in something other than jeans. These days, however, American groups are more show conscious while the English pop stars have taken to jeans.

Through the mid-sixties, American rock was defining its own ambience and style. Through the flirtation with folk music in the early sixties many musicians found a unique source out of which to mold a new kind of rock, something distinct from what British bands were offering. Foremost among these were the Byrds, who transformed Dylan into rock more extensively than Dylan ever did himself. Their special talents allowed them to combine the prettiness of popular folk music with the drive and strength of rock rhythm. The results were usually among the best rock of the period. The Buffalo Springfield had a similar talent and were more adventurous as songwriters, as well. Veering more to the pop side of the music were the Mamas and Papas and Simon and Garfunkel; both groups became masters of the art of studio recording. While a bit too polished and successful to be called an underground group, the Lovin' Spoonful kept more of an informal image than any of their fellow groups. Somewhat less talented than the others, they were often the most spirited. And like the others, they enjoyed huge AM successes in 1965 and 1966.

Most of these groups were concerned with attaining conventional success. In later years their music would appeal to the FM audience, but for the time being they committed themselves to the pop process. Other groups less concerned with (or less capable of) obtaining conventional success were creating a true underground: the Paul Butterfield Blues Band, the Blues Project, and eventually, the San Francisco groups. That city's musical development proved to be a fascinating story in its own right.

THE SAN FRANCISCO ERA

During the early and mid-sixties, San Francisco had the advantage of being shielded from the music business people of Los Angeles and New York. Because there were no firm practices already accepted on how to handle popular music, people there were free to invent their own. Ballrooms emerged as rock's first answer to folk clubs, discothèques, and civic auditorium concerts with poor sound and lighting. The Fillmore West eventually served as a model for every rock club in the country, and it is interesting (maybe even absurd) to recall that there was little regular presentation of rock in New York City until Graham decided to open the Fillmore East.

In companioship to Fillmore, KMPX started a new form of FM radio in San Francisco which quickly spread to other big cities. In two years time FM became more important than AM in affecting album sales and, more importantly, in successfully providing rock audiences with a style of radio and an outlet for music which suited their needs. The mass acceptance by rock audiences of FM, with its superior fidelity and variety, make it clear that the seventies will see the further demise of AM programming. In cities like Boston (WBCN) and Detroit (WABX and WKNR) as well as on the West Coast, FM stations have already destroyed the primacy of AM radio for good. A new federal regulation requiring all 1971 cars carrying radios to have both AM and FM bands will hasten the process considerably.

In the mid-sixties San Francisco was the only city to develop a consciousness about the importance of rock. That cultural awareness was the cushion for all other developments. Rock was not only viewed as a form of entertainment; part of that collective outlook held that music was the essential component of a "new culture." The almost religous fervor that surrounded rock in 1966 and 1967 was occasionally frightening. Like the infatuation with drugs, there was a sense of discovery going on that made it seem like nothing could ever be better and that nothing would ever change. Things were so good, who could ever get tired of them?

Moby Grape was the best performing band to come out of San Francisco, although few people in their native city recognized it, perhaps because there was a little too much Hollywood in the group for the new audiences and new performing style. Their first album for Columbia was by far the best first album from a San Francisco group. Regrettably, with so much talent in the group, they went the way of all hypes and spent three years trying to catch up with an unbelievably inflated press. Janis Joplin, who came to national attention in the summer of 1967, was typical of a number of San Francisco musicians who had immigrated from Texas and the Midwest.

But the two most important groups to come out of the

city were the Jefferson Airplane and the Grateful Dead. Together they defined an American style of improvised music that was quite different from the blues bands (Butterfield) that preceded them and the English groups (Cream) that would come after them. The Airplane on record confined themselves to an elongated fabric of folk-rock. Live, however, they jammed often and at length. Unlike British groups, their jams seldom centered around blues but instead displayed a more intellectual and complex approach that was loud but not hard. The Dead did involve itself more with blues and, later on, country, but they too specialized in cerebral improvisation. Both bands have grown considerably since they first became popular. *Volunteers* was an undeniably powerful statement about America after Chicago while the Dead's "Casey Jones" shows them ready to adapt to anything. Both groups are something of a national institution and come closer to permanence than any other American bands.

THE UNDERGROUND

In the wake of the success of San Francisco groups, American businessmen saw the potential in this new approach to popular music, dubbed it "Underground Music" and started responding to what had already become a fact of life for hundreds of thousands of young people. In three years' time the audience would number in the millions.

During the late sixties, literacy, the first sign of civilization, struck rock hard, first in the form of Crawdaddy and Richard Goldstein's writing in the *Village Voice,* and then in the pages of *Rolling Stone.* Dissemination of news and publicity to the new audience became an amazingly efficient process, thereby accelerating the pace of change within the business itself.

All of these new conditions helped to make possible the second coming of British rock groups, the British underground acts. In 1966, a harbinger of the future occurred.

JON LANDAU

Having missed the boat in San Francisco, Atlantic records decided it had to expand from its R&B base and sign some of the English groups. This led to meetings with Robert Stigwood, the notorious English impresario. Stigwood offered Atlantic a package of two groups. One was put forward as the new Beatles, the latter was forced upon the company as part of the deal. The former was the BeeGees; the latter was Cream.

Cream legitimized the whole new development with unimaginable force. In New York a new booking agency, Premier Talent Associates, evolved to specialize in British groups and following the pattern of Cream's success helped establish the modern concept of a tour. It entailed extensive promotion of new releases on a regional basis. In each of the major markets of the country the group would appear at the local club, usually gaining FM airplay (where they would often turn up to do interviews), coverage in the local underground press, and word of mouth publicity from those who saw them.

This last was ultimately decisive. The tie-in between new releases, FM airplay, and appearances in selected markets was successfully used to build Jeff Beck, Jethro Tull, Joe Cocker, and Led Zeppelin. It became a formula still rigidly adhered to today.

As in the late fififtes and early sixties, towards the end of the decade the formula seemed to be taking precedence over creativity. A group of people emerged, sometimes producers, sometimes managers, sometimes engineers, who understood rock well enough from a technical point of view to manipulate it with above average success. Technological changes within the recording process itself helped to make this possible.

During the late sixties eight- and 16- track tape recorders became the standard of the industry. These machines not only improved the quality of recorded sound but made it easier to program. Producers and engineers, increasingly the equivalent of movie director and editor (or cameraman), have greatly increased their roles in the recording process. The negative consequence is a potential reduction in spontaneity and feeling. Overdubbing as a recording technique has virtually eliminated the need for musicians to play together at all. Mixing, in turn, offers vast opportunities to affect the sound of the record after the actual recording has been done. Together they make it possible to formalize and standardize recorded sound to a higher degree than ever before.

Cream more than any other group established the importance of improvisation and instrumental facility as bases for new rock. They had no talent for and did not rely on singing or song writing. The core of their live performance material was blues although Cream was not merely a blues band—at their best they combined that musical form with rock in an expert and exciting way. At their worst, they indulged in a narcissistic display of technical virtuosity. Among other things, they institutionalized rock "jams" and long cuts, and they may well have pulled it off better than anyone who has tried them since.

Jimi Hendrix was the other major artist who helped elevate the importance of instrumental rock. While Cream maintained a detached image of themselves as craftsmen, Hendrix flaunted his decadence and outrageousness in an almost vaudevillian style. And even more than Eric Clapton, he challenged people with his extensions of the guitar into all sorts of realms that had been overlooked, ignored or undiscovered.

The children of Cream and Hendrix—Jeff Beck, Ten Years After, Led Zeppelin, Grand Funk and Mountain—were outgrowths of blues bands and used blues as the framework for developing individual styles. Beck was perhaps the first to take the more exhibitionistic elements of the approach and turn it into a virtual parody of improvised music. Ten Years After's Alvin Lee followed Beck with a primitive form of showoffishness that created brief moments of excitement and long hours of tedium.

Led Zeppelin has by now become the most popular of all the late sixties British bands. Like their predecessors, they build their style on doubling bass and guitar figures, thereby creating a distorted emphasis on the bottom sound range. It is a completely physical approach to sound that usually works better live than on records. Zeppelin's demeanor, like that of most of these groups, was loud, impersonal, exhibitionistic, violent and often insane. Watching them at a recent concert I saw little more than Robert Plant's imitations of sexuality and Jimmy Page's unwillingness to sustain a musical idea for more than a few measures.

I got a sense that the real mood of the band is ennui. I sat there thinking that rock could not go on like this. There are those who are prepared to buy it now, but there is no future in it, and that is why groups like Zeppelin take it all in now. They have no place to go, no place to grow into, no roots anywhere. And so there they were in front of 15,000 people, going through the motions—their "act"—in order to pick up a paycheck. Fifteen thousand people sat through it all hoping that somehow their expectations would be fulfilled. They weren't because in the words of a fine Bob Dylan song, "nothing was delivered."

THE FESTIVAL BUSINESS

The changes of the late sixties were illustrated best at the three major festivals that took place between 1967 and 1969. The Monterey International Pop Festival signaled the decline of the then existing rock establishment and legitimized the underground. Out of Monterey came Jimi Hendrix, Janis Joplin, and the Who, as well as increased mass acceptance of some San Francisco bands and Otis Redding. These relatively new names entirely overshadowed the AM stars: the Association, Simon and Garfunkel, Scott McKenzie, and even the Mamas and Papas. One could witness the underground culture at its point of transformation into mass culture.

The Woodstock Music and Art Fair, held only two summers later, signified the ultimate commercialization of that same culture. A fitting end to the sixties, it showed the country just how strong in numbers the rock audience had become, and just how limited its culture was. It was the last assembly, if not the only one, of virtually every name of any consequence to have emerged since Monterey and was held in front of the largest audience ever assembled. After it there was no place left to grow, no way for things to get any bigger, nothing that could be more exciting or gargantuan.

The energy and intensity of interest could only be imitated cheaply then parodied, and from bathos it went through pathos to tragedy: at Altamont, the anticlimax of it all, an audience once naively optimistic turned rancid with cynicism, a cynicism that was but a reflection of the stars whom they admired. The vibrations that emanated from the Stones' free concert showed at least a healthy sign that people had not forgotten how to be critical of both themselves and those whom they admire. And yet somehow one realized it couldn't be made up. Altamont showed everyone that something had been lost that could not be regained.

The summer of 1970 saw exploiters and manipulators trying to pull off Woodstocks all over the country. The incompetence of Woodstock, an incompetence (and resultant spontaneity) which was worshipped in the media, could not be institutionalized as a fixed part of the program by the new promoters.

The rock business has had a bad case of elephantiasis and everything that had been swept under the rug was now coming into the open: the greed, the hustle, hype and above all, the lack of a long range commitment to the music or the audience on the part of many groups, managers, agents and record companies. More and more, it looked like people trying to take the money and run. And when decadence comes into the open, decline cannot be far behind.

INNOVATORS AND IMITATORS

Presley was forced to look at his reflection in the face of Frankie Avalon. The Stones saw themselves parodied by the

JON LANDAU

Doors. And Bob Dylan must have tired long ago of that sincerest form of flattery, imitation.

Cream created the instrumentally oriented trio and then had to watch it come back to them in the form of Jeff Beck, Zeppelin, and finally (one hopes, finally) Grand Funk Railroad. In these last three there is a chronological pattern moving from bad to worse. With Grand Funk we finally reach a sort of nadir with the expectation that people must inevitably turn their attention elsewhere.

Zeppelin, and lately Grand Funk, stand as the current word in English hard rock (despite the fact that Grand Funk is an American band). Blood, Sweat and Tears are the opposite of Zeppelin's parody of sexuality. This group is the slick, castrated, middle of the road rock that only Columbia could do justice to in its marketing. Andrew Sarris, in one of his more charitable moments, said of director Stanley Kramer, "He will never be an original, but time has proven that he is not a fake." No one will ever say the same for Blood, Sweat and Tears.

Creedence probably sells more records than anyone else these days and are uniformly respected for their diligence and taste, as well as their ability to make catchy 45s. They may well be the best popular band in America, but if rock was where it should be that statement would be ludicrous. When a competent and talented, but unspectacular band such as this represents the height of the scene, something has surely gone wrong.

Crosby, Stills, Nash and Young may never perform together again. They were the latest contribution to the soft sound within the rock hierarchy. While gifted in any number of areas and capable of doing spectacular live shows, their records have been contrived without direction. The sense of an organic unit working tightly together seldom intrudes, which is why it is so easy to believe talk about their breaking up.

The Who were one of the truly inspired groups of the mid-sixties. After expending so much energy just getting known in this country, they have finally reduced what was once a blazingly exciting concept into their own set of rules and formulas. *Tommy* has made the Who a permanent institution, and wonderfully so. Unfortunately, it seems that their most innovative days are behind them.

The Band, like Creedence, seems to have almost everyone's respect and have created one unquestioned masterpiece, *The Band*. However, they have not ignited the massive enthusiasm common to some of the biggest bands precisely because of their conservative, thoughtful approach to performing. Also, there is no single personality upon whom public interest has focused. On *Stage Fright* they show signs of believing their own publicity a bit too much with the result that they are trying to sound wise before their time and have become too tight as well. They will continue making important music, but they are in many ways an isolated phenomenon.

Of all the major groups of the sixties still performing, Sly and the Family Stone is among the best musically. His influence on contemporary music has yet to be fully understood. He is the only major rock figure who has a deep following with both whites and blacks. He completely reshaped the content of R&B following the death of Otis Redding and the eclipse of Stax records. Motown, the greatest hit factory in the land, is currently in hot pursuit of his style. Unfortunately, his personal problems have complicated what could still be one of the most rewarding careers in the recent history of popular music. However, it is fair to say that his influence will last longer than anyone now imagines.

Such are the heavies in 1970. Omitted are Santana, Traffic, Jethro Tull, Ten Years After, the Doors, Steppenwolf, Three Dog Night and so many other names that could be pulled off the Billboard chart or a good agent's client list. But it is a fair cross-section: British and American, hard and soft, East Coast and West, and even a black man.

Every group on the list contains at least one exceptional

JON LANDAU

musician. Each one's music is stylistically well-defined. And yet something fundamental is missing. Certainly there are no names to equal Dylan, the Stones or the Beatles. With a possible exception or two, there are no legends, no passion, no glamor and no stars. And while a lot of the music is good, not too much of it is interesting and very little of it will have any impact beyond the lifespan of the group itself. For me, most of the names on the chart already conjure images of the past. The future lies mainly with an altogether different group of artists.

THE RETURN OF THE SOLO ARTIST

Rock in the late sixties was, ultimately, a harsh music. It most often communicated frenzy, confusion, anxiety, depression and anger. It often failed to give expression to the tenderer emotions. And among its most positive accomplishments were the acceptance of long rock improvisations and the breakdown of the three-minute rule for recorded music.

By the end of the sixties, countertrends, often springing from within these very groups, began to emerge. As the harsher forms became increasingly repetitious and unimaginative, musicians flirted with country music, old rock and roll, and new styles of production and arranging, often involving the use of a greater variety of instruments than are associated with rock bands. The solo artist, a concept that had all but been abandoned with the decline of the folk revival of the early sixties, was revived by the likes of Delaney and Bonnie, Leon Russell, Dave Mason, Neil Young, Rod Stewart, Elton John, Van Morrison, Eric Clapton, Joni Mitchell and James Taylor.

This group of artists is almost as diverse in character as any listing of rock groups but there are important distinctions to be made. In general, they are a more reflective, relaxed, sometimes even pastoral, group of artists. The elimination in many instances of the banks of amplifiers and the breaking of the group bond returns the accent to a single person's feelings and thoughts. In many ways it allows for a far greater range of emotional expression. The soloists are without a doubt the new *auteurs* of popular music.

As yet only three have achieved economic parity with the larger rock bands: Joe Cocker, James Taylor and Neil Young. Cocker stands like a storm in the middle of this new sea of tranquility, a magnificent anomaly. His tour last spring with the Leon Russell group of musicians was an exciting and sometimes spectacular event, as it matched one of the fine vocalists of the moment with what was at the time the best performing band in rock. The results, captured to a surprisingly accurate degree on *Mad Dogs and Englishmen,* gives us one of the few truly joyful albums of the year as well as an inspiring bit of contemporary musicianship from beginning to end. The Cocker tour not only had musicianship and artistry, but a grapes and wine decadence and glamor that was inspiring in itself. He and his colleagues carried on like true stars: they oozed with confidence and self-assurance.

It was all so refreshing, and yet inherent in its overlarge structure was its own inevitable self-destruction. It had one great quality that had been missing from so much of the music of the last two years: spontaneity. And yet one could see a hint of desperation underneath the smiles that seemed to say, "Get it while you can."

The backbone of Cocker's tour was composer-singer-pianist-arranger-producer Leon Russell. Russell worked regularly and especially on the Cocker tour with a fabulous group of West Coast musicians and free lancers that included drummers Jim Gordon and Jim Keltner, bassist Carl Radle, guitarist Don Preston and hornmen Jim Price and Bobby Keys. Many of these same men had toured earlier with Delaney and Bonnie, a white country soul duo with a distinctive style. Out of that association came organist Bobby Whitlock who has now joined with Radle and Gordon to form the Dominoes in Eric Clapton's new band, Derek and the Dominoes. Many of these same musicians accompany Russell, Clapton and Dave Mason on their solo albums.

JON LANDAU

Russell himself is a genuine talent. His "Shoot Out On the Plantation," "Hummingbird" and "Delta Lady" are among the finest songs of recent years. His piano playing, with its flashes of Earl Hines, is about the best to be heard these days and while his singing is erratic, it is also intensely personal.

Eric Clapton was a leader of the band scene in the sixties and has taken a larger role with his new group than he ever did with Cream or Blind Faith. Not yet accomplished as a singer or as an arranger, he still ignites occasional sparks that make it clear his best days are still ahead of him. Delaney and Bonnie are talented musicians who have yet to find themselves. Each of their five albums, especially *From Delaney to Bonnie,* has had its moments, but never enough of them. Dave Mason is bound to be one of the really bright faces of 1971. His first album displayed excellent songs and arrangements from beginning to end. His only shortcoming is an apparent tendency towards cuteness.

Sensing the danger of overproduction, many of the new solo artists have reacted the opposite way. Traveling alone or with small groups, they are more concerned with feelings of intimacy, naturalness, warmth and honesty. They seldom try to intimidate, overwhelm or to energize an audience physically.

Of the soloists to appear so far, James Taylor is probably the most influential and most talented and certainly the most popular in this vein. He is establishing the style of the genre in the early seventies. Contemplative, reflective, natural to an often painful degree, unpretentious, not inordinately humble, he comes before audiences as Dylan did in the early sixties and asks people to accept him for what he is. He refuses to try too hard but will always meet his audience halfway. The music of his *Sweet Baby James* is embellished in a subtle way that leaves him in the foreground. What solos there are are thoroughly de-emphasized as the lyrics and voices are once again made central. "Country Road" is an almost perfect song, with its deceptively simple beginning, its barely noticeable syncopation on the chorus, and its clear lyric line.

However, at the end of the album Taylor reminds us over a delightfully rocking Russ Kunkel on drums, that "Oh, my soul, I'm sure enough fond of my rock and roll."

Neil Young reflects a different mood than Taylor, a mood much more enriched by sophistication. Taylor's music is often painful; Young's is confused. His new album *After the Goldrush* is one of the best to be released this year and should serve to further define the contemplative approach just emerging. His languid and plaintive style is obvious emotionalizing at its best. His "Oh Lonesome Me" is a minor masterpiece.

Rod Stewart is different from both Taylor and Young because his background is so closely tied to the British rock band scene. Even now he continues to lead a schizoid existence. On the one hand he records and tours with a fine little British funk group, the Small Faces. On the other he has released two superb solo albums which comprise a much more intimate and personal statement. *Gasoline Alley* is an exceptionally brilliant piece of work which shows Stewart blending all manner of folk and rock styles into a very cohesive statement of his own. Particularly startling are his superb renditions of Elton John's "Country Comfort," his own "Gasoline Alley" and his stylized rendition of Eddie Cochran's "Cut Across Shorty." At times he blends the styles of Sam Cooke, Bob Dylan and Ewan McCall, but on *Gasoline Alley* he has emerged as a true original.

Van Morrison will undoubtedly be one of the major figures of the seventies. *Moon Dance,* one of the major releases of recent years, was a work of brilliant originality. It combined a soul-styled approach to melody and arranging with a simple and personal style of lyric writing. Morrison's voice—his phrasing, timing, tone quality and diction—are close to the summit of rock singing from any period of time. The richness of feeling in his work should set an example for every practicing singer-songwriter.

Elton John bears some resemblance to Morrison in his use

of soul devices in his composition. He has a fine voice and has thus far collaborated with an excellent lyricist, Bernie Taupin. The production on his first album was big but John used it to his own best advantage. An excellent pop piano player, his music has a depth missing from most group rock. His two best songs, "Country Comfort" and "Border Song," have been covered beautifully by Rod Stewart and Aretha Franklin respectively.

Some of the new solo artists are reminders of their own past. Figures like John Sebastian were closely tied to the first folk revival of the early sixties and are now completing some kind of musical odyssey. Through the years Sebastian has learned how to play on people's sentimentality and desire for tranquility in an almost cynical way. While his voice is rather meagre he has developed a cult based on his capacity to accept virtually anything as being groovy, warm and loving.

Randy Newman, Harry Nilsson, and Neil Diamond, in increasing order of commercial musical styles, all offer something more substantial in the solo vein. Joni Mitchell has developed the ability to express the mood of frustrated intellect in a time when thought is so undervalued to an ever-expanding degree. Melanie has emerged as the female counterpart to Sebastian in sentimentality. Carole King has come out from behind her writing career and is a beautiful pianist, arranger and singer. Her legendary talents as a songwriter are now revealed as but part of an unbelievably whole musician. And Laura Nyro, one of the most talented but confused artists of the period, may find the new mood of the audience more sympathetic to her erratic but superb talents than that of the sixties was.

The dozens of solo artists will begin to have larger show business potential than do rock groups. Johnny Cash has sold more albums than anyone else last year as he parlays his legendary background into a model for the nation's most primitive forces. Tom Jones and Glen Campbell have cleaned up in the old Sinatra market. And, in what is probably the most revealing fact of all, Elvis Presley found this year to be the right one to wage a full-scale comeback attempt. For what time could compare to the present for the return of the most stylized, personalized and possibly the most talented, of all the rock stars?

In the range of the popular solo artists, seen as a group, certain traits are clearly manifested.

There is a greater focus on songs and singing than on any form of virtuosity, particularly instrumental virtuosity, which is a quality that few of them possess. And because the work of so many of these artists is so precise and compressed, it is often best presented through records rather than live appearances. In fact what has happened, as it always has when popular music is at a crossroads, is a return to the basic facts: the singer and his song.

As the image of this type of performer jells, we can expect an increasing number of press releases that jabber about honesty, restraint, quiet, countriness and reflectiveness. And while the approach of these artists is easily parodied, those adjectives fairly describe the best of them. Before their day is over we are in for a lot more of them than anyone has already imagined. On the basis of the evidence thus far, can anyone doubt that this is a reason for some excitement and enthusiasm over the future of rock music?

Thus, the most easily identifiable major shift of early 1970 is that the R&R band scene introduced in 1963 by the Beatles and which dominated pop music through 1969 is in the initial stages of decomposition.

THE BLACK MUSIC SCENE

The black music scene has not gone untouched. The popular stars of the last few years have all gone into decline and no replacements are on the horizon. Aretha Franklin stopped making personal appearances though she is making a comeback. James Brown has lost some of his overwhelming drawing power at the box office and Motown performers continue to be locked into their plastic nightclub performing style. Only the incredibly popular Jackson 5 come before us with something wholly original to say.

In recording, the most stunning fact of recent years has been the decline of Stax records. When Stax left the Atlantic fold, the rights to Otis Redding and Sam and Dave, reverted to Atlantic Records. Since that time they have discovered they suddenly were without major stars. Perhaps the lone and not particularly strong exception is Isaac Hayes whose sentimental, talky "soul" versions of pop hits has connected with the black middle of the road audience, one of the few things keeping the company going.

Atlantic's black music has gone into something of a decline as well, as Wilson Pickett no longer turns out hit after hit; and many of those he does are not comparable to his great era. Aretha has been fair to middling, although it now looks like she is on the comeback trail with her fine version of "Don't Play That Song" and "Border Song." Sam and Dave have tragically parted company while people like Percy Sledge are in danger of drifting into obscurity. Joe Tex has started imitating Isaac Hayes to no avail and singers like DeeDee Warwick just aren't distinctive enough. Only Clarence Carter keeps churning it out, and his records are straight pop AM raido pieces by now. The problem at Atlantic revolves around the lack of a contemporary, original recording style of what used to be called soul artists, and in the failure to develop new personalities.

Those two problems do not plague Motown at the moment and they are justifiably as hot as ever. They have already developed the major new soul group of the seventies, the superb Jackson 5. Norman Whitfield continues to turn out contemporary, Sly-influenced, repetitous rhythm records on people like Edwin Starr and the Temptations. Stevie Wonder has recently developed into not only the brilliant singer heard on "Signed Sealed and Delivered," but with that record and the Spinner's "It's A Shame" a fine producer as well. The latter is the best single to come out of the company in recent months.

It is important to remember in discussing the work of black artists that they are dealing with an increasingly homogenized market in which the old class of R&B and soul records is merging more and more with the basic pop market. Secondly, it is a music still basically oriented to the 45 rpm record and AM radio. Consequently, the immediate pressure to find big stars is not as great as the need to find songwriters and producers who can turn out consistently commercial singles. No one has greater success in developing such production teams than Motown, but towards the end of the sixties the team of Kenny Gamble and Leon Huff seemed like a good pair of challengers.

Gamble and Huff, who are based in Philadelphia, are independent producers who have worked with the Intruders, the O'Jays, Dusty Springfield, Archie Bell and the Drells and Jerry Butler. Their two albums with Butler, *Ice on Ice* and *The Iceman Cometh*, represent some kind of zenith in the pop production of soul artists. Their integration of strings, horns, choirs and timpani into unbelievably well-recorded arrangements of their own melodic and lyrically sensitive songs was often astounding. Unfortunately, they and Butler have parted ways and the potential of their work may never be realized. Without Butler, whose singing is possibly the most sophisticated in all of pop music today, their productions lose their focus. Often they sound contrived and the worst of it is beginning to sound like a parody of their earlier work. Like so many producers before them, they have reduced what was refreshingly original to something trivial through repetition. The fire is gone and only another "Western Union Man," "Never Gonna Give You Up," or "Only the Strong Survive" is going to light it again.

As an offshoot of the Gamble and Huff development, other producers using the same studio and band have made interesting records in Philadelphia. Of them, the best are

JON LANDAU

done by the Delphonics, who are the masters of the trendy "sissy soul" sound. Masters of falsetto harmony, they have produced a succession of fine pop records culminating in their hit, "Didn't I Blow Your Mind This Time."

Of the other independent producers, the American studio in Memphis has gone into an entirely pop bag and has been almost unbearably successful at it. Rick Hall scores with occasional hits, but nothing new of consequence has emanated from there beyond his superb record of Carter's "Patches." The other studios in the South, with the exception of Atlantic's Criteria in Miami, have been cool.

While it may be sacrilegious to say it, the most influential black artist of recent years, with the possible exception of Jimi Hendrix, has undoubtedly been Sly and the Family Stone. In the early R&B days it was not uncommon for songs to have one chord. Sly has revitalized that concept and recharged it with contemporary rhythms and a group singing approach that is a pure delight. His versatility and capacity to synthesize seems almost endless. Both the singing and the rhythm have been completely absorbed by Motown, with the Temptations making greater use of the former and the Jackson 5 modeling themselves on the latter. Without "Dance to the Music" there never would have been "I Want You Back." His influence has been vast. Even Lulu has cut her Sly imitation of "Hum A Little Song From My Heart."

The Jackson 5 stand as something of a phenomenon amidst all this. The voice of 12-year-old Michael Jackson is so fresh and pure that it would sound good singing anything. As it is they give him the absolute best R&B being composed today and provide him with the best vocal and instrumental arrangements anyone has heard anywhere lately. The only thing keeping the Jackson 5 from establishing a new hegemony over the entire R&B scene is their youthfulness.

As with white groups, recounting the names and companies and hits only serves as an ultimate reminder of the lack of cohesiveness of this scene. The major problem is how to deal with the black record buying public when it has merged so tightly with the AM pop market. Will black record buyers ever start buying albums in preference to 45s? And are well-produced records more important than the perennial need for major personalities? On this last point, the stark fact is there are none. Sly came close but he blew it. Isaac Hayes is a fad. The Motown artists are all too limited on stage. Only Jerry Butler has real possibilities, and thus far it hasn't happened. There is no James Brown or Otis Redding to set it all right these days. There is no one with a personal vision to offer this time around. No matter how good some of the records are, the black scene remains business as usual right now. It many ways it is a cynical business indeed.

THE BIG THREE

Through most of the sixties three figures conjured up the mood of the music: the Beatles, the Rolling Stones and Bob Dylan. Not only was their music important but they fulfilled the mythic need for leadership in the period. Every era requires strong innovators and personalities to give glory to the movement; revered figures who achieve universal respect and can be held up as models to aspiring musicians as well as to audiences. Heroes. And perhaps the thing that tells us most about the changes going on in rock are the changes that overcame the heroes of the sixties.

While an enormous financial success, the Stones tour of 1969 will ultimately account for their decline as a pop myth. They simply could not live up to their own introduction: "The greatest rock and roll band in the world." People enjoyed themselves but they knew it wasn't that different, that much better, that much more exciting. As Michael Lydon noted, at each concert there was more applause at the beginning of the first number than at the end of the last. And yet the Stones knew that if they hadn't toured they would have suffered *more* precisely because it had been so long since they had communicated in the flesh and there were

JON LANDAU

millions of kids who wanted to see them who hadn't even heard "Satisfaction" when it was released in 1965. Even God has to deliver a miracle from time to time just to keep the customers satisfied. Indifference is the enemy of all deities, religious or secular.

Dylan's dilemma is much deeper. The source of the rock intelligence, the originator of the contemporary rock lyric, the synthesizer, the opera singer, the solo artist, the true outsider: he has so much to live up to, so many expectations to fulfill. And yet, like the Stones he has been caught by his past. *Self Portrait* was such a disaster precisely because it wallowed in the past. *New Morning* was a refreshing step away from the emptiness of its predecessor but not quite a large enough one. Dylan's problem is one of time. He is older than most of us and it's beginning to show in his music. That isn't necessarily bad, but who can say that it is necessarily good. He has been around long enough to see an approach that he gave definition to in the early sixties revived in the early seventies: the force of a single personality. The question facing him is whether or not the students still need their teacher.

And the Beatles: as Dylan traversed the line from underground folk hero to national and international rock star, the Beatles went from international rock stars to underground folk heroes. They played all roles to all people and were ultimately accepted by the Queen and Timothy Leary, AM and FM, black and white and by musicians of all types and in every field. Their separation, when it finally occurred, was a result of the inability of so much talent to be contained within the limits of a group. And yet it is certain that no single member of the group on his own will enjoy anything approaching the popularity or influence of the Beatles as a group.

When they began, the Beatles were superb exponents of a simple adolescent rhythmized form of popular music whose life style addressed itself to its audience's needs as perfectly as Presley had to his. And like Presley they achieved unanticipated and incalculable popularity in a brief period of time. With success undoubtedly weighing heavily on them, they did not chance to move into an openly rebellious stance, preferring instead to play the part of a flea riding an elephant. Their rebelliousness, while entirely real, was always gentle and they preferred to kneel rather than fight.

By comparison, the Stones were a more violent and openly defiant group. The media could never adjust to them and as a result a young audience could feel that they belonged to them and them alone. The Stones did not share themselves with adults in witty and clever movies. Parents would find themselves saying about the Beatles: "Well, they are cute." When Jagger finally made it to the screen in *Performance,* the adjective most commonly used to describe him was "loathsome."

The Stones music was blues-based instead of pop-based. There was no chance of them recording "A Taste of Honey" or "Till There Was You." They seemed to be flaunting their anger when the Beatles sometimes seemed to be concealing it, and as a result the audience learned to love the Stones in quite a different way than they did the Beatles.

Dylan, the American, stood apart from groups and came before his earlier audiences as a self-proclaimed prophet. His anger was the most blatantly obvious of the three, as his tone, his lyrics, and his music were all designed to express it explicitly. Many songs from his earliest period were filled with hatred ("Masters of War") and his political anger often carried over into other areas ("Ballad of a Thin Man") in his later works, only to mellow by the time he arrived at *John Wesley Harding.*

What rebelliousness there was in all three entities is tamed today. Little they do appears outrageous any longer, and in the case of Dylan and the Beatles (except for John Lennon), that appears to be the way they want it. Having grown older, they seem to have grown wiser and are less intensely engaged

JON LANDAU

in the conflicts that dominated their earlier music. It all sounds very mature, in fact quite often too mature, too self-accepting, too accepting of things as they are.

Only the Stones continue to play with defiance, but after their last American tour it's hard to take that too seriously. Rather one gathers that the Stones harp on the past in their live presentation because they have no place else to go with it. If Jagger is not outrageous, what then is left of the Stones? Unlike Dylan they cannot cope with, or do not have, the luxury of change at that level. Their music however, continues to grow, often dramatically so. It is just that the context now seems to be more theatrical than lifelike.

The truth of the matter is that the names of the sixties have become anomalies. No one looks to them for direction, no one copies them and few are still influenced by them. Despite the high level of its musical content, *Let It Bleed* had virtually no effect on pop music today. Jimmy Page and Robert Plant are more to be emulated by every flourishing high school band in the country than Mick and Keith. While there are still those who imitate the old Dylan—Arlo Guthrie is perhaps foremost among them—who has been affected by the Dylan of *Self Portrait?* And with the exception of Badfinger and other isolated instances, the last group to strive for the Beatles style was the Bee Gees. The work of the rock triptych is consumed and passed over with reverence and awe but not with the enthusiasm of past years.

None of this is meant to imply that the individuals involved will no longer create great music. They surely will. Rather it is in their relationship with an all-adoring public that change is most visible. Their music has changed—whether for better or worse—and with those changes their audience has too. Whatever happened to Bob Dylan, the Rolling Stones and the former members of the Beatles in the sixties, it will not be the shape of things in the seventies. They were once more than musicians. They were once Gods.

The alternatives are not well defined, and there is

confusion at all levels of the music industry about the direction rock is taking. For the men who stage live shows, now often unable to afford the superprices of the super-groups, the question of the day is where the stars of tomorrow are coming from. The clubs and medium-sized concert halls are in trouble. "Who are the big groups to emerge over the summer?" asked an agent in one of the largest independent booking agencies. The answer was none. Club owners are now headlining acts they might well have passed over for second billing a year ago. Some clubs have closed, others closed for the summer, and in many cities where music is being presented regularly, business is very, very soft.

Because of the current economic recession customers seem to be concentrating more money on fewer attractions, whether buying records or tickets. As a result, a handful of acts have become incredibly popular, while it has become harder than ever for a middle-level band to get along or a new band to get off the ground. For the past two and a half years, since the success of *Sgt. Pepper,* the album sweepstakes has begun to look like the singles game, with many companies shotgunning it: releasing large numbers of albums on the assumption that someting will catch on. While they may have been right in the short run, in the long run they have saturated the market, making it harder for talented new musicians to break through the mass of pap at the rate of a 150 new albums released *every* week along with 200 new singles per week.

THE RAT RACE

It's now widely assumed that sooner or later the audience will be unable to absorb any more of a particular kind of music, and everyone in the business is searching desperately for what's coming next. If someone *were* to find the next thing, though, it's inevitable that he would rush it too fast, and record it to death before it had a chance to grow into

JON LANDAU

anything at all. Once there were dozens of talented musicians who only needed to get inside a studio to do something interesting; now there are few who don't get a chance to record something years before they are prepared for it. There was a time when going to see a band play on a weekend could be something to look forward to for days. Now it can often be an invitation to depression.

Rock and roll is madness and the method that has been imposed on it is too rational, too businesslike, and too orderly, and if something doesn't break loose soon, it will kill off what energy is left for a good long time. Rock, the music of the sixties, was a music of spontaneity. It was a folk music—it was listened to and made by the same group of people. It did not come out of a New York office building where people sit and write what they think other people want to hear. It came from the life experiences of the artists and their interaction with an audience that was roughly the same age. As that spontaneity and creativity have become more stylized and analyzed and structured, it has become easier for businessmen and behind-the-scenes manipulators to structure their approach to merchandising music.

The process of creating stars has become a routine and a formula as dry as an equation. But thankfully, if history is any judge, it is only a matter of time before adhering to that equation will reach a point of diminishing returns and those who stick to it will pay the consequences. For while equations don't change, the audiences, musicians and music, do change.

A cycle is coming to an end. Rock's first phase, which truly began with "I Want to Hold Your Hand," ended with the break-up of the Beatles. And amidst the economic tightening in the industry, and the changing character of the audience, something new is forming. Whether or not it will lead to something basically different than the music of the last six years cannot be discerned as of yet, but the change is now.

There is a new audience that grew up on the music of the sixties that is going to require and demand a music for the seventies. No one yet knows what that audience will want or what the musicians will give them. But one thing is certain: that audience *will* have music. For whether we know it or not, we are all committed to music. And whether we believe it or not, it is too late to stop now.

JON LANDAU

Rock, Recordings
and Rebellion
IRVING LOUIS HOROWITZ

In the sociology of music, most analysis seems to start with the musician instead of his music. That is, standard stratification variables of class and racial backgrounds, urban life styles, regional and sectional characteristics and so forth are generally employed. Some very useful work has been done within these categories, but my own feeling is that to arrive at a somewhat deeper understanding of the sociology of music, we should begin with the musical product and end with the social sources and background of music. Aside from the priority of the art object over the art producer or art consumer, there is an additional strategic advantage: namely, establishing a bona fide among those who know the music you are talking about, even though they may know little or no sociology.

The gap between the esoteric knowledge held by musicians and the exoteric belief systems held by listeners is exceptionally wide. Unlike the fields of politics, psychology and economics in which everyone fancies himself an expert, professional distance between musician and listener is easily established. In music, the notational system by which the creative process is expressed is so removed from the knowledge of ordinary listeners that communication between artist and audience, at the verbal level at least, is difficult and sometimes quite impossible. My starting point, then, will be the product and the place where artist and audience interest meet most significantly—the market, the recording. The record is to the musician what the book is to the academic scholar. It is the recognition of his importance to a wider public. It is the focus of his musical energies, all directed toward making the recording different from all others, or at least different enough to be purchased. The musician measures success precisely in terms of the aesthetic worth of the product and the sales of that product to a nonmusician audience, or at least an audience beyond his known circle of friends in the musical world.

The recording represents the transformation of an ephemeral idea into a copyrighted product; a musical moment into a durable commodity. Jazz, and especially rock, are both essentially twentieth century aesthetic concepts, but they emerge coincidentally with a market system that defines worth in terms of saleability—specifically, the sale of the recording. The jazz ambience has been less willing to accept this fact, and has therefore hesitated to fully exploit the medium through which the artist speaks to a wider audience. The rock subculture, being thoroughly convinced that the recording is an expression of worth, has been more innovative; the use of electric guitars, Moog synthesizers, the use of amplifiers as musical instruments, and so forth, are all clearly pegged to the product as record. Thus, what starts as an effort at bottling and selling the ephemeral idea, ends with the market product, the record, beginning to determine the musical structure, and the ephemeral idea itself.

The recording not only provides legitimacy to rock performers by proving their worth in market terms, but also warrants their authenticity. Rock music listeners usually hear a group first on recordings; then, later on, they see the group in person. The recording provides the audience with an

IRVING LOUIS HOROWITZ

objective standard of measurement for determining whether the live performance is better than, the same as, or worse than the recorded performance. The live performance also enables the performing artist to advertise his new disc, or new album. Few performances fail to include an announcement to the effect that "the next number is from our new album on our very own label, and can be heard again if you like the live performance." In other words, the crucial item of exchange between artist and audience is clearly the recording, rather than, as it was 50 years ago, sheet music.

The recording is important to rock groups for other reasons as well. In their live performances, musicians are constantly involved in electronic processes. Though the music is reasonably, or as some may declare, unreasonably simplistic, the electronic apparatus they must learn to manipulate is quite complex. Because of this relative isomorphism between rock music and technology, the impulse to define success in terms of the recording is not simply or even primarily a desire for wide communication with an amorphous audience, nor is it a pecuniary drive unique to musicians; rather, it stems from realization that the gap between the engineering of sound and the creation of music has narrowed to a remarkable degree. Thus, the legacy of dodecaphonic and electronic music has not been lost in classical experimentation, but has been absorbed, though largely unconsciously, in the rock tradition. The recording situation allows the musician maximum control in the manipulation of technology, and thus, in his artistic creation.

Finally, by starting with the recording, we can encompass the whole gamut of social actors in the music business: the recording company, the booking agents, the performing artists, the engineering and recording experts, publicists and propagandists and pushers of all sorts. For this reason, I shall simply examine a series of recordings that illustrate the theme of this paper: the relationship of modern jazz to hard rock. The selection of recordings will not be exhaustive or exclusive; but rather representative and illustrative of major trends and tendencies. But first, let me review the background of jazz and of rock, and the similarities and discontinuities between the two.

There is a parallel between the history of societies and the history of their arts. Just as there is a historical continuity in science, there is also a historical continuity in the scientific-technical aspect of the arts (it was not mere chance that perspective became consolidated during the Renaissance—Europe was discovering the third dimension in painting).

While the sociologist studies the social, historical, economic and cultural events which account for the development of an intellectual and artistic movement such as the Renaissance, the musician can translate the manifestations of that movement into specific expressions: Humanism gives birth to tonal language, and ecclesiastic modes which lack the lyricism of the new language are rejected. The counterpoint extends its methods toward new horizons which are part of that expression. Another example might be provided by the translation of Enlightenment absolutism into music in the form of the homophony of the classical period. Or the ideas of freedom in the French Revolution which are echoed in the chromatics and the gradual development from sonata form to the cyclical form of the Romantic movement.

Jazz also underwent, in the course of 80 years, the change of a dynamic society, reflected in its schools and innovations. The jazz musician—black or white—gradually acquired a certain lucidity regarding the sound materials with which he was working. The mixture of rhythms and modes of African polyphony mingled with the tonal homophony of the European colonizers. The resulting synthesis was jazz, and the perception of musicians (who are always in the forefront of society regarding the apprehension of sounds materials) became wider. What makes such an analysis difficult is the fact that jazz never existed in pure form. (For example, Bix Beiderbecke "discovered" Debussy.) The important thing is

IRVING LOUIS HOROWITZ

that musicians such as Thelonious Monk, Charlie Parker and Dizzy Gillespie achieved results similar to those of Bartok and Stravinsky by the way of instinct and the extension of tradition. Lennie Tristano and Ornette Coleman, on the other hand, opened the door to tonal dissolution. They were all the product of a complex period—from World War II until the present.

But this tonal dissolution involved, in extramusical terms, the dissolution of the musical audience. The deeper the music, the further removed jazz became from the dance tradition. Into this void of a music without audience, and a form without content, the rock musician emerged. At first clumsily, almost foolishly in the form of sexual exhibitionism and musical inanities—such as in the performances of Elvis Presley and Jerry Lee Lewis. Indeed, the Sha-Na-Na now make a living parodying such "music of the fifties." Yet, even in its early days, rock provided direct percussive expression to dance needs, and reestablished communion between artist and audience without retreating to the absurd banalities of the fox trot, the Vienna waltz and the Virginia Reel.

The first stage in the development of rock was the sacrifice of musical complexity for the sake of capturing an audience; the second step was to solidify that audience by message music—by an appeal to the rising political consciousness of a generation no less than by an appeal to dance forms that were clearly generational in character. Only when both these stages were reached, did the third stage of musical innovation involving atonalities, electronics and art music become possible. It might well be that rock is doomed to replicate the cycle of jazz, with its attendant separation from the dance form and its ultimate loss of mass audience, but in the meantime a new art form has been born.

Although technical perfection for the most part remains an unfulfilled goal in rock music, there are notable successes. Among them are the rejection of complication for its own sake, the return to a more direct expression of emotions and an attempt to move beyond a jazz scene thoroughly lacking in extramusical direction (with the possible exception of men like Archie Shepp and John Coltrane—although they have yet to generate a significant audience for their message) by introducing lyrics of political and personal significance.

More significantly, the history of every art form can be formulated as the following: Each new form of expression requires a new technology for its fulfillment. And here there is a complicated syndrome at work. For on the one hand, the young harbor a powerful resentment for a technological idiocy that has brought mankind to the brink of nuclear, bacteriological and chemical warfare. On the other hand, the musical requisites of rock involve a remarkably advanced form of technology, the implications of which are only now being drawn. In the larger societal situation, there is a demand on the part of many radical young people for simplicity, and a utopian longing for nature and mother earth, rather than society and grandfather pollution. But the young's rejection of these aspects of the larger society is radically different from their response to the new music. The rock scene is extraordinarily concerned with technological innovation.

A young sociologist, Paul M. Hirst, has recently taken note of this fact in an article entitled "The Economics of Rock" that appeared in *The Nation* in March 1970. His summary comment is quite appropriate to our discussion:

> The contribution of modern technology is important. All phases of rock music have become increasingly tied to technology, from concert staging and recording techniques to record retailing and audience management. Musicians and their audiences regard better amplifiers, microphones, tape recorders, film techniques, record packaging, outdoor festivals and speaker systems as a natural and desirable part of their environment. They assume, with accustomed indifference, that the gadgets they've grown up with are to be used when

needed, and simply ignored when irrelevant. Most young people including "dropouts" and "dissenters," are neither alienated, as some have argued, by such signs of the age as television, moon shots and atomic weapons, nor are they particularly impressed. They seem only "natural" to a generation which ahs always known them. While this attitude is now starting to be challenged by a growing concern for our environment, it is still too early to pronounce today's vanguard youth seriously hostile to modern gadgetry. Persuasive evidence that we are still far from a wholesale "back to nature" movement is the overwhelming popularity of rock and roll, and all the technology it encompasses.

The importance of this youth ambivalence to technology can hardly be overestimated. It points up their dialectical attitudes toward technology, not simply a foolish concern on the part of the young for a return to musical primitivism or sectional chauvinism.

The jazz musicians, especially the followers of Gillespie and Monk, are most resistant to technological invention. In fact, they tend to think that any device not to be found in a nineteenth century symphony orchestra is by definition not a musical instrument. However, it is not primarily at the technological level that objections are registered, but rather at the sociological level. The new electronic phase upsets the existing professional status arrangements. It introduces new personnel and makes new demands on established performers. Only the recent herculean efforts of Miles Davis, that ever-inventive figure, have moved beyond this technological Ludditism; and interestingly, as the composition of his new group shows, beyond racial exclusivism as well.

With respect to the tonal dissolution that jazz is said to have exhibited, my own feeling is that this is more myth than reality. The jazz musician has tended to use shifting tonal centers rather than to move toward the kind of tonal dissolution advocated by Berg or Schoenberg. In this connection, I would say that many rock musicians have done much the same kind of things as their jazz predecessors. They have not worried about formal invention as much as they should have. But this may be because musicians in active creation rarely concern themselves with their place in the history of modern popular music.

The problem here is not one of integrity but of musicality. The rock musician is concerned about the dance elements in his output—that is, the relationship between sound and movement. I have the distinct impression that the modern jazz musician has come to envision himself very much like a member of a chamber ensemble. This is reflected in the behavior of the Modern Jazz Quartet and in the Charles Mingus quintet, which often make outrageous demands of silence on the audience. The jazz musician has come to expect a non-emotional response to emotion; which in some sense is precisely what the rock culture is in rebellion against. The jazz generation has become the older generation. It has done so inadvertently by absorbing the general culture (and the genteel values) of classical music, with its fixed separation of artist and audience.

Music expresses its times and its anxieties, but certain expressions of these anxieties are more effective and others less effective. The anomaly, the contradiction, of an all-black group like that run by Archie Schepp or John Handy is that they are listened to by a largely white audience. This certainly lends a note of doubt to the belief that theirs is an effective form of black protest. It more likely alleviates white guilt. In this sense, the rock scene, being generational rather than racial, suffers less from the kind of black-white contradiction that has plagued jazz from its inception. Unlike jazz, hard rock is basically a white music. A strong connection does exist between soul music and hard rock, but hard rock is a sound apart: white, youthful, disengaged, sexually blunt and for the most part ideologically closer to pantheism than to socialism. But even though rock music is a white music, it makes no affirmation of being white, nor does it even covertly affirm supremacist tendencies that were prevalent in previous white sounds from Paul Whiteman in the twenties to Elvis Presley in the fifties. The best rock musicians have been unabashed in their praise of the black traditions of their craft, and unashamed to express such continuities in musical terms. This makes it possible for rock to achieve an intellectual integrity, and perhaps ultimately a synthesis, that has always been one giant step beyond the nonideological and undisturbed jazz musician.

No more than a decade ago, recordings were being made for "square" audiences who loved the classics and hated jazz. It is a sign of new generation fissures that the jazz audience has moved over into the camp of the squares, seeking comfort and solace in its "art" music over and above "pop" music. The tradition of the new, it seems, must always be less than welcomed by participants and advocates of established cultural traditions. This only proves that staying young beyond one's chronology is a complex and often painful undertaking and that those who even make the attempt subject themselves to criticism if not downright ridicule. As Marty Balin and Paul Kanter of the Jefferson Airplane explain: "One generation got old/One generation got soul."

The following selection of rock albums is based on considerations of innovation and invention that hopefully reveal certain jazz qualities: high improvisation, solid arrangement, awareness of social roots and tradition, novel harmonies and rhythmic patterns and so forth. It may not be the best hard rock of the last few years but my own guess is that were such a list compiled, even the *cogniscenti* would agree that the following albums are outstanding.

Country Joe and the Fish! Electric Music for the Mind and Body (Vanguard VRS09244). Like many groups, this one is uneven; but some of the cuts, like "Grace" and "Porpoise Mouth" are a remarkable cross between Ravel of the Bolero and Schifrin of the Jazz Mass. This group has come a long way from its original adolescent recordings. They retain a radicalism of extramusical purpose with a certain musical integrity which prevents them from becoming commercial in the bad sense. They have the old jazz concern for the negative consequences of being popular without point. And they act out that concern by wonderfully outrageous assaults on political moguls of Americana. Perhaps this group sounds fresh because they manage to be political without falling into prepackaged ideological traps.

This group has the unique ability to "secularize" rather than "sacralize" their sound and lyrics. Direct assault is made on all forms of mystification from astrology to drugs to political conformism. And by the careful avoidance of a simple-minded "heavy" sound, the lyrical aspects of their performances remain clear and uncluttered. Because of their premature radicalism, Country Joe and the Fish have not had the advantages of a big recording label, but rather have joined performers like Joan Baez and Pete Seeger on a label of distinction and taste. The young listeners have caught up to this group politically, and it has now become a question whether this group can meet the pace in creative musical terms.

Barry Goldberg: Two Jews Blues (Buddah Records BDS05029). Goldberg is a major figure from the musical underground, who never quite surfaced. His arrangements and work for the Mother Earth group make them rise beyond the pedestrian. In this particular album, he is free to experiment much more. He knows more about jazz and is better able to integrate the jazz tradition than nearly any other hard rock soloist (with the possible exception of John Kahn and Skip Prokop). The key cut here is "Spirit of Trane"—a veritable review of Coltrane and the movement from "waves of sound" hard jazz to a similar technique in hard rock. The title of the album is strange. This is not a religious mish-mash of talmudism; but the work of a hard-driving, alienated third generation Jewish soul who knows where it's at from the street-black viewpoint. He is an important ideological variation on the theme of Jewish alienation from wealth and Jewish identification with suffering of the poor.

Rolling Stones: Beggars Banquet (London PL-539). This is probably the key album by the Stones—musically and politically. Everything works well, especially the lyrics by Mick Jagger and Keith Richard. I doubt that this group will ever replicate this achievement; certainly their more recent album performances are much weaker, more eclectic and confused in direction. It is hard to remain a "Street Fighting Man" when one is so rich and famous, or fall in love with a "Factory Girl" and make cheap Hollywood films. But this album is a direct musical assault on the conservatism of the Beatles, on the freakout and copout approach they have come to represent. The Stones remain a real group, while the Beatles have become a recording session. The quality of their performance reveals the difference between gigging musicians and studio musicians. Perhaps the jazz element is less profound than the traditonal blues and folk elements in the Rolling Stones—but the roots are there; and this is a critical album to an understanding of what the hard rock revolution is about, and particularly how that musical revolution develops a political awareness.

The juxtaposition of the Stones with the Beatles is hardly accidental. They compare and contrast in critical respects. Both represented the two major British groups of most of the sixties; both developed international reputations by simulating an amalgam of American sounds from rock to jazz; and both produced individual performers of such noteworthiness as to transcend the customary group identities. But the gulfs and the gaps are even more noteworthy: The Stones represented radicalism in extramusical content, while the Beatles moved steadily toward a conservative ideology disguised by a continuing faith in the drug scene. The Stones recorded for London Records while the Beatles recorded for Electric Musical Industries, a subsidiary of the American-owned Capitol Record Company. Once the level of musical capabilities of the Stones became equal to that of the Beatles, the choice between them had to be made on extramusical grounds; and in effect the two groups came to symbolize the two main tendencies of the youth culture, at least within an Anglo-American context. Needless to say, beneath the manipulation of conflicting political symbols was the common drive for financial payoff. Radical lyrics and conservative lyrics, the political culture versus the drug culture, the folk style in contrast to the mystical style—all seemed to coalesce in these two groups and in this way their audiences were able to simulate as well as absorb the larger political and economic struggles going in the world.

The Beatles: Revolver (Capitol T-2576). The one really great album the Beatles made, *Revolver* holds together musically, without the freakish, bizarre qualities of the later albums, and the amateurish childishness of the early *werke*. It has things that hard rock needs more of: above all, a sense of humor and a range of emotions that fall somewhere between love and hate, rather than at the poles of expression and the precipice of emotion. From a jazz viewpoint, the best cut is "Tomorrow Never Knows"—although the entire album swings hard and clean. Also this recording is not over-engineered, the way nearly every Beatle album has been since 1966.

The tragedy of the Beatles is commercialism with a vulgar vengeance. Business interests, pressures to make movies, discover new talent, all the mawkish things that musicians are better off leaving to their press agents have come, sadly, to be the hallmarks of the Beatles. The choice between a drug culture and a political culture has become increasingly urgent. And the Beatles have, in the main, opted in favor of heroin and against heroism.

The Beatles evolved from a hip youth cult, strongly identified with the aspirations of English working class

IRVING LOUIS HOROWITZ

sectors, to an international recording and commercial combine. In this not so mysterious magical tour, they created the basis of their dissolution as a group. Individual performers became key, personal mawkish styles became exaggerated, and the process of arranging and orchestrating became completely detached from the group itself. The collapse of the Beatles was heralded by their final album, in which a Mantovani-like string ensemble was dubbed into simple musical lines to create a thoroughly outmoded sound typical of the late forties and antithetical to the needs of the late sixties. And this drift signified a decisive break with a major portion of the youth culture as it exists, and a mystification of life processes that took on all but the formal apparatus of conservative Christian symbolism of a rather unsophisticated variety. The urge for peace was drowned by demands for piety; and under the circumstances, perhaps the dissolution of the most famous of all rock groups was inevitable.

Big Brother and the Holding Company: Cheap Thrills* (Columbia KCS-9700). This album presents a major event—the best jazz singer since Ma Rainey and Bessie Smith in the white form of Janis Joplin. She is the real thing, and her album illustrates a key facet of the new music: the role of the collective. Although Joplin is clearly the most viable commercial variable here, the group rather than the individual vocalist is featured. When this essential aspect of the new sound was forgotten, and Joplin attained dubious star status, the group dissolved; and in part, so did Joplin. "Piece of My Heart" and "Ball and Chain" are brilliant. If only Aretha Franklin could have such a supporting group instead of the cheap Mantovani style backup that makes a mockery of her great talent. The musicianship here is first class, and Joplin and the group led by Albin, Getz, Gurley *et al,* are really fine.

Perhaps the most revealing description of Joplin is contained in what probably was meant to be high flattery—the program notes for her Canadian "Festival Express" perform-

*This article was written prior to Janis Joplin's death in October 1970.

ances in the summer of 1970:

> Janis Joplin will probably explode some day. It's inevitable. She'll be up there on stage, shrieking and stomping and wailing over some old Big Mama Thornton blues tune, a white girl trying to sound so black her voice comes in all colors. And she'll laugh her hooker laugh as she smooths down her hooker clothes, as she calls them, that ersatz combination of feathers and frills, ankle bracelets and satins and ribbons. It'll happen at one of those incredible moments when Janis suddenly sounds like she's singing in the wrong decade. It'll happen with a bottle of Southern Comfort nearby, and some guy nearby, and . . . well, you know. It'll happen when she'll be trying for that one note that's never been had before. When she'll be singing harder, higher and faster than anybody has sung before. It'll happen because it will be the only thing left for her to do. It'll happen that way.

In point of fact, Joplin is expected to "explode," since of all white singers, her conception of music comes closest to the black sound, and her extramusical conception of black life is the suicidal model so typical of past blues singers. That black life has changed, and black aspirations have become antithetical to such neurotic models only makes Joplin an anomaly, albeit a tragic one, living out in vicarious white form the long since dead "black experience."

The Iron Butterfly: Ball (Atco SD-33-280). This is an unusual group. They incorporate many elements from Bach to Shankar. They have an eclecticism that derives from a strong identification with the drug scene and the return to astrology and related antiscientific trends. They have not quite jelled yet; perhaps they never will. Or perhaps they are into a mystical bag that a supreme rationalist must question if not reject. But the mystique of the new music is an important cultural element linking drugs to resistance. They are on the right track in terms of innovative possibilities. Listen to "In the Crowds," "Fill With Fear" and "Belda Beat" for some

IRVING LOUIS HOROWITZ

idea of the Butterfly's direction. This is not a polished group, but it is a major attempt to make a new music that integrates vocals, orchestration and invention, with the entire drug culture.

Creedence Clearwater Revival: Bayou Country (Fantasy 8387). This is a powerful group, coming out of the Arkansas country and blues tradition. They exhibit the benefits of amplification and engineering effects, at the same time leaving intact certain driving musical values. This is hard rock of the sixties, like the Jazz Messengers represented hard jazz in the fifties: uncompromising devotion to the role of rhythm, with melody and harmonic invention playing a lesser role. And like the Blakey machine, CCR tends to get themselves into a groove from which there is no escape. This is a highly repetitious group. But can they ever swing and drive! They have the conviction and uncompromising drive that the jazz feeling is all about. "Proud Mary," "Bootleg" and "Keep on Chooglin" are major attempts to universalize what in the past were regionalisms. This is the best of healthy nonsubjective hard rock; just as the Butterfly is the best of the subjective wing—if one can speak in such a strange language about music. Creedence's move backward to a Bill Haley's Comets sound indicates a return to musical history to escape from the hard tasks of creativity, not an unusual decision in this competitive environment.

The Band: The Band (Capital STAO 132). If the appelation "Bob Dylan's back up group" or the publicity in *Time* magazine does not do this group in, then we will have a major musical event. That we probably have already. It remains to be seen whether or not The Band can sustain themselves; for here the ideology of country and western music is fused with the more radical ideology of hard rock. "The Night They Drove Old Dixie Down" is perhaps one of the best and yet one of the most disquieting events in the rock scene—since it represents a veritable *Gone With the Wind* in musical terms. Like the book and movie, "The Night They Drove Old Dixie Down" portrays both the antiwar sentiments and regional passions that inflamed the South in the aftermath of the Civil War.

The frustration of white rebellious youth with the black scene is nowhere better evident than in the current celebration of The Band. Dylan's integration of the country and western sound has also taken on elements of working class populism (listen to the Johnny Cash *San Quentin* album), but they remain poorly articulated in extramusical terms. Musically, there is no doubt, however, that The Band has it. This is a polished professional group in every way, with a universally appealing good story on every record side, and with a moral lesson behind every story—also near and dear to the youth culture of today. All of this is attractively presented in precise musical terms. This album grows and does not wear on the listener, because sophistication rather than simplicity underlies every note and every line of music. I cannot imagine a firmer grip on musical invention that relies so heavily on the country and western blues traditions. This is a "rural" music, and its extraordinary reception indicates a strong longing for utopia and the future that is really the past. But the music is worth paying attention to—since the elements of creativity are all present. No musical revolution is ever a perfect expression of the age—but some groups well express the longings and confused hopes of revolutionists— and this The Band does remarkably well.

Carlos Santana: Santana (Columbia CS-0891). Santana offers a hard rock equivalent to the Afro-Cuban jazz rhythms which gripped many of the more popular varieties of music in the fifties. It has a similar percussive emphasis, with a variegated, inventive use of bongos and congas augmenting a rich texture of guitar and organ. Unfortunately, like the Afro-Cuban materials, there is a tendency toward musical repetition, and the broad use of rhythmic color at the expense of the more serious elements in contemporary rock. Further, while the instrumental portions tend to be innovative, the vocal arrangements tend to be cheap and banal. This group would

IRVING LOUIS HOROWITZ

do well to distinguish between good taste and ethnicity. But this is a problem common to hard rock in general.

To get a good idea of what this group can do at their best, two sides stand out: "Treat," which offers very good jazz blues variations; and "Soul Sacrifice" where the work on piano and organ by Carlos Santana and Gregg Rolie is superb. The work of Santana, like that of Don Ellis, can better be appreciated in live performance than on recordings. Their fantastic percussive inventions too often transcribe poorly on records. Here too, this can probably just as easily be said about most top quality rock groups. Just as in jazz, the element of spontaneity and creativity of live performance is a central factor in the rock scene; groups that fail to innovate soon fail to attract wide audience support. What is important in Santana specifically, is the satisfactory marriage of different musical traditions. Santana is the "hard" equivalent of such "soft" musicians as Jose Feliciano. He represents, in a strange way, the merging musical consciousness of the Chicano. He is doing for the California Spanish-speaking peoples what Mongo Santamaria, Machito, Prado, Puente and others did for the Puerto Rican young a decade earlier in the New York area. These marginal outsider groups employ the dominant cultural expression of the age—be it rock or jazz—to give form to their special impoverished status in American society.

Ten Wheel Drive: Construction No. 1 and *Brief Replies* (Polydor 24-4008; 24-4024). This musical organization is probably the closest thing in the rock field to a pure jazz concept. They feature a brilliant, rough-hewn blues singer, Genya Raven, who manages to combine superb musicianship with her vocal talents. Like Janis Joplin and Bonnie Bramlett, she has listened closely to the black singers from Ma Rainey and Bessie Smith, to Billie Holiday and Ella Fitzgerald. The tenor saxophone of Dave Leibman is strongly reminiscent of Coltrane, and when given the opportunity do so, as in "Interlude: A View of the Soft," he is uniformly clean in his execution. The hard driving ensemble work at times overwhelms individual solo efforts, but the unusual Basie-type arrangements are so distinctive as to offset the absence of conventional rock progressions; although they are subtly expressed through the guitar work of the group.

The superior work of the ten-tet is enhanced by the trumpet, tenor sax, trombone and other instruments not customarily found in the rock band. The problem is a lack of integration: the winds and woodwinds want to play jazz, while the guitars want to play rock; and even the tight arrangements do not so much solve as disguise the disparity in traditions. On both these albums, which both emanate from the same period—1969-1970—there is an awareness of a unique attempt at "jazz rock"—a driving rock base over which is added a jazz chording with a rock or blues solo. On such tunes as "Tightrope" Genya sounds like Janis; while on "Candy Man Blues" she can sound like Bessie Smith might have with amplification.

Ten Wheel Drive is everything that Blood, Sweat and Tears is not: spontaneous, driving and yet highly disciplined. The group writes its own materials; and the work of Aram Schefrin and Mike Zager (two of the ten wheels) is very consciously attempting to bridge the jazz and rock traditions in a meaningful way. Even if all the pitfalls have not been cleared, the attempt is remarkably sound, and far beyond the usual cliché-ridden efforts to introduce simple blues phrasing into rock presentations. The lyrics also provide some good and tough East Coast elements; and these can be heard to advantage in "I Am A Want Ad" and "Home in Central Park." Like their West Coast counterparts, this group is archetypical of much that is happening, rather than a special musical force unto itself. If the East Coast sound is hard, intellectual and rationalistic, it still lacks one major ingredient of West Coast rock: a specified anger with direction.

Sly and the Family Stone: Stand! (Epic BN-26456). This is an exciting musical unit; one of the few interracial groups around, it manages to get beyond some stagemanaged rent-a-nigger or rent-a-whitey type of sound meant to appease naive liberal audiences. Musically, this is a hard swinging unit, strong on the blues tradition, and perhaps at times better in extramusical sentiment than in musical performance. Yet, this group has a tremendous driving quality, with a rich musical liturgy. Frankly, their less ideological materials are the most musically engaging, such as: "Sing a Simple Song," "Sex Machine," "You Can Make it if You Try." What a weird anomaly this group is: raising the banner of black and white forever, while everyone is running about taking up black separatism and cultural nationalism. Perhaps this is what makes the group so well-liked. They appeal to the middle class and essentially liberal youth-musical constituency who comprise a large part of the rock audience. However, their musical integrity would make them worth hearing whatever the peculiarity of their ideological or racial constellation. And who knows but that the slogan next year won't be togetherness instead of separateness. We old liberals clearly need such an option, and Sly and the Family Stone provide one.

The Grateful Dead: Workingman's Dead (Warner Bros. 1869). The Grateful Dead are perhaps more linked with the fate and fortune of California-based rock and roll than any other group. In that sense, their movement from funky Memphis-styled rock and roll, to an abstract expressionist "acid rock" phase, through a country-blues style is indicative of the toughening up of the rock sound generally, and the growing disenchantment of American youth with a purely non-political and drug-oriented subculture. The *Workingman's Dead* album, which, although not as "heady in its solos as the earlier *Live Dead* album, has a sense of returning to the folk and blues traditions charted by The Band but with a firmer extramusical content. Many of the problems earlier encountered by the Grateful Dead: repetition in solo lines, lack of rhythmic and melodic definition, absence of a clear extramusical statement in the lyrics, have been satisfactorily resolved in the newer Dead recordings. And if any group has demonstrated a selfless dedication to free concerts, free drugs and free love, it has been the Dead—for ironically, although they lack the technical proficiency of the Jefferson Airplane, they seem to capture in their music the very probings, albeit partially understood, that characterize the most civilized city in America, which must yet remain part of the most uncivilized country in the industrial world.

Jefferson Airplane: Volunteers (RCA Victor LSP-4238). This is one of the most exciting and innovative recordings made by an American group. Grace Slick is a marvelous singer, and for this album, the regular members of the Airplane have been augmented by such superb performers as Stephen Stills of Crosby, Stills, Nash and Young and Jerry Garcia of The Grateful Dead. This group gets better with every album and politically more serious. From "We Can Be Together" to "Volunteers (Got a Revolution)" this is powerful statement of radical youth. As a literary sentiment, the group might sound contrived, but not as a musical expression. They exhibit a sectional West Coast element—West Coast radicalism—fuzzy and even bizarre ("Up Against the Wall Motherfucker"), but nonetheless, generous and nonsectarian. Anyone can join the movement led by the Airplane. The West Coast with its culture of civility is remarkably receptive; and the militance ultimately becomes a part of humanism. But this album cannot and should not be reduced to ideological content; its musical essence is paramount. In so many ways, this recording summarizes the best of the hard rock scene—the professionalism of The Band, the drive of Creedence Clearwater Revival, the radicalism of the Rolling Stones, the racial egalitarianism of Sly and so forth.

To understand the Airplane is to appreciate what the culmination of the moralizing sixties offered. That this moral energy may blow up into a paroxysm of money-grubbing was made clear at the strange final "concert" turned mass-movement of the Rolling Stones on their recent United States tour. The group of Hell's Angels they hired "to protect them from the audience" beat to death a listener while the Stones were playing "Sympathy for the Devil" and while a member of the Jefferson Airplane was doing his best to save the victim's life. Theatricality has turned bitter and acrimonious in the seventies. The hard rockers, like the hard boppers before them, are not sure of their audience, either its size or substance. There are difficult years ahead, and maybe the music I have just been speaking of will appear obsolete and absurdly out of tune in the upcoming period, as jazz now seems to so many members of the present anti-American generation.

Clearly, any devotee of the rock music scene has his own favorites. The jazz aspects of Mike Bloomfield and Al Kooper, the endless inventiveness and seriousness of Eric Clapton, the Jelly Roll Morton piano playing of Leon Russell, the remarkable early efforts of Canned Heat, or the "blue-eyed soul" of Delaney and Bonnie—all of these can and do have their partisans, and each can be said to reveal definite jazz sources for inspiration. But the individual performer or performance is secondary. The hard rock scene at its best is a musical trip that seeks to get beyond an ego trip. It is not a study in priestly "influences" (one of the most decadent and wasteful forms of energy among followers of jazz—and sometimes the musicians themselves—was to track down a musical ancestry with relentless energy, as if the absence of lineage was the same as the absence of legitimacy) but a vast movement toward the redefinition of American culture. And the redefinition is a task uniquely performed by the young, since it is they alone who combine invention and exaggeration, reason and motion, word and sound, music and politics.

Hard rock may be done in by popularity, commercialism and festivals. More likely it will collapse from internal ailments: becoming too artsy-craftsy or removed from the dance form that gave rise to jazz and rock alike, and thus distancing itself from the folk sources of its original inspiration. But in the meantime, this is the most significant music having a mass social base yet to appear in American society.

IRVING LOUIS HOROWITZ

About the Authors

Howard S. Becker is professor of sociology at Northwestern University. He is the author of *Outsiders: Studies in the Sociology of Deviance* and editor of *The Other Side: Perspectives on Deviance*, and most recently, *Making the Grade: The Academic Side of College Life.*

Morroe Berger is professor of sociology at Princeton University. In the sociology of art, he has written an introduction to *Madame de Stael on Politics Literature and National Character*, which he also translated and edited.

Robert Faulkner is assistant professor in the sociology department at the University of Massachusetts. He is the author of *Hollywood Studio Musicians*. His current interests include studying the work and careers of symphony musicians, and professional hockey players.

Nat Hentoff is associate professor of the Graduate School of Education at New York University, staff writer for *The New Yorker*, and columnist for *The Village Voice, Jazz & Pop*, and other publications. Among his books are *The Jazz Life* and *Jazz Country*, and most recently, *The New Equality.*

Irving Louis Horowitz is professor and chairman of the department of sociology at Livingston College, Rutgers University. Among his recent

289

books are *The Knowledge Factory* and *The Struggle Is the Message.* He has written on the subject of music for *Psychology Today, New Society* and *trans*action magazine, of which he is editor-in-chief.

Howard Junker is a former associate editor of *Newsweek,* and a contributor to *Esquire, The Nation, Playboy* and *Rolling Stone.* He has recently finished an anthology, *An Apocalyptic Reader,* and his autobiography.

Jon Landau has been writing about rock since 1966 and is currently record review editor of *Rolling Stone.* He has produced several rock albums and is finishing work on a collection of his writing to be published in 1972.

Neil Leonard is associate professor of American Civilization at the University of Pennsylvania. The author of *Jazz and the White Americans,* he has written several articles on jazz and is completing a book about literature and the other arts.

Charles Nanry is assistant professor of sociology at Rutgers University and Director of the Institute of Jazz Studies there. (For more information, see the cover.)

Richard Peterson is an industrial sociologist and professor of sociology and anthropology at Vanderbilt University. He is interested in the music industry and has written articles and books on social problems and change.

Robert A. Stebbins is associate professor of sociology and former chairman of the department of sociology and anthropology, Memorial University of Newfoundland. He is the author of *Commitment to Deviance: The Nonprofessional Criminal in the Community.*

Chris White is an assistant professor of music at Rutgers University (Newark campus). For 15 years he was a professional musician and worked with the Dizzy Gillespie Orchestra, Nina Simone, and others.